My24 X

GENERAL BURGOYNE
in Canada and America

ABOUT THE BOOK

Michael Glover has written a definitive biography of John Burgoyne which sets him squarely back in the context of his career and upturns most of the clichés which have been written about his campaign in Canada and America. Dilettante, playwright and courtier, lover, Member of Parliament, Burgoyne was lampooned by the rugged and rustic Americans as "Gentleman Johnny"—significantly a term of derision. His good looks, cultivation, social graces, high connections, his dislike of gloomy American winters, his annual returns to the London season, which he regaled with his urbane Sheridan-type comedies, did not endear him to the colonists. Burgoyne was one of the few British generals chosen on merit and flexible enough to fight a winning war. Although the British government made him a scapegoat for the loss of the British colonies, he was a remarkable military innovator. He was also a brilliant negotiator, as he demonstrated in his "surrender with honour" at Saratoga, a "gentleman's agreement" which the colonists betrayed. A romantic character, who eloped with the daughter of the Earl of Derby and lived happily with her for twenty-five years, a whig Member of Parliament, he was also a close friend of the Abolitionist Charles James Fox and father of several illegitimate children.

ABOUT THE AUTHOR

Michael Glover served as an officer in the British Army in the Second World War and has since written some thirteen books on military subjects, including *Wellington As Military Commander*, *Legacy Of Glory* about Napoleon in Spain and *The Peninsular War*. An Englishman with an American great-grandfather, much of his writing has been devoted to myth-breaking.

GENERAL BURGOYNE

in Canada and America

Scapegoat For a System

MICHAEL GLOVER

GORDON & CREMONESI

FOR DICK *IL MIGLIOR FABBRO*

Designed by Heather Gordon-Cremonesi
Set in 11 on 12pt Caslon and printed in Great Britain
by W & J Mackay Limited, Chatham

ISBN 0-86033-013-3

Gordon Cremonesi Ltd
New River House
34 Seymour Road
London N8 0BE

6001871322

Contents

Acknowledgements

Many people have helped me in the writing of this book but I must particularly express my gratitude and obligation to Professor Richard Glover whose advice and guidance have been invaluable. I have also had much help and encouragement from Professor David Curnow and Miss Sheila Gullick.

The help I have received from my wife and daughter is, as always, beyond computation.

Michael Glover
Avenis Green
February 1976

"One thing should be remembered in the course of this Inquiry, that these transactions should be considered as they appeared at the time."
Lieutenant General John Burgoyne MP
to the House of Commons,
26th May 1778

List of Maps

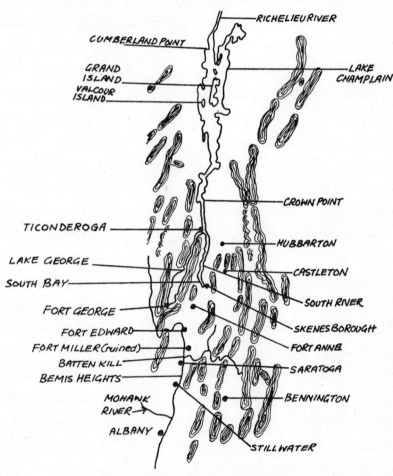

1a. The Campaign of 1777: North of Albany

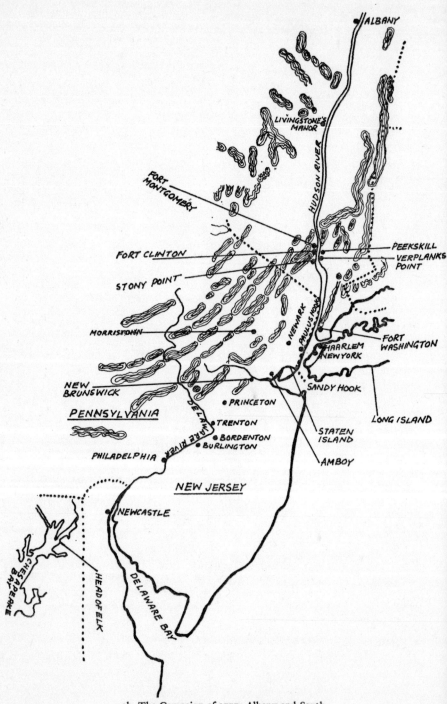

1b. The Campaign of 1777: Albany and South

Prologue

On 13th October 1777 Lieutenant General John Burgoyne called an extra-ordinary Council of War. On the previous day he had brought his generals into consultation. Since then the situation had deteriorated and now he extended the membership of the Council to include all field officers and captains commanding corps. This meant that, including staff officers and aides-de-camp, nearly forty men were present and, since there was no building capable of accommodating so many within the constricted boundaries of the camp, the Council had to be held in the open air. Occasionally an American roundshot whistled overhead. Around the gathering, the army was deployed in hastily fortified redoubts. The southern flank was protected by the lower reaches of the Fishkill stream with the village of Saratoga near its mouth. The Fishkill was fordable in places despite the recent heavy rains. To the west was a line of low heights crowned by earthworks. The line of them was carried round on the north until it met the broad Hudson's river which covered the army's rear.

Sombrely, without a trace of his usual cheerfulness, Burgoyne explained the army's situation. "The enemy in force, according to the best information he can obtain, to the amount of upwards of 14,000 men and a considerable quantity of artillery, are on this side of the Fishkill and threaten an attack. On the other side of the Hudson's river, between the army and Fort Edward, is another army of the enemy, the numbers unknown; but one corps, which there has been opportunity of observing, is reported to be about 1,500 men. They have likewise cannon on the other side of Hudson's river, and they have a bridge below Saratoga church by which the two armies can communicate."

On the previous day the generals had decided that the army should abandon its baggage and artillery and slip away during the night on the sixteen mile march to Fort Edward, keeping to the west bank of the Hudson. However, the scouts sent out to reconnoitre the road returned with the

I

information that "the enemy was intrenched at the fords of Fort Edward and likewise occupied the strong position on the Pine Plains between Fort George and Fort Edward."

As to the British army, the regular infantry amounted to less than 2,000 British and 1,600 German rank and file. At the reduced rations which had been issued for the last ten days the remaining stock of provisions would last for another week although there was no more rum or spruce beer. There was no definite news about the force which was coming up the river from New York to cooperate with them. According to the only message which had been received from them, they should have started their advance four weeks earlier. "The intelligence from the lower parts of the Hudson's river is founded upon the concurrent reports of prisoners and deserters, who say it was the news in the enemy's camp that Fort Montgomery [120 miles to the south on the Hudson] was taken."

Burgoyne "expressed his readiness to undertake at their head any enterprize of difficulty or hazard that should appear to them within the compass of their strength and spirit." No one present could doubt that he meant it. In the past month they had seen him exposing himself fearlessly in two general actions. Six days earlier he had been shot through his hat and through his waistcoat. His reputation for courage and enterprise went back for a decade and a half. He had also the gift of inspiring the devotion of the soldiers he led. If anyone could command them in a desperate thrust through the rebel lines, Burgoyne could do it.

In their hearts the officers knew that they had come to the end of the road. The British believed, perhaps unjustly, that their German allies could no longer be trusted. They were beginning to desert in batches and it was thought that they "meant to have given one fire and then clubb'd their arms" in token of surrender. Some of the British regiments were in little better case. There were reports that the Forty Seventh were "not to be depended upon", and that the Sixty Second, who had lost 368 out of the 541 rank and file who had set out from Canada, were "disheartened by the situation of their post and not equal to their former exertions". Many other officers believed that their men would only "fight upon *that* ground if attacked".

The general knew of this and said to his Council that, "he had reason to believe that a capitulation had been in the minds of some, perhaps of all, who knew the real situation of things". He, therefore, put to the assembled officers two questions. The first was, "whether an army of 3,500 fighting men, and well provided with artillery, were justifiable upon principles of national dignity and military honour, in capitulating in any possible situation".

The officers gave their opinion in order of seniority, starting with the most junior. All agreed that circumstances might arise in which capitulation would be justifiable.

The second question followed logically. "Is the present situation of that nature?"

Only one voice was raised against surrender. The first officer who spoke was twenty-year-old Midshipman Edward Pellew, who commanded the detachment of sailors serving with the expedition. He "pleaded earnestly that his own small party might not be included in the proposed capitulation but be permitted to make the best of their way back. He had never heard, he said, of sailors capitulating and was confident he could bring them off. But their escape would have cast a very undeserved discredit on the army and the proposal was properly discounted. Burgoyne said that what sailors could do, soldiers might do; and if the attempt were sanctioned for the one, the others must throw off their knapsacks and take their firelocks. As Mr Pellew still clung to his proposal, for he felt confident of succeeding, the general took him aside and, having represented to him the impossibility of drawing off the army, convinced him of the impropriety of permitting the attempt by a small part of it." The general was undoubtedly right but the midshipman lived to become the most famous of Nelson's frigate captains and, in the fullness of time, Admiral Lord Exmouth.

When he had the unanimous agreement of the Council, Burgoyne sat down and wrote a letter to be taken to the rebel outposts:

"Lt. General Burgoyne is desirous of sending a field officer with a message to M. General Gates upon a matter of high moment to both armies. He requests to be informed at what hour Gen. Gates will receive him to-morrow morning."

That evening a reply came back through the lines:

"Major General Gates will receive a field officer from Lt. Gen. Burgoyne at the advanced posts of the Army of the United States at ten o'clock to-morrow morning; from whence he will be conducted to head quarters."

The War of American Independence was to drag on for five more years but on 13th October 1777 the British chance of winning had evaporated.

By any standard General John Burgoyne had an extraordinary career. In his youth there was romance—a runaway marriage between a penniless captain of dragoons, the son of a ruined gambler, and Lady Charlotte Stanley, daughter to the Earl of Derby. This led to twenty five years of blissfully happy marriage and his acceptance by the earl as a satisfactory son-in-law— neither of them the commonest results of elopements. Then his professional talents attracted the notice of William Pitt and Burgoyne was given a chance to attain real military glory. His victory at Valencia de Alcantara made him a popular hero in London and Lisbon. Next he turned to politics, being sent into Parliament initially through the influence of one of his junior officers.

While still pursuing both his political and his military careers, he turned to the stage with his play *The Maid of the Oaks* and, later, *The Heiress*. Between these two plays came his command in America, a misfortune but, as will appear in due course, not one of his own making. The Convention of Saratoga ended his active military career but he continued in public life both as a conscientious member of Parliament and as a playwright until his death. In the last years of his life, a widower since before Saratoga, romance returned. He begat and acknowledged a new, illegitimate, family of four children. The eldest of them was to become a distinguished soldier in his own right—Field Marshal Sir John Fox Burgoyne, Moore's chief engineer at Coruña, the officer Wellington wished to have at the head of his engineers in 1813. In his old age he was Lord Raglan's Engineering Adviser in the Crimea, a war in which his own son won the Victoria Cross in the Royal Navy.

Any man with a career as varied and distinguished as John Burgoyne the elder might expect to occupy an honourable place in his nation's history. No such acknowledgement has come to Burgoyne. His own generation made him the scapegoat for their defeat in America. Modern writers, with two distinguished exceptions, have held him up to ridicule.

It is, of course, true that Burgoyne's defeat at Saratoga was one of the decisive battles of the world and that, for Britain, its consequences were disastrous. It gave new heart to rebels who in two seasons had seen their main army routed twice—at New York and Brandywine—and three of their main cities—New York, Newport and Philadelphia—fallen into the hands of their enemies. Worse still it emboldened the war-hawks at Versailles. France came into the war as the declared ally of the rebels. Spain followed in 1779, Holland in 1780. The rest of Europe—Russia, Austria, Prussia, Sweden and Denmark—formed themselves into an Armed Neutrality that left no doubt where their sympathies lay. Simultaneously, French intrigues in India involved Britain with the powerful Mahratta Confederation and with Hyder Ali of Mysore. As a result of Saratoga, Britain was to stand more alone in the world even than she did in 1940. It is no wonder that Burgoyne's contemporaries sought a scapegoat.

One would have expected that historians would have come to a more equitable verdict. It is a shock to find in an otherwise balanced and carefully researched book such a statement as that "The choice of Burgoyne was the worst ministerial error of the campaign." There can be no doubt that Burgoyne was chosen on his military abilities both as a trainer of troops and as the only available general who had to his credit a victory, albeit a small scale one, in independent command. By contrast historians have shown a remarkable leniency to Sir William Howe whose conduct was the real cause of what happened at Saratoga.

What made Saratoga a disaster for the British was not in fact Burgoyne's surrender. In a desperate situation, not of his own making, with his army on the edge of starvation and surrounded by enemies of more than three times his own strength, Burgoyne turned to diplomacy. Playing the weakest imaginable hand, he secured from his American opponent, General Horatio Gates, terms of striking generosity. His troops, under their own officers, were to be repatriated on condition that they should not serve again against the colonies. Had these terms been honoured, Britain would have lost little. The advantages she might have obtained from the operations of Burgoyne's army had already been squandered by Howe's irresponsible failure to carry out his share of the plan. The repatriated regiments would have been available to replace others in garrison in Britain, Gibraltar and Minorca—vital posts with war against France and Spain looming. As it turned out, the Americans went back on their word. The Continental Congress deliberately rejected the formal instrument which their general had negotiated and signed. It was primarily perfidy that made Saratoga the disaster it was.

It is natural that Americans should commonly gloss over the manner in which the Congress flouted the terms their general had granted. No country likes to dwell on records of national dishonour. One may still wonder why they need go to such lengths to portray Burgoyne as a buffoon, a figure of fun. Armies usually recognise "urgent private business" as reason enough for granting leave to officers outside the campaigning season. What then can be made of an author who describes Burgoyne as "a typical man of fashion, passing his winters at Bath 'on account of his health'. In the springtime he would hasten to the front, take command of an army that had been nursed all winter by lower officers and undertake some dashing adventure." Could it be that the author was ignorant that Burgoyne returned to England in the winter of 1775–76 on the King's direct orders, even if his inclination was also to return since his beloved Lady Charlotte was dying; or that when he returned in the following winter it was with the leave and encouragement of his Commander in Chief and because he had to settle his dead wife's estate? The same author adds gullibility to ignorance when he states that in the campaign of 1777 "thirty waggons were required for Burgoyne's baggage". The source of this allegation can only be the Brigade Order, issued by Burgoyne's second in command, General Phillips, which refers to "about thirty wagons on the road loaden with baggage *said to be* the Lieutenant General's". It is perfectly clear to anyone who has read this order that

Phillips knew perfectly well that these waggons were not Burgoyne's but contained baggage which other officers were trying to pass off as Burgoyne's. Had this not been the case the order would hardly have been issued.

It is surely needless to add further examples of how Burgoyne has been pilloried by men from whom one might have expected better. The reader should, however, be warned against taking at its face value the venom which Horace Walpole expresses against Burgoyne. This is sufficiently explained by Burgoyne's honourable attempt to frustrate a "job" planned by the diarist's nephew, Major Edward Walpole. Horace Walpole was too partisan a family man to forgive such an act as that. It should also be noted that the nickname "Gentleman Johnny", of which so much use has been made in ridicule, was in fact bestowed on him in affection by his own troops. Far from being a denigration, it was a high compliment, a tribute paid to the character of a fair-dealing, considerate officer, by men who had learned to trust him. One could wish that more commanders were able to earn such a distinction from that most perceptive of critics, the private soldier.

That said, one may turn to the two recent authors who have seen Burgoyne in a favourable light. They are unexpected bedfellows—George Bernard Shaw and Sir John Fortescue—the most flippant of Irishmen and the greatest of English military historians.

Shaw's kindly representation of Burgoyne may be no more than one playright's sympathy for another, but Shaw is full of surprises and there is evidence that he had done some research into eighteenth century military matters. He knew, for example, the number of live rounds allowed annually to the British soldier for musketry practice. It may well be that Burgoyne may not have been very different from the urbane, intelligent figure portrayed in *The Devil's Disciple*.

Sir John Fortescue is, of course, the author of many unconventional opinions but he had a knack of studying very thoroughly many documents which conventional historians rarely consult. To these documents he brought an understanding of war rare among academic men. This combination made his opinions uncommonly likely to be right. It would be suitable to close this prologue with his verdict on 1777. "As to Burgoyne's campaign at large, it seems to me that no more honourable attempt by British officers and men to achieve the impossible is on record. Burgoyne was denied a court-martial . . . but was allowed to defend himself before a Committee of the House of Commons where, in my judgement, he vindicated himself completely. A stronger man might indeed have retreated, whatever his instructions, after the reverse at Bennington; but Burgoyne's instructions ['to force his way to Albany' for his intended 'junction with Sir William Howe'] were undoubtedly positive[1] nor could he tell how far other operations might be dependent on his advance . . . Even more to his honour is the unfailing loyalty of his troops towards him."

Fortescue's veredict seems sufficient excuse for a re-examination of John Burgoyne and the circumstances which led to Saratoga.

PART I

The System

CHAPTER 1

Britain in the Seventies

The Britain in which John Burgoyne grew to middle age was inconceivably different from the Britain of the twentieth century. It would scarcely have been recognisable to those born ten years after the end of the American war. It was predominantly an agricultural country, almost always self-sufficient for food. The great majority of the population lived in small self-supporting villages. The bread they baked in their own ovens was made from wheat grown in the surrounding fields. The meat they ate came from animals grazed on the nearby commons. The beer they drank was brewed in the village. The woollen cloth they wore was spun from the village's own sheep. Few men, and even fewer women, ever went further from their birthplace than the few hours' walk to the nearest market town, itself scarcely as large as a twentieth century village.[1]

Within the village lived a tightly knit community, held together by custom and kinship. At its head was the squire. There were great lordly squires who spent much of the year in London but most squires were little more than substantial farmers. Like the villagers they were born and brought up in the village. They, and their sons, would be educated at a nearby grammar school. They would know every man, woman and child in the village. As Justices of the Peace they represented both the law and the executive of the kingdom. Since the squire and the vicar, who was more than likely to be one of the squire's relations, were among the tiny minority of the villagers who could read and write, they represented almost the only link between the community and the outside world. Their authority was undisputed but with it went a responsibility for their own people which was all-embracing. While they represented the power of the government they also, in their own persons, fulfilled many of the functions of the welfare state. Doubtless there were some bad and negligent squires but the great majority were honest, kindly, hard-working patriarchs who took their responsibilities as seriously as they took their privileges. As long as Britain was predominantly a village society, it was a system that very few of the villagers would wish to change.

There were larger towns but, in all England, there were only two with a population of more than 50,000—Bristol with 75,000 and London with three-quarters of a million. Norwich had 50,000 and so did Manchester if the count included Salford and the other little towns growing up round it. Birmingham, Hull and Sheffield each had between twenty and thirty thousand. Leeds, Nottingham, Chester and Worcester were the only other English towns with populations of more than ten thousand.

Soon towns were to grow. By 1775 the requisites for the Industrial Revolution were ready to hand but the great change had not yet got into its stride. Hargreaves had patented the spinning jenny in 1765. Arkwright's water frame had followed four years later. Crompton's "mule", combining the capabilities of the inventions of Hargreaves and Arkwright, was not available until 1779. Water was still the primary source of industrial power. Steam could not be applied to factories on a substantial scale until the eighties when James Watt produced the reciprocating action steam engine. In 1775 only five million pounds of raw cotton came into the country annually and Britain had to import cotton cloth. By 1789 32½ million pounds of raw cotton would be imported each year and the export of manufactured cotton cloth was a major activity.

Even if the capacity to produce on a large scale had existed, the means to transport raw materials and finished goods were lacking. Roads, though better than those on the continent of Europe, were appalling. On the Great North Road men had to be hired in parts to stop a coach overturning. In 1755 an advertisement appeared in Manchester for a "flying coach" claiming that, "However incredible it may appear, this coach will actually (barring accidents) arrive in London in four and a half days after leaving Manchester." Off the main roads pack horses were more useful than wagons. Canal building was only beginning and, for the transport of heavy loads such as coal, only coastal shipping was available. Not only was this paucity of transport a bar to industrial expansion, it heightened the isolation and parochialism of the countryside.

There were some six and a half million people in England and Wales. Scotland added a million and a quarter. Ireland, which was bound to Great Britain by a common Sovereign and little else, supported a population of three million. The British Isles were a very small unit on which to base a world-wide trading empire which already controlled much of North America, India and the West Indies.

Fortunately the small population, about half that of France, was strikingly hard working, enterprising and self-reliant. At the same time it was prepared to accept a social system which put all effective power into the hands of a minority who held it by right of wealth, hereditary or acquired, or by administrative ability. Although the urban minority were given to bursts of violence in times of economic distress, it was an astonishingly easy country to govern, so easy that its system of government had grown up piecemeal over the centuries, retaining old forms with only the minimal adjustments necessary to cope with slowly changing circumstances. As a result it was a confused mass of archaism and pragmatism. Very few parts of it were defensible on logical grounds but it worked more than adequately so long as too heavy a strain was not thrown on to it. Until the American colonies were lost there were few people who wished for any significant reform.

Politicians of all persuasions were given to lavishing superlatives on what George III, in all sincerity, described as "The beauty, excellence and perfection of the British Constitution as by law established". Since the constitution was unwritten, it was difficult to know what this admirable disposition of affairs actually was and the politicians' views of its provisions tended to vary according to whether they were in or out of office. It was generally agreed to rest on the twin pillars of the "Glorious Revolution" of 1688, which replaced the Catholic James II with his Protestant daughter Queen Mary and her husband, William III, and the Act of Settlement of 1701, which secured the Protestant succession to the House of Hanover. Both events were primarily concerned with ensuring that there should be no more Papist sovereigns, perhaps the only political question which could have produced so much interest and unanimity among the whole of the British population. The constitutional provisions of the Act of Settlement were far from forming a basis for anything as concrete as even an unwritten constitution although, somewhere along the line, the independence of the judiciary had become common ground.

The relative powers of the Executive and the Legislature were far from clearly defined. It was generally agreed that the King was the chief executive. He chose the ministers and, as far as it was practicable, laid down the policy they were to follow. The Legislature, the two houses of Parliament, controlled how far it was practicable since they alone could find the money necessary to implement it. It was a sensible compromise whereby the King was left with effective direction of affairs and Parliament stopped him going too far in any direction. Parliament, in fact, was mainly concerned with keeping taxation low and with ensuring that there was not more government than was absolutely essential. As Lord Shelburne remarked, "A powerful negative is the great requisite of all governments: for Providence has so ordered the world that very little government is necessary." Before the Industrial Revolution this was a perfectly tenable view with which all politically conscious men of the time would have agreed.

The ways in which members were elected to the House of Commons were diverse. There were 588 seats and the size of the constituencies varied from seven voters (Old Sarum) to 20,000 (Yorkshire), the largest urban constituency being Westminster with 10,000 voters. Methods of election varied from straightforward nomination to hard fought contests with free beer for the voters and, frequently, broken heads for those who voted against what appeared to be their duty. The largest number of nominations lay with the Crown, in effect the government in power. Crown nomination held good for about thirty seats, for the most part coastal towns with either dockyards or custom houses where all or most of the voters were government employees. The Duke of Newcastle in his heyday could nominate four members and have a considerable say in the choosing of three more, and, in all, various of the King's subjects, peers or commoners, could nominate or strongly influence 205 seats. John Wilkes, while sitting for the notoriously corrupt borough of Aylesbury, remarked that "fifty-six of our members are elected by only 364 persons." Some seats were, to all intents and purposes, hereditary. The Yonge family represented Honiton for 101 years through twenty-nine parliaments. It must be remembered, however, that the members nominated by borough patrons, as distinct from those nominated for Crown boroughs, were as likely to be independent in their views as those who fought elections, frequently more independent since they did not have to concern themselves with the selfish local interests of their constituents.

Some boroughs had the franchise embodied in the holders of municipal offices or in the freeholds of certain properties. Such closed boroughs would elect those who would do most for the town. Tewkesbury in 1753, resolved to "chose no members but such as will give £1,500 each towards mending the roads".[2] Members elected in such a way were expected to give the closest attention to the concerns of their constituency but, on wider issues, no member would consider that he had a "mandate" from the voters which could interfere with his right to vote as his judgment dictated. As Edmund Burke explained to his Bristol constituents, "Parliament is not a *congress* of ambassadors from different and hostile interests; which interests each must maintain, as an agent and advocate, against other agents and advocates; but parliament is a *deliberative* assembly of *one* nation, with *one* interest, that of the whole; where, not local prejudices ought to guide, but the general good, resulting from the general reason of the whole. You choose a member indeed; but when you have chosen him, he is not member of Bristol, but he is member of *parliament*." Daniel Cole put it more bluntly when he addressed the people of Nottingham, a borough with two thousand voters, an eighth of the total population in 1784. He declared that he would do everything he was able in the service of the town but "he declined entering into the discussion of political questions, as they very frequently caused confusion."

It is clear that with every member elected to use his own judgment there was no place for political parties in anything approaching the modern sense. There were loose groupings, based on common interests or family ties, but none of them could contemplate achieving a majority in the House and few of them were large enough to form a cabinet. There were a small number of men who could fairly be described as professional politicians, men who were in Parliament for what they could get out of it in the way of offices, real or sinecure, or for honours. These men, together with those who sat for the Crown boroughs, could be counted upon to support the government in power. So too could the forty-five members who represented Scotland, where the franchise was notably corrupt even by the worst English standard.[3] Nevertheless, a bare majority in the Commons required 279 votes and no combination of professionals, Crown nominees and Scots was enough to give a majority to even a coalition of the various groupings.

The backbone of the House was the hard core of independent country gentlemen who belonged to no group but sat because they thought it was their duty to their country, their neighbours and themselves to do so. Many sat for county seats, more for boroughs. Some had pocket boroughs of their own, others held them for a proprietor, frequently a relation. They had no interest in attaining office; any favours they sought were small ones—an ensigncy for a son, a living for a nephew. They disapproved of political parties (which they referred to as "factions") and were beyond the reach of bribes. They followed what they conceived to be "a patriotic line". In Shelburne's words, they "desired to see an honourable, dignified government conducted with order and due economy".

Without the support of this loyal but amorphous body of members no ministry could hope to survive. Their natural instinct was to support government because it consisted of the King's "confidential servants". As long as ministers were seen to have the King's active support, the independent gentlemen were prone to support it. This was especially true under George III since the policies which appealed to him were almost always those which appealed to the independent gentlemen. As one of them wrote in 1762, "I like the King and shall be with his ministers as long as I think an honest man ought." Conversely, a ministry which lost the King's support would soon lose that of the independent gentlemen and with it their majority.

To get and maintain a majority in the House under these conditions required in a Prime Minister very special skills. Offices, sinecures, pensions and other favours had to be distributed with discrimination and, above all, tact. Little of this was, by the standard of the time, corruption. Even among the professional politicians there were few men who could be bought. There was a general belief that there were many who deserved "gratifications" for long and faithful service or because their circumstances were insufficiently affluent to allow them to continue in public life at a time when members of parliament were unpaid. Some outright bribery was practised but the amount was far smaller than has been represented, and far more important than any pecuniary gratifications was the Prime Minister's need to maintain friendly relations with members. Misunderstandings had to be patiently explained, minor appointments made with infinite tact. The emollient word was of greater significance than disbursements from the Secret Service Fund. The offer of a bribe to an independent gentleman was more likely to do harm than good.

Whatever skills in the management of members a Prime Minister had, the deployment of them must consume a great deal of his time. Even allowing for the small amount of government done in eighteenth century Britain, it was as much as one man could do to run the country and maintain his majority even in peace time. When the country was at war it was impossible. The Duke of Newcastle, who had a real talent for managing majorities and a passionate interest in doing so, managed to bumble along as Prime Minister for two years of peace but as soon as the Seven Years War broke out in 1756 it became obvious that he was out of his depth. The obvious choice as a war leader was William Pitt but, being of a dictatorial disposition, he was as incapable of managing Parliament as Newcastle was of running the war. National necessity forced the two men, who detested each other, to join forces. The Great Commoner directed military operations and the Duke saw to it that he had the necessary Parliamentary support. Between them they had brought the war to a victorious conclusion even if Parliament's reluctance to continue voting high taxes deprived Pitt of the total victory he had intended.

It was inconceivable that Pitt and Newcastle should continue in the same government after the peace. Even if they had been prepared to serve together, they would not have been acceptable to George III, who came to the throne in 1760. The new king may have been inspired by his mother's injunction to "Be a King!", but the kind of king he intended to be was that which he believed the constitution called for—the chief executive of his country. He was well content to govern through ministers acceptable to Parliament but he was not prepared to lend the vast influence of the Crown to distort the inclinations of Parliament in favour of policies dictated by a clique of Whig magnates, policies of which he disapproved and which the independent gentlemen supported only from a sense of loyalty to the Crown. In particular he was determined to bring back into the mainstream of public life the Tory squirarchy, now the loyallest of his subjects whom a generation of Whigs had blackened as Jacobites and Catholic sympathisers.

Unfortunately, George III underestimated the difficulties facing him. The independent gentlemen, Whig or Tory, did not want to govern the country. They saw their role as preventing others from misgoverning it. He underestimated the difficulties of keeping up a working majority. He might have achieved this if he had had the services of a skilful political manager. The old Duke of Newcastle could have done the job and would willingly have done so since his passion for management was far stronger than his party allegiance. The king disliked Newcastle and shuffled him off to lesser posts, finally discarding him altogether. Sadly the old Duke wrote to Bute, who succeeded him, "You thought it was an easy thing to govern this country thro' the King's favour. Now I can tell you that altho' I had full possession of the late King as you have of the present, I found it necessary to take the great connexions of the country with me, which you are endeavouring to break and oppose; but take my word for it, you will find your seat at the Treasury an uneasy one if you don't change your plan."

The consequence of this miscalculation was a period of seven years weak and unsettled government following the Peace of Paris in 1763. Four prime ministers—Bute, Grenville, Rockingham and Grafton—followed each other in rapid succession. They had little in common except an inability to manage Parliament, a determination to reduce taxation and a vascillating policy towards the American colonies. The King disliked them all except Bute and backbenchers in both houses viewed them with increasing suspicion. Deprived of their fifty year hold on power, the Whigs lost such cohesion as the possession of office had given them. They broke into bickering factions united only in opposing what they described as extensions of the influence of the Crown. While it had been at their disposal the royal patronage had been a pillar of the constitution. When it was distributed by other hands it became a menace to the liberties of free-born Englishmen. Liberty, to the Whigs, meant the distribution of royal favours by Whigs. In 1770, when the Grafton ministry finally petered out, King and country were thoroughly disgruntled with incompetence and faction. With something approaching all-party agreement the leadership of the government passed to Lord North.

The eldest son of the 1st Earl and 3rd Baron of Guilford, Frederick North was two months short of his thirty-eighth birthday when he took office as First Lord of the Treasury. Under his courtesy title he had sat in the House of Commons for the family borough of Banbury since he was twenty-two. He belonged to none of the political groupings but had held minor office under Newcastle, Bute and Grenville. In Grafton's ministry he had been Chancellor of the Exchequer, an office of less consequence than it became in the following century. He was a classical scholar and spoke French, German and Italian with fair fluency, but he would have been happiest as a back-bencher among the independent gentlemen.

Two factors forced him into office, his poverty and his talent. He had great financial expectations but very little money during his father's extended lifetime. Lord Guilford lived to be eighty-six and "although his estates are £10,000 a year has not made any further allowance to Lord North except £300 a year to Mr North [Lord North's eldest son] while he was at Oxford." Nor had his wife brought him money and he had to mortgage his estate for £6,000 at the time of his marriage. Since his wife bore him six children who survived, he needed office to be able to live.

Having achieved office he displayed abilities unbecoming to an independent member. He understood and could explain government finance and he showed a mastery of the House of Commons. "In opening a budget, he was esteemed peculiarly lucid, clear and able." He could not only explain finance, he could manage it. In the first four years of his premiership he put the country's finances on a sound footing which they had not achieved since before the Seven Years war. Moreover, he was transparently honest. Richard Cumber-land, who admired North although he thought himself ill-used by him, re-corded that, "He kept his hands clean and empty."[4]

He was no orator but he was an immensely fluent and effective speaker in the House of Commons. Charles Fox said of him, "there exists not within these walls, nor in the kingdom, a more complete master of language, nor one who can more plausibly discourse on any subject." Nathaniel Wraxall said that he "was powerful, able and fluent in debate, sometimes repelling the charges made against him with solid argument, but still more frequently eluding the weapons of his adversaries by the force of wit and humour[5] . . . He seldom or never took notes, trusting to his memory for retaining the principal facts which occurred during the previous discussion."

He was the ideal man to keep the independent members in support of the government because, apart from his financial talents, he had so much in common with them. He was also extremely likeable. To quote Wraxall again, "His natural affability rendered him so accessible, and the communi-cativeness of his temper inclined him so much to conversation that every member of the House found a facility in becoming known to him. It was impossible to experience dullness in his society." Richard Cumberland agreed. "I do not know a person to whose society a man of sensibility might have given himself with more pleasure and security than to Lord North; for his wit never wounded, and his humour never ridiculed; he was not disposed to make an unmerciful use of the power which superiority of talents en-dowed him with, to oppress a weaker understanding; he had great charity for dullness of apprehension." Gibbon called him "one of the best companions in the kingdom", and Horace Walpole, who disapproved of him but could not dislike him, wrote that "he is indolent, good humoured, void of affectation of dignity, void of art; and his parts and the goodness of his character would have raised him much higher if he had cared either for power or applause."

Among his many attractive qualities was his modesty. He once remarked that the First Lord of the Admiralty in his own cabinet had "conceived such a mean opinion of my intelligence and all my suggestions (perhaps deservedly) that I do not think it would be of any service for me to write to him". Nor would he admit that, as First Lord of the Treasury (and concurrently Chancellor of the Exchequer), he was even *primus inter pares* with his cabinet colleagues. After having led the government for nine years he told Charles Fox that, "if the hon. gentleman supposes me to be the first, or sole minister, I do assure him he is mistaken; I know of no such minister in this country, and do therefore hope the hon. gentleman will consider me in two lights, namely as acting at the head of a very important department, where I acknowledge I am solely answerable for whatever is transacted, and as acting with others in his Majesty's confidential councils." At the same time he was at pains to stress that, "I do not mean to fly from that state of responsibility attached to my office, nor from the general responsibility which I am bound to with others, as one of his Majesty's confidential servants."

This diffidence sprang in large part from the indolence which Horace Walpole mentioned. North believed that tiresome questions would go away if they were ignored. His predecessor's government had discredited itself by a great expenditure of parliamentary time and legal lucubration in trying to solve the problem posed by the antics of John Wilkes. They failed and North inherited the problem. He ignored it and, as he had hoped, Wilkes found his own level as a minor, egocentric irritant.

In larger questions, North pursued the same policy and frequently he was successful, although in doing so he sometimes distressed the independent members who liked identifiable solutions to problems of state. Some began to deplore "the want of a more general plan; in all affairs since Lord North's administration this has been the case. Members who are independent and not obliged to follow the minister are often at a loss what part to take, for want of a thorough knowledge of what is to be the next measure."

In the early years of North's administration the American colonies were relatively quiet. This led him to the belief that, if left alone, the American problem would solve itself.

Despite Lord North's indolent optimism, a schism between Britain and her American colonies was inevitable. The difference in their outlooks were wide and growing. England was a settled country, prosperous, thriving on overseas trade, predominantly agricultural and relatively free from fears of invasion. She had evolved a form of government which, though frequently absurd and inconsistent, suited her circumstances and state of development. The thirteen colonies, although they occupied only a narrow strip on the eastern seaboard of North America, were settled, as far as they were settled, by a thrusting, pioneering people. They were preoccupied with making good, and increasingly resentful of a form of government evolved to meet other circumstances. To the British, trade with America was important but less so than trade with the East or West Indies. For more than a century it was more important to Britain that France or Spain should not control America than that she should do so herself. Equally, the colonists had until 1763 been kept acquiescent to an irksome control from London by the presence of the French in Canada.

The British regarded the colonies with a kindly indifference. They assumed that, since most of the colonists were of British origin, they would accept a set of rules which the English had devised for their own very different circumstances. They overlooked the fact that a high proportion of the colonists, starting with the Pilgrim Fathers, had crossed the Atlantic with the avowed aim of escaping from the English system. Many of the later immigrants had been Irish, who admitted no reason for blessing the English. Another large section were Scots fleeing from the vengeance and economic distress which followed the suppression of the Forty Five.[6] Nor could much sympathy for the Mother Country be expected from the 1,400 convicts who, according to Edmund Burke, were transported there each year.

The British would have continued their vague benevolence towards the colonies had they not cost the taxpayer so much money. Many merchants on both sides of the Atlantic were making large sums out of trade between Britain and America, but British expenses in the colonies, chiefly for defence, amounted to the equivalent of a shilling on the Land Tax, and the people who had to pay the Land Tax were exactly the class of person who became members of parliament. To them the issue was straightforward—the colonists were not paying their share. As Lord North put it, just before war broke out, "The annual taxes borne by the people of Great Britain amounted to ten millions sterling; and the number of inhabitants he supposed to be eight millions, therefore every inhabitant paid at least 25 shillings annually. The total taxes of the continent of [North] America amounted to no more than £75,000; the inhabitants were three millions, therefore, an inhabitant of America paid no more than sixpence annually."

Every British government since the peace of 1763 had endeavoured to reduce expenses in America and to increase the share of them paid for by the colonies. George Grenville made the first move in 1764. He halved the duty paid by the colonies on molasses from the West Indies. He may have expected that this move would be greeted with acclaim on the other side of the Atlantic but, being a tidy minded man he insisted that this duty be paid, the collection having for many years been "executed in the most shameful and negligent manner". Thus, he raised an outcry by damaging the large and influential smuggling interests which did little to impress the British taxpayer.

Grenville followed this, the next year, by proposing that all documents required in official transactions should be stamped. He undertook that all money raised in this way should be used only for defraying defence costs in the colonies and added that he would withdraw the proposal if, within twelve months, the colonists would produce an equal sum by taxing them-selves. This resulted in no proposals from the Americans for raising money, but produced the slogan, "No taxation without representation."

Since each of the thirteen colonies had its own legislature which could have raised the revenue required, this cry made little appeal to the British taxpayer. The inhabitants of Manchester and Birmingham had no represen-tation in the House of Commons and they were paying higher taxes than those expected from the people of Boston and Philadelphia without attempt-ing to subvert the constitution. Moreover, from the British point of view, the colonies were represented in Parliament by a vocal and effective lobby. After 1763 there was always at least one MP born in America; there was a solid block of merchants in the House whose predominant interest was trade with the colonies and each of the colonies had a paid agent in the House in the way that today Trade Unions have subsidised members to press their claims. On top of this there were a number of members who, through military, naval or civil service in America had ties of family, marriage, sentiment or interest in the colonies.

This colonial lobby went into action very efficiently when Lord Rocking-ham succeeded Grenville in 1765. The Stamp Act was repealed, less perhaps from sympathy with the colonists than from the widespread dislike in the House for Grenville, who had proposed it. However, the right to tax the colonies was reaffirmed. To omit the reaffirmation would have been to deny the complete supremacy of Parliament which was the ark of the Whig cove-nant. Moreover, the British taxpayer would never give up hope that the colonies could be made to pay their way, and no government that rejected that hope could expect to survive. The reaffirmation saved the government's face but to the colonies the repeal of the Stamp Act was all important. They had learned that the British would give way if they met firm resistance. Rockingham had tried to appease the colonies and had succeeded only in convincing them of British weakness.

When his health permitted, the moving spirit in the government which followed Rockingham's, was William Pitt, now Earl of Chatham. He was still regarded as a hero in America and had supported the repeal of the Stamp Act. He made no attempt to impose direct taxation but met different problems. Under the Mutiny Act of 1766 the colonies were obliged to billet troops and to supply them with rations, fuel and candles. Both Massachusetts and New York refused to do so. New York asserted that she would be willing to provide for the soldiers if ordered to do so by the King, but not at the behest of Parliament. This put all those who sympathised with the colonies in a dilemma which was repeatedly aggravated until 1775 as the colonies asserted their allegiance to the King but denied the supremacy of Parliament. Had they declared that taxation was an unjustifiable extension of the royal prerogative, they would have had the support of at least a substantial minority in parliament. As it was, the small and disunited minority who supported the colonies had constantly to walk a tightrope to avoid denying their most cherished belief, the supremacy of Parliament.

Lord Chatham soon retired into melancholia. His colleague, Townshend, the Chancellor of the Exchequer set about reducing the £428,000 a year that the colonies were costing Britain. He introduced a number of import duties but aroused so much opposition that his successor abolished all of them with the exception of that on tea. The colonists replied with a boycott on tea (though they continued to smuggle it in large quantities) and were confirmed in their belief that they could bully any British government.

In the first three years of North's ministry relations between Britain and the colonies were almost peaceful. There was the ugly incident of the Boston "massacre" when a handful of British soldiers opened fire in self defence on a voracious mob, and in 1772 the revenue cutter *Gaspée* was set on fire off Rhode Island and her commander desperately injured. North's emollient inactivity smoothed over both incidents. There were signs of a reaction against mob violence in America and the colonies resumed their habitual internecine quarrelling. Pennsylvania was at daggers drawn with Connecticut, New York with New Hampshire. In the Georgias there was fighting between frontiersmen and the settled coastal inhabitants. In England men began to think that a *modus vivendi* had been reached with the colonies.

That this was an illusion was shown when Lord North agreed with the East India Company that, to restore their ailing finances, they should be allowed to import tea into the colonies. The Company were to pay the duty of 3d a pound and the result would be to reduce the price of a pound of tea from £1 to 10/-. On the face of it, this was a sensible proposal which would benefit everyone except the smugglers. What the British government overlooked was the special emotional significance that had become attached to tea in the colonies. Afraid that the people of Boston would react as half-heartedly to a boycott on tea as they had to the earlier boycott on British goods,[7] the radical leaders forced the issue by destroying the tea on board the ships in the harbour.

The Boston tea party made it clear in England that appeasement had failed. Law and order had broken down in Boston and showed signs of doing so throughout Massachusetts. It must be restored and Boston must be forced to compensate the East India Company for their losses. This much was common ground to all parties in Britain. Lord North, always opposed to extreme measures, put forward what Edward Gibbon described as "a most lenient prescription". His proposal was "A Bill for removing the custom house and taking away the privileges of the harbour of Boston." This bill was not challenged to a division at any stage of its passage through Parliament. Even Colonel Barré, the most prominent and vituperative advocate of American claims, said in the House that, "the Americans ought to be punished for their ingratitude, that he would co-operate with Lord North on this measure." North wrote that, "there was a good deal of speaking but very few speakers declared themselves against the proposition."

A second bill was described by Gibbon as "the utmost attempt towards a new settlement, seemed to be no more than investing the Governor [of Massachusetts] with a larger share of executive powers, the nomination of civil officers (judges however for life) and some regulation of juries." The suspicion that juries were to be tampered with, although inserted only to secure a fair trial for British soldiers brought before civil courts, caused a ripple of opposition to the second bill. Nevertheless, it was passed by 239 votes to 64. Appeasement was at an end but the British were still determined to administer only minimal sanctions to restore orders. As the King summed up the general feeling, "Perseverance and the meeting of difficulties as they arise with firmness seem the only means of, either with credit or success, terminating public affairs."

The American reaction astonished Britain. It was to be expected that the Bostonians would resent the closure of their port but it was quite out of character for the thirteen colonies to cooperate with each other in resisting the will of Parliament. As the year wore on, the news in England became more and more serious. In September the King could write, "The dye is cast, the colonies must either submit or triumph; I do not wish to come to severer measures but we must not retreat." Two months later, he wrote, "The New England governments are in a state of rebellion; blows must decide whether they are to be subject to this country or independent."

No one in Britain wanted war with the colonies but very few favoured returning to appeasement. A snap general election at the end of 1774 consolidated support for North's government and, by implication, for continued firmness. As Gibbon, newly elected MP for Liskeard, wrote, "For my own part I am more and more convinced that we have both the right and the power on our side, and that, though the effort may be accompanied with some melancholy circumstances, we are now arrived at the decisive moment of persevering, or of losing for ever, both our trade and empire."

Those who opposed taking firmness to the point of war could, at their strongest, scarcely muster one vote in six in the House of Commons. "There was," wrote Horace Walpole, "no union among them. Lord Rockingham's was the largest party, the rest were small detached squadrons—all disunited. The Rockinghams were so low and inactive that they saw they had no chance till affairs, expecially in America, should grow worse." Rockingham was a high minded but ineffective nobleman who had gathered round himself the remnants of the Whigs who had followed Newcastle, the "Old Whigs". Two men, both notable parliamentary speakers, made the Rockingham splinter groups significant—Edmund Burke and Charles Fox.

Burke, an Irishman with a background of dubious financial transactions, was a master of the high-sounding sentiment and the written word. His reputation as an orator stood high but his oratory was lengthy and involved. It earned him the nickname of the "dinner bell". As his friend Oliver Goldsmith wrote:

". . . Too deep for his hearers, still went on refining,
And thought of convincing, while they thought of dining,
Though equal to all things, for all things unfit,
   Too nice for a statesman, too proud for a wit."

Burke, who liked to pose as the conscience of the nation, consistently supported the American cause but, since he was the paid agent of the province of New York, he could not be seen to be demonstrably disinterested. Moreover, the sophistry whereby he upheld Parliament's right to tax the colonies but added that it was inexpedient to do so, was unlikely to appeal to independent gentlemen paying the land tax.

Burke's greatest contribution to the American cause was in bringing Charles James Fox into the ranks of the Opposition. While Burke could make magnificent set speeches (usually to an empty House), Fox, an orator himself, was a great House of Commons man. He could influence votes with an improvised phrase and was the only member who could rival Lord North in the rough and tumble of debate. Fox had many personal friends in the House, notably North himself, but his public image was not one to create confidence. Walpole recorded that, "he would not give up his dissolute life, sat up all night and was seldom out of bed before two in the afternoon".

When he resigned junior office to join the opposition, "his character was so decided that the mob believed he was turned out for robbing the Treasury."

Only one man had the prestige to rally the opposition and made it effective, William Pitt, Earl of Chatham. He, however, refused to contemplate anything that smacked of an organised political party. Again and again, the Rockinghams approached him in the hope of forming an alliance. Chatham was uncooperative, believing that sooner or later the King would be driven to calling him to form a government on his own merits alone. Burke spoke feelingly of "those reserves he never fails to have as long as he thinks that the [King's] closet stands a jarr to receive him. The least peep into that closet intoxicates him, and will to the end of his life." Walpole agreed when he noted that, "Lord Chatham might have commanded the opposition but his intractable mind, his unsociable obstinacy and his scorn of owing anything but to himself had estranged them." It did not help that Chatham's principal adherent, Lord Shelburne, although probably the best intellect in politics, suffered from the insuperable disadvantage that no one trusted him.

When war came, therefore, Britain was united in support of it. North, who was more than ready to continue to apply "lenient prescriptions" in the hope that something would turn up, found himself driven to maintaining a firm attitude by the pressure of his supporters in and out of parliament. The Secretary at War, who was opposed to fighting and doubtful of the result, had to admit in January 1775 that, "nothing can be more zealous in support of the power and authority of Parliament than the present House of Commons; many members who generally oppose government in other points, cordially support it in this. I have reason to believe the same spirit prevails in town and country." Only among dukes was there a majority for continuing to try to conciliate the colonies.

CHAPTER 2

"They have a great resource in our incapacity"

Parliament and people had willed the use of force in America. They had not willed the means to apply that force. Neither the machinery of government nor the army were in any condition to bear the strains involved.

The machinery of the executive was fit for light duties only. The King stood at its head but no one could define how far his powers stretched. In ordinary times Parliament could control his actions by refusing to give ministers a majority. George III had the great strength that his views largely coincided with those of the independent members of Parliament and, far from controlling ministers, Parliament was driving them further than they wished to go. Left to himself Lord North would never have precipitated war, but he was driven to it by pressure from the King above and from Parliament below. A strong man would have resigned but North was not a strong man. He took the easiest way out and stayed where he was.

In normal circumstances the King could not have forced his ministers to act against their judgment. He had a keen sense of his constitutional limitations. As Lord Hillsborough, who resigned the American Secretaryship in 1772, said, "The King . . . will always leave his own sentiments and conform to his ministers, although he will argue with them, and very sensibly; but if they adhere to their own opinion, he will say, 'Well! Do you chuse it should be so? Then let it be.'" In 1775, times were not normal. King and Parliament were in alliance and it was a combination ministers could not resist.

Ministers were, of course, the King's confidential servants. They were paid out of the Civil List. The cabinet was an *ad hoc* body, about eight strong. It conducted the bulk of its corporate business while the port was circulating after the weekly cabinet dinner. The First Lord of the Treasury usually presided and reported any decisions to the King. If the discussions were largely concerned with the business of one particular minister he was likely to report the discussion to the King instead of, or as well as, the Prime Minister. There was, in peacetime, very little government done and the after dinner discussion tended to be mainly about foreign policy.

Although the Prime Minister was in charge of the Treasury,[1] most of the members did not have departmental responsibilities. They were the great officers of state, the Lord Chancellor, the Lord President of the Council and the Lord Privy Seal, dignitaries who contributed general advice and who normally owed their places to their positions in the various parliamentary groupings which lent their support to the government. The only executive ministers were the Secretaries of State and the First Lord of the Admiralty.[2] The Secretaries of State were the only ministers who could authorise action. Only they could give authority to act to the Treasury, the Admiralty, the Ordnance or the Navy. They were responsible to Parliament for the results of such authorisations and they normally gave them in accordance with cabinet decisions and after receiving the King's approval.

Although foreign affairs took up most of the cabinet's time there was no Foreign Secretary. Until 1768 there had been two Secretaries of State, presiding over the Northern and Southern Departments. The names denoted that in the past they had dealt respectively with the Protestant powers of northern Europe and the Catholic powers of the south. For home affairs they dealt also with the north or south of Britain, although their powers to authorise action were world wide and one could act for the other. As the known world expanded, so did the responsibility of the departments. The Cape of Good Hope and the East Indies became the responsibility of the Southern Department. Curiously William Pitt had directed the victorious years of the Seven Years war from the Southern Department although most of the operations were taking place in Germany and North America, both the responsibility of the Northern Department.[3]

In 1768 a third Secretaryship had been established to the accompaniment of a great Whig outcry that such a move was unconstitutional. Its responsibilities were the colonies on either side of the Atlantic, the small trading posts in west Africa and the much larger settlements on the west of the ocean— the West Indies, the thirteen American colonies, Nova Scotia and Canada. All this had previously been dealt with, subject to the authority of the old Secretaries of State, by the Board of Trade. The first Colonial Secretary, Lord Hillsborough, had been President of the Board of Trade when he was made Secretary and he continued to hold both appointments, as did his two successors. This had the unfortunate side-effect that the two "ancient" Secretaries of State affected to believe that the American Secretary was a lesser minister than themselves and continued to exercise powers over America, which properly belonged to their new colleague. Since a war with the Americans could only be coordinated by the American Secretary, it was regrettable that the holder of the office from 1772 to November 1775 was Lord Dartmouth, a mild and well-meaning nobleman who was as little equal to organising a war as he was to resisting the encroachment of his fellow Secretaries.

Since one of the functions of the Secretaries of State was the issuing of orders to the Royal Navy, it is reasonable to ask why the First Lord of the Admiralty should be a member of the cabinet. There is no logical answer to this question. It was a practical matter because experience had shown that the Navy could always find a professional reason for evading a cabinet instruction if they felt they had not been fully consulted in advance. It was, therefore, convenient always to have the First Lord present and in agreement with the course of action decided upon.

While there was, in peacetime, very little for ministers to do, economy dictated that they should have only the slenderest means of doing it. The office staff of the American Department, even after it had been expanded to meet the pressure of war business, consisted of the Secretary of State, two Deputy Secretaries, six clerks, a porter and a "necessary woman". The office of the Secretary at War, on whom depended most of the army's administration, totalled less than twenty and was the third largest of all government departments, exceeded only by the Treasury and the Admiralty.

It was a very precarious administrative base from which to conduct a complicated war involving tens of thousands of soldiers and sailors fighting three thousand miles away across an unpredictable ocean, a war in which information from the theatre of operations was never less than a month in arriving in London.

All governments, and particularly that of island Britain, are tempted to keep down taxation by reducing the strength of their armies. Britain had undertaken little in the way of military operations since 1763 and, since each of the governments in power in the intervening twelve years had been dedicated to economy, the army had been ruthlessly reduced. When war with the colonies broke out in 1775 the Adjutant General, who was in the best position to know, asserted that, "taking America as it at present stands, it is impossible to conquer it with our British army. To attempt to conquer it internally with our land forces is as wild an idea as ever contraverted common sense." It was not that he doubted the capability of the army to deal with any force of comparable size; his point was that the peacetime army, and any foreseeable expansion of it, was too small for the job.

The establishments[4] for 1775 called for an army of 45,123 men, comprising 28 regiments of cavalry, three of Foot Guards and seventy regiments of infantry of the line,[5] one of which, the Forty First Foot, was composed of "invalids". There were a further twenty independent companies of "invalids" to garrison fortresses. The line battalions of infantry consisted of only 410 rank and file[6] at full strength. In fact no battalion was less than 10% under strength. The eighteen regiments in America (including Canada) should have had 8,580 men of all ranks. In fact there were no more than 6,991.

Apart from the troops in America, the army had to find garrisons for Gibraltar (7 battalions), Minorca (5) and the West Indies (3). A substantial force had to be kept in Ireland, both for internal security and external defence, and a guard had to be mounted on the south coast of England in case France and Spain attempted to take advantage of England's preoccupation with America to mount an invasion. Moreover, in the absence of a police force, troops had to be available to deal with civil disturbance in any part of the kingdom, and military help was always needed to prevent smuggling. It was impractical to use many of the army's 6,879 cavalry for operations in America. There was good cavalry country in parts of the colonies but to attempt to ship cavalry horses across the Atlantic would only result in killing the horses on the long sea journey.[7]

It will be noticed that in speaking of the strength of the army reference has only been made to cavalry and infantry. There also existed 40 companies (batteries) of artillery and a small but skilled body of officers of the Royal Engineers.[8] Neither artillery nor engineers belonged to the army. They had separate establishments in both Britain and Ireland and in each country they had distinct political heads in the Masters General of the Ordnance. The Ordnance corps had their own establishments of medical officers and chaplains and their transport and supply arrangements were dealt with separately from those of the infantry and cavalry.

Neither the army nor the Ordnance corps had any transport and supply arrangements of their own. These services were the responsibility of the Treasury, and the Treasury had no peacetime military transport, and the supply of rations was handled by sedentary commissariat officers who made contracts with provision merchants in garrison towns. On the outbreak of war the Treasury would engage additional commissaries, who could hardly be other than inexperienced, appoint them to overseas expeditions and rely on them to arrange with foreign contractors to provide rations, fuel, wagons, draught horses and drivers. The only permanent vehicles in any of the military forces were the limbers of the artillery and even these could not be moved until the Treasury had hired horses and civilian drivers.

The pay of the forces also emanated from the Treasury, but between that august body and the recipients was the Paymaster General, a senior member of the government in his own right. Medical services were the responsibility

of a multitude of archaic bodies which were in a perpetual state of bureau-
cratic war with each other.

As if to ensure that an army set about with so many organisational
hazards should be as ineffective as possible, the army (meaning the cavalry
and infantry) had no head, except in so far as the King was able to attend to
its concerns. In the early years of his reign George III took a close and
wholly beneficent interest in his army, but he was a busy man and could not
spare the time necessary for a full-time commander in chief. It was the
custom for such a personage to be appointed only in time of war and the post
had been left unfilled since the death of the last incumbent, the Marquess of
Granby, in 1770. No further appointment was made until the American
war had been in progress for three years. In 1775 the nearest the army had
to a professional head was Lieutenant General Edward Harvey, the Adjutant
General. Although he sat in Parliament for Harwich, a Crown borough, he
seems to have been an honest and conscientious staff officer, despite Walpole's
sneering description of him as "the King's confidential tool for the army".

Nor did the army have a political head, comparable to the First Lord of
the Admiralty.[9] The nearest equivalent was the Secretary at War, a minister
below cabinet rank. His concern was entirely with the administration of the
army. He prepared the Army Estimates and presented them to Parliament
but he had no say in what the army did or where it went. He prepared commissions for the King to sign but had no direct influence in deciding who
received them.

This chaotic superstructure was not merely a matter of chance or misplaced economy. It was the deliberate choice of the nation. Men in 1775
would have heard from their grandfathers of the traumatic time when Crom-
well placed England under military rule and when James II tried to overawe
London with a Papist army encamped on Hounslow Heath. The fear of a
military *coup* was far from dead a century later, and a decentralised army
seemed a small risk to take against the chimera of authoritarianism.

The very existence of an army in peacetime seemed to some to be a
threat. Dean Swift had written that, "A standing army in England, whether
in time of peace or war, is a direct absurdity. For it is no part of our business
to be a warlike nation, otherwise than by our fleets. In foreign wars we have
no concern, further than in conjunction with our allies, whom we may assist
by sea or by foreign troops paid with our money." In the seventies, Burke
could still assert that, "An armed, disciplined body is, in its essence, dangerous
to liberty."

It has always been a British belief that, with the Royal Navy as a shield, an
army could be improvised when the need arose. When, in presenting the
Army Estimates for 1774, the Secretary at War proudly announced that,

"the expences of the army were not so much as the last year by £1,004",
Mr Dowdeswell, who had been Chancellor of the Exchequer in Rockingham's government, countered by saying that, "our keeping up so large an
army now was no stroke of good policy; that at the commencement of the
last war there was not the force we had now, yet we proved successful."

One of the results of the intense suspicion with which the army was
regarded was that there was no permanent formation larger than a regiment,
which in practical terms meant a battalion. Brigades were formed only for
active operations and there were no trained staff officers to direct them,
regimental officers being taken out their units to act on the staff as the need
arose.

Regiments were almost the private property of their colonels who could,
and sometimes did, make a handsome profit from their commands. There
were a number of legitimate perquisites, particularly the clothing account
whereby the grant for the mens' uniform for the year was paid into the
colonel's private account well in advance. Thus colonelcies were precisely
the kind of "gratification" which politicians were anxious to distribute to
their supporters. Throughout the eighteenth century there was a constant
struggle between the politicians and those who valued the efficiency of the
army. Successive kings tried to use promotion to a colonelcy as a reward for
military efficiency. Parliamentary managers, especially the Duke of Newcastle, claimed that they could not maintain their majorities without being
able to dispose these valuable places.

Even the existence of a Commander in Chief was no guarantee that
military considerations would predominate. The Duke of Cumberland
certainly used the appointment of colonels for political ends, and the Marquess
of Granby was liable to have promises "exacted" from him "in the midst of
riot and dissipation". George III fought hard against political colonelcies. He
"would not let Lord North dispose of the principal regiments, or let him
know how he himself designed to dispose of them." "Lord North remonstrated about the large number of military preferments which the King himself bestowed; a practice, he said, that loosened military discipline, as officers
did not look up to the Minister, nor could he engage the attachment of
country gentlemen when they found he had not credit to provide for their
sons and relations in the army." It is true that in the early days of his reign the
King deprived General Conway of his regiment for voting against General
Warrants in the House of Commons but he was given another regiment four
years later and although he was the most constant critic of the American war
and of North's government, Conway retained the Colonelcy of the Royal
Horse Guards from 1770 until his death twenty-five years later.

If colonels were the proprietors of their regiments, many of their officers also had a proprietorial interest since they owned their commissions. That they did so was, like so many of the army's peculiarities, the result of parliamentary meanness. To raise a regiment by voluntary recruitment was an expensive business. Parliament had always been reluctant to find the necessary money and, instead, farmed the task out to colonels who subcontracted to the captains of companies, who in turn subcontracted to subalterns for raising a given number of men. All officers, therefore, held shares in what amounted to a military joint stock company. When the original shareholders wished to retire they naturally expected to recoup their investment. Since Parliament would not find the money to buy them out, there was no alternative to allowing them to sell their commissions to younger aspirants. Successive kings had tried to abolish the system but, since until 1870 Parliament would not provide the necessary funds to end it, they had to content themselves with making ineffective efforts to regulate it.

Since commissions were not heritable property, a commission lapsed with the death of the holder. Thus a number of free vacancies always occurred. It was the custom that ranks vacated by the death of the holder in action should be filled by regimental seniority. Death vacancies from other causes—illness, accident and old age—were at the disposal of the Crown and were, for the most part, filled by seniority or merit. In peacetime such vacancies were few and made fewer by the absence of retirement pensions. Since most army officers were poor men they could not afford to retire unless they had commissions to sell. Non-purchase officers, therefore, had to continue serving until they died. Occasionally a special dispensation was granted to a deserving officer to sell a commission he had not purchased to enable him to leave the service, but such exceptions were rare. The result was that regiments had too many elderly officers. The proportion of purchase to non-purchase officers clearly varied according to the number of deaths that had recently occurred. In 1775 the army had suffered no significant vacancies for twelve years so that the proportion of purchase officers was high. It needed a war to create a large number of free vacancies. It would, however, be an error to suppose that purchase officers were in any way inferior to those with free commissions. There were good and bad in both categories.

It is often asserted that the British officer corps was "a preserve of the aristocracy". This cannot be true.[10] The great majority of officers were the sons of officers (including, of course, the sons and grandsons of officers who were ennobled for their military prowess, such as the Stanhopes and the Cadogans). They were steady, conscientious men, content to devote their lives to their regiments and accept a very small wage for a lifetime of service. For most of them the height of their ambition was to be the captain of a company or a troop. There seems to have been astonishingly little resentment when the rich minority purchased promotion over their heads and went on to command battalions and, eventually, to become general officers by seniority.

The soldiers who served under them were the dregs of the population. The conditions under which the private soldier served were such that no man would enlist unless driven to it by desperation. War might induce a small number of romantically minded patriots to join but in peace it required appalling social or economic pressures to persuade a man to take the King's shilling. His pay would be eightpence a day (sevenpence on the Irish establishment) but by the time he had paid for his rations, his uniform, his "necessaries" and a number of other deductions he would be fortunate if he had a penny a day left to him. This would be paid to him every two months in arrears. There were very few barracks and those there were were grossly insanitary. Most of his home service would be spent billeted on an unwilling publican who would lose no opportunity of cheating him out of his meagre rights. He was despised by the civilian population and forbidden to walk out in the public parks.[11] There was always the chance of being posted to the West Indies where his chances of surviving fever would be poor. Discipline could be harsh, though less so than in the navy. He was not forbidden to marry, although he enlisted for life, but he would know that if his unit was ordered overseas only six wives from every company could accompany the battalion overseas. If his wife was one of the six to be chosen, she would face unknown dangers and hardships. If she were not chosen, she would be left unprovided for in Britain. No marriage allowance was payable and there was no system whereby the soldier could remit to her any savings from his meagre pay. It is no wonder that recruits were "the scum of the earth" but, to continue the same well-worn quotation, "it is astonishing what fine fellows we have made of them". Out of the unpromising material from which the ranks of the British army was filled, the officers, aristocractic or plebian, purchased or not, fashioned incomparable troops. Off duty they were deplorably given to drunkenness; on active service they looted like brigands, but in their loyalty to their colours and to their officers, in their steadiness under fire they had no peers in the world.

When war broke out the government had a serious problem to increase the number of recruits. The usual procedure was to offer a bounty of three guineas to each man who would enlist and, in times of hardship, there were usually enough shiftless and thirsty men prepared to bind themselves for life to a hard and dangerous trade. Unfortunately for the army in 1775, times were not particularly hard and recruits were difficult to come by. Even in Ireland, traditionally the most promising reservoir for the army's raw material, it was hard to raise men and it was depressingly reported that "we have hitherto found that recruits raised in Ireland desert so fast while they continue in that kingdom, or in the neighbourhood of it, that not above half those enlisted are ever brought into the public service." Naturally the bounty system was wide open to abuse at a time when the population was unregistered. It was all too easy for a man to collect a bounty, desert and re-enlist in another regiment. He would be unlucky if he was ever caught however often he repeated the process. In 1787 a man was hanged near Ipswich who "made the extraordinary confession that he had enlisted forty nine times . . . and had obtained three hundred and ninety seven guineas as bounty money thereby." Nor was recruiting made any easier by the fact that the East India Company was also recruiting an army in Britain. In 1775, Lord North requested the Directors "to stop or at least diminish their recruiting for a short space of time". He feared that, "such an application would be unsuccessful", and he was right. The Company made only minor concessions.

The other method of expanding the army was to raise new regiments. It was known that more recruits were forthcoming for such temporary units. Unfortunately such a course was certain to inhibit recruits from joining existing units which had to be brought up to war strength. Moreover, if a rich man raised a regiment he expected to have the nomination of the officers, and this led to men being promoted to ranks to which their merit and experience did not entitle them. The King, who regarded the raising of new regiments as "a very disagreeable measure", set his face against the practice as long as he could. "I cannot consent that what should appear as spontaneous acts arising from a feeling of the justice of the contest should be turned into apparent jobs to give unreasonable rise to young men." When necessity forced him to accept the practice, he insisted on maintaining "the principle that no man is to get more than one step".

Since sufficient British troops could not be raised to deal with the colonies, German mercenaries had to be hired. This was the traditional remedy for Britain's chronic shortage of troops, but the step was greeted with howls of humanitarian outrage from the colonists, the Earl of Chatham and the King of Prussia. Most of this moral outrage was spurious. No one, except perhaps Jacobites, had complained when Germans had been brought to Britain to put down Scottish rebels in 1715 and 1745. The Americans had been glad enough to have Hessians hired to defend them from the French in the Seven Years War and few men had hired more mercenaries than Lord Chatham, although he attempted to deny that he had ever done so. King Frederick had some grounds for his complaint. Soldiers in substantial numbers were deserting from his army to obtain the better conditions of service in the Brunswick and Hessian contingents for America.

In July 1777, General Clinton remarked to General Howe at New York that "No rebellion could be quelled by armies on the defensive." Britain could not put down the American revolution merely by occupying territory and defending it. She must act on the offensive and either destroy the rebel army in general actions or so divide the enemy army that it ceased to be an effective force. The colonists had the advantage that they could stay on the defensive, and they were much assisted in doing so by the topography in the main theatres of operations.

To make the British problem more difficult, the weapons of the period were far more suited to defence than to attack. On both sides the principal weapon was the musket. The British model, which was also widely used by the rebels, was a long clumsy weapon with a 46-inch barrel and which weighed 10 lb 12 oz.[12] It fired a lead ball, three-quarters of an inch in diameter, which would disable a man at three hundred yards if it hit him. The problem was to hit him. The range at which a skilled soldier could count on hitting a man was sixty yards. The musket's rate of aimed fire was three rounds a minute and the procedure for loading was long and complicated, so that, while he performed it, about forty-five seconds in every minute, the soldier was defenceless. Even when the musket was loaded and aimed, it was by no means certain that it would fire when the trigger was pressed. The quality of powder available left much to be desired and the flint, which set off the explosive charge, would fail to give an adequate spark once in every seven firings even in dry weather. To obtain substantial fire-effect with muskets many of them had to be fired at the same time in the same direction. This meant that the troops had to be lined up shoulder to shoulder and trained to fire volleys. They made a magnificent target.

Since the rebels could remain on the defensive, they could place their main trust in the shovel and the felling axe. They could throw up earthworks or stockades. Behind them they could remain in perfect safety. The penetration of a musket ball fired at packed earth at a range of sixty yards was one and a half inches. In a tree trunk it would make a slight dent. Behind their defences the rebels could wait until the range was right, appear briefly over the parapet, fire their volley and disappear to safety while they reloaded.

They could also use the rifle. Rifles were even longer and clumsier than muskets, but they were accurate up to two hundred yards and, in the hands of a marksman, even further. The Pennsylvania rifle, the model principally used in the early years of the war, threw a ball half-an-inch in diameter. Although frailer than the musket and much more expensive, it was, by contemporary standards, a precision weapon. Its disadvantage was that it was very slow to load. The ball had to be forced down the four foot barrel with its seven or eight deep spiral grooves. One round a minute was a good rate of fire. The rifle was an excellent weapon for a man firing from behind cover. For a soldier in the open (as he would have to be in an attack) it was almost useless.

The traditional counter to fortification was the use of heavy artillery. Twelve- and twenty-four pounder guns could batter down any earthwork or stockade, given time, a supply of ammunition and a position from which the guns could bear on their target. The last needed to be out of rifle range, as all battering guns had a flat trajectory and could not fire from behind cover.

Battering was a slow business. On good roads siege guns moved at a snail's pace. On improvised tracks it was difficult to move them at all. The rate of fire was slow. Twenty-four pounders could fire only one round a minute, since every time they fired the gun and its carriage recoiled several yards and had to be hauled back into position. It could take days to breach a substantial earthwork, longer even than it took to break down masonry, and it could only be done by daylight. To fire at night would only waste irreplaceable ammunition. If the breach and the attack was not completed by nightfall, the gunner would find the earthwork largely replaced by dawn.

When a breach had been made, it must be assaulted. This meant the infantry going forward across open ground under fire from the defenders on the flanks of the breach. The attackers could fire a volley; they could reload on the march and, perhaps fire a second. Neither would be very well aimed and, if they lost their shoulder to shoulder formation, their fire would lose its effect. In the end, everything depended on the seventeen-inch steel bayonets fixed on the muzzles of the muskets. For bayonets to be effective the men still had to be in close formation. There is no point in sending out skirmishers with fixed bayonets. Artillery could clear the way but only massed infantry with fixed bayonets could capture fortifications. There was no other effective weapon available.

The British army was not ignorant of America. Many officers had served there in peace and war. They knew the great distances involved, the endless series of good defensive positions available, the poor roads, the vast tracts of forest. They also knew the frontier farmer's skill with the rifle—indeed they probably exaggerated it. At the same time experience had given them an unjustifiably low opinion of the colonist as a soldier. Too often in the French wars, American militia had behaved badly and had been ill-supported by their provincial governments. There was a facile assumption that these faults would repeat themselves when they faced British troops.

Most of all the British underestimated the sheer size of the opposition. All the early plans were based on the assumption that a substantial body of loyalists would rally to their support. Many did and far more would have done, could they have been certain of protection for their families and their property. The expectation broke down because, when the fighting started, the small minority of active rebels were the men in possession. British protection could extend no further than Boston Neck. Each time the British advanced, recruits enlisted in large numbers. Each time the British retreated, the recruits deserted. Their only option was to leave their farms to be destroyed and their dependents terrorised. Had the British started the war with a number of bases firmly held, they might have built up a loyalist army large enough for their needs. As it was they started with only a single base, which was barely tenable.

British soldiers started the war with a wholly justified confidence in their abilities as fighting men. They believed that, soldier for soldier, they had no equals in the world. Two incidents in the Seven Years War seemed to prove this fact. One was Wolfe's capture of Quebec. It was a dashing exploit, the kind of romantic incident that every schoolboy learned and remembered. Yet Quebec had been "a damned close run thing". James Wolfe was one of the luckiest generals in history. From the start he had naval cooperation of a kind no general could expect until a hundred and fifty years later. The landing at Anse de Foulon was accomplished with great skill but only succeeded by quite uncommon good luck. The greatest good fortune came later. Had Montcalm decided to retire within the fortifications of Quebec, there was little that Wolfe could have done about it. The city walls were defective, but they could have withstood the battering of any guns Wolfe's men could have manhandled up the cliffs. Wolfe's communications with the fleet and his supply ships depended on a single, steep, rough path. The army could not have been fed for a week on the Heights of Abraham. To make matters worse, the admiral was insistent that the fleet must leave the St Lawrence in a few days, before ice blocked its retreat. As it happened Montcalm elected to come out and fight without even waiting for his whole army to be concentrated. Had he not done so Wolfe's only course would have been to climb down the cliffs and re-embark.

The other incident was totally different but went far to convince the British that there was no limit to what their infantry could achieve. Six weeks before Wolfe took Quebec, an Anglo-German army under Prince Ferdinand of Brunswick faced a somewhat larger French army under Marshal Contades at Minden. Ferdinand had devised an elaborate concentric attack on the French on 1st August 1759. This was disjointed from the start because Contades was simultaneously making a complicated movement. The day might well have passed in profitless manoeuvring except that, for reasons which have never been fully elucidated, a brigade consisting of six British and two Hanoverian battalions marched straight at the French. What happened is best described by an officer of the Twelfth Foot in a letter home.

"Now began the most disagreeable march that I ever had in my life, for we advanced more than a quarter of a mile thro' a most furious fire from a most infernal battery of eighteen 18-pounders, which was at first upon our front, but as we proceeded, bore upon our flank, and at last upon our rear. It might be imagined that this cannonade would render the regiments incapable of bearing the shock of unhurt troops drawn up long before on ground of their own choosing, but firmness and resolution will surmount any difficulty. When we got within about 100 yards of the enemy, a large body of French cavalry galloped boldly down upon us; these our men, by reserving their fire until they came within about 30 yards, immediately ruined, but not without receiving some injury from them . . . These vistants being thus dismissed, without giving us a moment's time to recover the unavoidable disorder, down upon us like lightning came the Glory of France in the persons of the *Gens d'Armes*. These we almost immediately dispersed without receiving hardly any mischief from the harmless[13] creatures. We now discovered a large body of infantry, consisting of 17 regiments, moving down directly on our flank in column, a very ugly situation; but Stewart's Regiment [Thirty Seventh Foot] and ours wheel'd, and show'd them a front . . . We engaged this corps for about 10 minutes, kill'd them a good many and, as the song says, the rest ran away.

"The next who made their appearance were some regiments of the Grenadiers of France, as fine and terrible looking fellows as ever I saw. They stood us a tug; notwithstanding we beat them off to a distance, where they galded us much, they having rifled barrels and our muskets would not reach them. To remedy this we advanced, they took the hint and run away. Now we were in hopes that we had done enough for one day's work and that they would not disturb us more, but soon after a very large body of fresh infantry, the last resource of Contades, made a final attempt upon us. With them we had a long but not very brisk ingagement, and at last made them retire almost out of reach, when the 3 English regiments of the rear rank came up and gave them one fire, which sent them off for good and all."

The six battalions had gone into action 4,434 strong. They lost 78 officers and 1,252 other ranks but, as he rode away in the midst of his routed army, Marshal Contades was heard to remark, "I never thought to see a single line of infantry break through three lines of cavalry, ranked in order of battle and tumble them to ruin." It was not surprising that British officers had a high opinion of their infantry's capabilities.

The British did not only learn from their victories. Four years before Minden, before the Seven Years War had actually been declared, a force of regulars and Virginia militia were advancing on the French post at Fort

Duquesne (Pittsburgh). The Virginians were under Colonel George Washington and the whole force was commanded by Major General George Braddock. Having forded the Monongahela river and got to within six miles of their objective, the advanced guard was ambushed in "an open wood free from underwood with some gradual risings, so open that carridges [sic] could have been drove in any part of it."[14] The advance guard, much harried by an invisible enemy, was ordered to retire by its commander. In doing so they fell into disorder and mingled with the main body who were coming up to their support. The whole body stood gallantly and hopelessly under a heavy fire for two-and-a-half hours. Then, with their ammunition gone and most of their officers fallen, they broke and fled. Braddock was mortally wounded and died murmuring, "Another time we shall know better how to deal with them."

After the disaster at the Monongahela river, a light infantry company was added to every infantry battalion. They were trained by George Augustus, 3rd Viscount Howe, and the Swiss, Colonel Bouquet, to operate in open order, to take advantage of cover and to act as a screen round the main body of the army. Usually the light companies from all the battalions in a force were grouped together into light infantry battalions, and before the end of the war they had shown themselves superior to any French or Canadian Indian enemy. As soon as the war was over, economy demanded that each battalion should be reduced by one company. Since the light infantry company was the junior company in every battalion, every light company in the army was swept away in 1763.[15] Fortunately wiser thoughts prevailed and the companies were re-established in 1770, but much valuable experience had been lost in the interregnum. In 1774 a training camp was organised at Salisbury where seven light companies were put through the "exercise" under Major General William Howe, brother to the Viscount. Nevertheless, the training of the British light infantry was not as good in 1775 as it had been in the earlier war.

Much has been made of the shortage of British light infantry in the American war. There were occasions when they were deficient in both numbers and training but, taken over all, they did almost everything that could be expected of them. Their shortcomings were not a decisive factor. The great British shortage was of sufficient "battalion" infantry who could be used to storm a defended position. What was needed was men with bayonets to make up for the offensive weapons which did not exist. In an assault, light infantry have some marginal value to draw fire and to keep down the heads of the defenders, although for this task they need rifles, the muskets of the light companies being little better than those of the rest of the infantry.

One lesson the British did not draw from the Monongahela river. They continued to give commands to the officer who commanded the advance guard in that action. He had shown himself as brave as a lion but he had neither conformed to Braddock's orders nor shown initiative. In 1774, as a (local) Lieutenant General, he was Governor and Commander in Chief of the Province of Massachusets Bay. His name was Thomas Gage.

PART II

The Man

CHAPTER 3

Dragoon and Guardsman

Wealth and social rank counted for much in eighteenth century England, but the governing classes were far from being a closed society. Any of the fortunate minority who could read and write could make their way to the top provided that they had talents and friends. John Burgoyne started life with few advantages. The grandson of an unimportant country baronet, there was no wealth for him to inherit, but he had talents and great charm.

An early Burgoyne had been a civil servant under Henry VIII. He was appointed one of the commissioners who supervised the surrender of monastic wealth and was rewarded with an estate at Wroxall in Warwickshire.[1] For the next century the family settled to being country squires, their importance being somewhat raised when they acquired, by marriage, a two thousand acre estate in Bedfordshire, Sutton Park near Biggleswade. The great grandson of the commissioner, an early John Burgoyne, born in 1591, found himself created a baronet at the age of fifty. He had done nothing to deserve this honour and it may be doubted if he had desired it, but the early Stuart kings, chronically short of money with which to govern their kingdoms, had unearthed an ancient statute whereby gentlemen in possession of estates of any considerable size were bound to accept baronetcies. Considerable fees were payable to the Crown for this promotion.

Sir John's eldest son, Roger, who was a lawyer, was elected to Parliament in 1640 as one of the members for Bedfordshire. His father joined him in the House, representing Warwickshire, five years later. Both men signed the Ordnance forming the Bedfordshire Committee of the Midlands Association and thereby took the rebel side in the Civil War, but both were moderate men and were ejected from Parliament by Pride's Purge, in 1648. Roger returned to the Commons for two years in 1656, the year before he succeeded to the title, but this was the family's last excursion into public life until the sixth baronet, another Sir Roger, was elected for Bedfordshire in 1734. Meanwhile the family tended their estates and, generation after generation, married untitled ladies, most of whom brought acceptable dowries. The Burgoynes were people of consequence in Bedfordshire but inconsiderable in national terms.

John Burgoyne, who was to lead an army to Saratoga, was born in Westminster on 4th February 1722, and was first cousin to the sixth baronet. His father, also John, was a captain in the army and the second son of the third baronet. Captain John Burgoyne married Anna Maria Burnestone, the beautiful daughter and co-heiress of a substantial London merchant. Her estate, however, was quickly dissipated by her husband, who was a lifelong and unfortunate gambler.

At young John's christening one of his godfathers was Lord Bingley,[2] whose wife, a malicious lady, put it about that her husband was the true father of the child. This piece of ill-natured tittle-tattle was enthusiastically retailed by Horace Walpole although the grounds for it were flimsy in the extreme. Those who knew Anna Maria Burgoyne thought it out of character and the rest of the Burgoyne family certainly treated him as if he were legitimate.[3] When Lord Bingley died in 1731, he left Mrs Burgoyne a legacy which enabled his godson to be sent to school at Westminster. Without this windfall there would have been no chance of going to so influential a school, for the unlucky Captain Burgoyne ended his days as a debtor within the Rules of the King's Bench Prison.

Westminster was one of the turning points of Burgoyne's life. The school was then at the zenith of its influence and provided a high proportion of the men who were to rule England and to command her fleets and armies until the end of the century. A few decades later Eton was to supplant Westminster as the nursery of English statesmen, but Eton never achieved the pre-eminence which Westminster held in the days of the Whig supremacy. For centuries the school had had close links with the Court and members of both houses of parliament sent their sons there at a time before the upper classes found it preferable to send them to boarding schools. In any mid-eighteenth century House of Commons at least one member in six would be an Old Westminster[4] and the proportion would be as high in the Lords.

When John Burgoyne went there in 1733, Lord George Germain (then Sackville) had just left, but his contemporaries included Lord Howe (who trained the original light infantry and was to be killed at Ticonderoga in 1758), Robert Monckton, who was to be Wolfe's second in command at Quebec, Thomas Gage, the future Commander in Chief in North America, and Edward Harvey, who was to be Adjutant General at the same time. Of the naval commanders who were to take prominent parts in the American war there were John Byron, Augustus Hervey and Augustus Keppel. Only one of the cabinet who were to send Burgoyne to America were actually at

Westminster with him, Lord Gower, Lord President from 1767 to 79, but Lord Rochfort, who held the two old Secretaryships of State in succession, had a brother there, and Lord Barrington, the Secretary at War, a future son-in-law. Of those who were to be prominent on the opposition benches were William Dowdeswell, later Lord Rockingham's Chancellor of the Exchequer, and Edward Maskelyne, who married Robert Clive's sister. Nor were the arts unrepresented. Burgoyne was at school with Roger Newdigate, who gave his name to the poetry prize, and with Thomas Sheridan, who was to become the proprietor of Drury Lane Theatre and the father of Richard Brinsley Sheridan. Another contemporary was the eldest son[5] of the 11th Earl of Derby. Although he was six years Burgoyne's senior their acquaintance was to have a major influence on the younger man's life.

Six years after leaving Westminster, Burgoyne was gazetted as a cornet of dragoons on 23rd April 1744. It is unlikely that he purchased this commission as there seems to have been no source from which he could have obtained the necessary £600. As it happened, the date of his cornetcy coincided with an augmentation of one cornet in every troop in the dragoon regiments serving on the continent. There were thus thirty-six free cornetcies available and it is probable that he received one of these.[6] Ten months later he was promoted lieutenant in the First (Royal) Dragoons. It seems unlikely that he purchased this vacancy either. He succeeded a Lieutenant James Surtees, and since that officer had taken five years to progress from cornet to lieutenant if is more than probable that he was promoted by seniority and would not have a purchased commission to sell. Burgoyne may, by this time, have acquired enough "interest" to press his claim to this vacancy but since, unlike most of his cavalry contemporaries, he took a keen interest in his profession, he would have been the kind of young man who would be recommended for promotion by patronage.

He did not reach his regiment in time to take part in the Fontenoy campaign, and soon after the battle the Royals were called home to deal with the Forty Five rebellion although they arrived too late to see active service. They did not return to the continent, although the war there continued until 1748. Instead, they were stationed on or near the south coast of England, guarding against a French invasion which never came.

During this time in the south of England, Burgoyne bought a captaincy in the Royals.[7] How he financed the transaction is unknown, but since he was an accomplished card player it may be the result of a successful coup at the gaming table. The officer from whom he purchased had not bought any of his ranks and was being permitted to sell as an indulgence after forty-four years of service.[8] He would not, therefore, be in a position to ask for more than the regulated price of £2,000.

In the next year, 1748, the regiment was sent north to suppress riots among unemployed weavers at Preston in Lancashire. Preston is within easy visiting distance of Lord Derby's seat at Knowseley. While calling on his school friend Lord Stanley, Burgoyne would have met his youngest sister, Lady Charlotte Stanley. The two fell in love, but the Earl and Countess of Derby did not regard a captain of dragoons with a penchant for gambling and not a penny beyond his pay as a suitable husband for their daughter. They forbade the match but in 1751 the couple eloped and got married.[9]

By that time Europe had been at peace for three years and there had been drastic cuts in the army. The Royal Dragoons had had their establishment cut from 500 to 285 all ranks. Their duties were "aid to the civil power" and "preventative duty"—patrolling the coast in the hope of catching smugglers. This meant that serious training was impossible. Seldom as much as a troop (about forty all ranks) was quartered in the same place. It was a disheartening situation for a young officer keen on his profession and anxious for distinction.

The Royals were posted to Scotland at about the time Burgoyne was married. Their task was to harry smugglers in the Firth of Forth, a notorious paradise for contraband. It was dreary duty for a troop commander and the Burgoynes were pinched for money. The Derby family had cut Lady Charlotte off without a shilling and Burgoyne's pay, fifteen shillings and sixpence a day, was far from sufficient for a high spirited couple. They decided to sell out of the army and live on the proceeds.

It was a good time to sell. Ten complete regiments had been disbanded at the peace and the displaced officers were pursuing rare openings to return to full pay. Vacancies were at a premium. It seems probable that Lieutenant Robert Winde, Tenth Dragoons, who succeeded to Burgoyne's troop in the Royals on 31st October 1751, paid more than the regulation price.

Soon afterwards Mr John and Lady Charlotte Burgoyne set out for the continent in search of cheap living. For a time they lived near Chanteloup in France, where they made friends with the young Comte de Stainville, later to become Duc de Choiseul and one of the greatest chief ministers of France in the eighteenth century. In his company they visited Rome where Burgoyne was painted by Allan Ramsay, the Scot who was to become portrait painter to George III.[10]

The Peace of Aix-la-Chapelle in 1748 had been no more than a European truce. Hostilities between Britain and France scarcely stopped in India, the West Indies and, above all, in Canada. In 1754 Colonel George Washington, while trying to resist French encroachments near Fort Duquesne, was forced to surrender to overwhelming strength at Fort Necessity. The British parliament voted a large increase to the army and in July 1755 General Braddock and his force met disaster on the Monongahela river.

War between France and Britain was not declared until May 1756, and by that time Burgoyne was back in London trying to get back into the army. On 14th June he was gazetted a captain in the Eleventh Dragoons, with a private promise of better things to come. Such reinstatement was unusual but by no means unprecedented. It may have been achieved through the influence of Lord Derby, who was by this time reconciled to his son-in-law, and it was almost certainly Stanley money which purchased the captaincy. There was some resentment in the army that Burgoyne should have been able to move straight back to a captaincy, although he had four years service in the rank, but there can be nothing discreditable in a man wishing to offer his services on the outbreak of war and, as a good and conscientious officer, the resentment would be more widespread among those who had hoped to purchase the same commission than among those who served under him. After two years with the Eleventh he was promoted to the Coldstream Guards as Captain Lieutenant.[11] Although his regimental rank was still only captain, the system of double rank in the Foot Guards meant that he had the rank of lieutenant colonel in the army and was thus liable to automatic promotion to the higher ranks with the mere passage of time.

Burgoyne did not have to wait long before seeing active service with the Coldstream, even if it was not of a very encouraging kind. The Duke of Wellington used to remark in later life that on his first campaign "I learned what one ought not to do, and that is always something." Burgoyne's first campaign gave him very much the same opportunity.

The elder Pitt, while being a great and effective war leader, had some unsatisfactory strategic quirks. One of them was believing that he could derange the French war machine by making large scale raids on the French coast, thereby diverting French troops from Germany and Canada. In September 1757 he had mounted an abortive operation against Rochefort. Nine months later he sent thirteen thousand against the Cotentin peninsula under the (third) Duke of Marlborough and Lord George Sackville. A few ships were burned near St Malo but the only other result was a good deal of ill-feeling between the naval and military commanders[12] and a number of vague accusations of timidity against the generals who were, in fact, only deserving of sympathy since they were totally without information about French dispositions. Pitt, however, was determined to renew the attempt but Marlborough and Sackville refused to take part in any more pointless buccaneering and were transferred to Germany, the raiding command being given to Lieutenant General Thomas Bligh, aged seventy three.

Burgoyne's unit, 1st Battalion, Coldstream Guards, had been ordered on the first expedition and on 9th May 1758 marched from the Tower of

London for the Isle of Wight. The journey took seven days, including a day's halt on the Sunday. Each night the troops camped on common land halting places being Esher, Ripley, "Godalmin", Petersfield and Southsea. Since there was no regimental transport, eighteen wagons had to be hired for the baggage and stores. For the long march from London to Southsea each wagon cost a shilling a mile, but from Southsea Common to "the place of embarkation for the Isle of Wight", the contractors charged 3/6d a mile. The battalion was camped for the Saturday and Sunday nights on Southsea Common where there was no water. A contractor had to be paid a guinea to bring enough for the battalion's needs. They crossed the Solent on 15th May and encamped at Newport, IoW, and it was here that Burgoyne joined them and took charge of the Colonel's company. They sailed on the St Malo raid in June (the contractors charging 5/- a wagon for the five mile journey from Newport to Cowes) and soon returned to Newport without having landed in France.

They sailed again at the end of July and, escorted by a naval squadron under Commodore Richard Howe, Bligh's force, twelve battalions of infantry and nine troops of dragoons, arrived off Cherbourg on 6th August. A French force of three thousand men was in the vicinity, but the Guards and the grenadier companies of the infantry of the line landed and drove them away. There was no further resistance and the whole force was put on shore. The docks, shipping and harbour defences of Cherbourg were destroyed and the troops indulged in an orgy of looting. They were re-embarked on 16th August.

Bligh's orders were to go next to Morlaix, thirty-five miles east of Brest, but he had been given discretion to attack other ports if Morlaix seemed un-propitious. He decided to attack St Malo from the landward side, possibly because strong westerly winds prevented the fleet from going towards Mor-laix. It was a most unwise choice. The attack on Cherbourg could only have brought French reinforcements marching towards that town. They would have to pass close by St Malo and would be available to resist him.

On 3rd September the fleet came into the bay of St Lunaire, twelve miles east of St Malo. It took three days to land the army in steadily worsening conditions, several men being lost in the surf. When the last man was ashore the commodore told Bligh that St Lunaire was unsafe for the ships. He pro-posed moving to the shelter of the bay of St Cast, ten miles away.

The army started its march to St Cast on the morning of 7th September. There were a few small parties of French troops who were swept away by the advance guard. The rest of the British army pillaged relentlessly. At dusk the leading troops came to the banks of the river Equeron. Bligh ordered the advance guard to ford it at six o'clock on the following morning, regardless of the fact that that was the time of high tide. The army was not across until the middle of the afternoon and no further progress was made that day. Another day's marching on 9th September brought them to Matignon from where Bligh sent his engineers to reconnoitre the beach at St Cast. It consisted, according to Burgoyne of "a circular bay, about an English mile in extent; the right is bounded by a steep hill, with a village on top; the left by a range of high rocks, which stretched a considerable distance into the sea. On the top of the beach ran a breastwork, cannon proof, that had been formerly thrown up to oppose a descent [from the sea]; beyond that was a plain of about a quarter of a mile, terminated by a range of hills on the side of which were two [redoubts] and the village of St Cast."

Next day at Matignon Bligh heard that a large French force was moving towards him. He immediately ordered the troops to march to St Cast and sent to the commodore asking him to make arrangements for immediate re-embarkation.

The French commander, the Duke D'Aiguillon, had divided his men into two columns each aiming to get between one of Bligh's flanks and the sea. They very nearly succeeded. As the troops reached the beach,[13] a French column appeared on the hill to the right of the bay. Commodore Howe had brought his frigates and bomb-ketches as close to the shore as he dared, to give fire support to the troops. As soon as the soldiers appeared on the beach, the boats of the fleet came to the shore to begin the embarkation. First, the dragoons went on board; then the infantry of the line. The rearguard consisted of the three battalions of Guards and nine grenadier companies. Under General Drury they manned the breastwork to cover the embarkation of the rest. Burgoyne wrote that, "about nine o'clock our bombs [ketches] began firing, and the first shells that were thrown took effect on the top of the hill with some success. When the enemy began to descend, which was about nine o'clock, the frigates gave him their broadsides and from this moment it was a continual fire till the whole affair was over. About ten the enemy opened a battery of cannon on top of the hill which did not hurt us much."

This French battery was, in fact, not firing at the rearguard but at the ships' boats in the bay, which caused havoc. It was only the example of the commodore and his officers which kept the sailors at their oars. Meanwhile the Coldstream held the right of the breastwork. Burgoyne and a brother officer saw "a very large body of the enemy pushing with great expedition upon the hill on the right, in the intention to flank us. Of this we immediately informed the generals, but received no orders how to act, and were obliged to determine on our own authority to wheel the divisions[14] we commanded to front the enemy. A short time afterwards I received orders to lead 300 men up the hill, but this was countermanded before I had got forty yards, and the whole battalion was ordered to occupy the rocks upon the left, towards which another column of the enemy was advancing."

By eleven o'clock the main body of the army was on board and Drury began to thin out the rearguard, sending the Coldstream and Third Guards to the boats. The First Guards and the grenadier companies of the line continued to hold the breastwork and for a time their musketry and the broadsides of the frigates kept the French back. Some of the remaining Guards were embarked but, as Burgoyne saw from the deck of a transport, the enemy "advanced with great resolution, and the ammunition of our men being wholly expended, they were obliged to quit the breastwork. From that moment all was confusion. Our men ran up to the neck in the sea; some pushed to the rocks in the sea; but the French had now gained the opposite side of the breastwork, where they were safe from the fire of the ships, and able to fire upon our defenceless men." General Drury was killed and the final remnant, about four hundred men, surrendered. The expedition as a whole lost seven hundred and fifty, killed, wounded and missing.

Pitt was hard put to it to claim this operation as a success. The guns captured at Cherbourg were paraded through Hyde Park and lodged in the Tower of London, but the French, although they censured their general for not capturing the whole of Bligh's force, were proclaiming a victory and had the spoils of war to prove it. Bligh was blamed for his conduct and deprived of his colonelcy of the Fifth Dragoon Guards, but the fault was really Pitt's for sending a septuagenarian with no military virtues except courage on so ill-conceived an expedition. Pitt, however, was always on the look out for promising young officers and, after his resourceful conduct at St Cast, Burgoyne was marked for promotion. In the following year it was decided to raise two regiments of light dragoons and he was appointed to the command of one of them.

Historians have uniformly assumed that Burgoyne was appointed Lieutenant Colonel Commandant[15] of the Sixteenth Light Dragoons through his family and political influence. The facts do not bear this out. By 1759 he was fully reconciled to his father-in-law but the political influence of the 11th Earl of Derby was very limited. The Lord Lieutenancy of Lancashire was almost hereditary in the family but outside that county the Stanleys were of far less consequence than they became in the following century. Their parliamentary influence was small. The earl could count on putting a kinsman into one of the two county seats for Lancashire but nine more years were to pass before they could command a single borough seat. This was far from sufficient to earn from ministers a "gratification" as substantial as the command of a regiment. On the Burgoyne side of the family, the only "interest" was that his step-cousin once removed was a Junior Lord of the Treasury. This would not have been enough to secure the command of a regiment, particularly in 1759 when Pitt was insisting on using the military patronage for military ends. It is far more probable that Pitt appointed Burgoyne to the Sixteenth because he recognised in him a serious student of soldiering who could show initiative in action.[16] This supposition is strenthened by the appointment to the command of the other new dragoon regiment of George Augustus Eliott, later Lord Heathfield, the "penniless son of a border baronet", who had no political interest whatsoever.

On 4th August 1759 George II sent to "our trusty and well loved" John Burgoyne, a beating order. "Whereas we have thought fit to order a Regiment of Light Dragoons to be raised forthwith under your command, which is to consist of four troops of three sergeants, three corporals, two drummers and seventy-one privates in each troop, besides commissioned officers, which men are to be entitled to their discharge in three years, or at the end of the war; These are to authorise you by beat of drum or otherwise so many volunteers in any county or kingdom of Great Britain as shall be wanting to compleat the said regiment to the above numbers. And all magistrates, Justices of the Peace, constables, and such others of our civil officers whom it may concern, are hereby required to be assisting unto you in providing quarters, impressing carriages, and otherwise as there shall be occasion."

The men were to be between eighteen and thirty years old and at least five foot four inches tall. Levy money at three guineas a head was to be paid to each recruit. To avoid unfair competition with other regiments who were in the market for recruits, it was forbidden to offer more than three guineas, as some rich colonels were tempted to do. "His Majesty has been pleased to direct that the pay of the regiment shall take place from the date of this beating order; and shall be allowed to you in aid of recruiting, on condition that you do render an exact account of the said levy money and pay that shall be issued by you, charging against it five guineas[17] for each man reviewed and approved, together with the subsistence of the non-commissioned officers and private men from the day of their respective attestations; and if there should be any balance remaining it is to be considered as a saving to the public. . . . It is required that the regiment shall be actually raised and approved (after being reviewed by a general officer) within four months hereto."[18]

Apart from the experience, lasting only five months, of the Fifteenth under Eliott, the raising of a light dragoon regiment was new for the British army.[19] Until that time the cavalry had consisted of regiments of horse and regiments of dragoons. The ostensible difference between these two categories were that horse always fought mounted while dragoons were supposed to dismount when necessary and fight as infantry. The actual distinctions were minimal since dragoons in any army have always shown a marked disinclination to fight on their feet and insist on considering themselves as full-blown cavalry. In Britain this tendency had been strengthened by a decision taken in 1746 that all but one of the regiments of Horse should be converted into dragoons.[20] The reason for this change was, as usual, economy, since dragoons were paid at a lower rate and rode less expensive horses. Naturally the converted regiments did everything they could to recover their lost status (and pay) and became more than ever reluctant to undertake the duties of mounted infantry. The existing dragoon regiments followed their example.

Light dragoons were intended to be the eyes of the army, undertaking reconnaissance and foraging raids in advance of the main body. Their horses were smaller than those of dragoons, being between fourteen hands three inches and fifteen hands one inch. Their horse furniture was correspondingly lighter. The light dragoon's principal weapon was "a short cutting sword, 34 inches long in the blade, with a light hilt without a basket." He also carried "a sort of carbine . . . with a bayonet but no sling; the carbine carried in a bucket.[21] In the left holster he had a pistol while on the right of the saddle was "either an ax, hedging bill or spade." The carbine was twenty-nine inches in the barrel, seventeen inches shorter than the normal infantry musket, and like the pistol, fired a ball which weighed 1/34th of a pound, compared to infantry balls which weighed 1/14th. Each light dragoon carried sixty-four rounds and each troop was allowed $11\frac{1}{2}$ barrels of powder annually for exercise, enough for each man to fire about 250 rounds. It was laid down that, unlike horse or dragoon, they were to be instructed in firing both carbines and pistols from the saddle at the walk, trot and gallop. The chance of hitting anything, even at a walk, must have been very slight.

Burgoyne realised that, if light dragoons were to act successfully, all ranks must be able to think for themselves. On forming the regiment he issued to his officers a "Code of Instructions" not "as the orders of the commanding officer, but as the sentiments of a friend, partly borrowed and partly formed upon the observation and practice."

He started from the premise that, "English soldiers are to be treated as thinking beings." There are, he wrote, "two systems which, generally speaking, divide the disciplinarians; the one is that of *training men like spaniels, by the stick*; the other, after the French, of *substituting the point of honour in place of severity*. The followers of the first are for reducing the nature of man as low as it will bear. Sight, hearing and feeling are the only senses necessary, and all qualities of reasoning become not only useless but troublesome. The admirers of the latter, who more commonly argue more from speculation than practice, are for exalting rationality, and they are commonly deceived in their expectations. The Germans are the best; the French, by the avowal of their own officers, the worst disciplined troops in Europe. I apprehend a just medium between the two extremes to be the surest means to bring English soldiers to perfection."

It followed from this that the regiment's officers must take every opportunity for "getting insight into the character of each particular man and proportioning accordingly the degree of punishment and encouragement". Neither officers nor non-commissioned officers were permitted to swear at their men since it would be "faulty, if for no other reason than it is condemned by the Articles of War". Officers were enjoined to treat their men in a friendly, kindly fashion while avoiding familiarity. "There are, however, occasions, such as during stable or fatigue duty, when officers may slacken the reins so far as to talk with soldiers; nay even a joke may be used without harm but to good purpose." Cavalry officers of the time would have been surprised not so much at the idea that they might crack jokes with their men as at the implication that they should actually be present at stable or fatigue duty.

When not on parade, the officers were to treat each other as equals. "Any restraint upon conversation, unless when an offence against religion, morals or good breeding is in question, is grating and . . . it ought to be the characteristic of every gentleman neither to impose nor submit to any distinction, but such as propriety of conduct or superiority of talent naturally create."

Burgoyne was also concerned with the education of his officers. "A short space of time given to reading each day, if the books are well chosen and the subject properly digested, will furnish a great deal of instruction. To those who do not understand French, I would recommend a serious and assiduous application until they attain it. The best modern books upon our profession are written in that language, and in foreign service gentlemen will find themselves at a great loss if they do not both write and speak it readily. I should be sorry, nevertheless, to engage them so far in that pursuit as to neglect the study of our native language. An officer ought to write English with swiftness and accuracy."

Any officer with a talent for drawing was urged to put it to use. "I would recommend him to practice taking views from an eminence and to measure distances with his eye. This would be a talent peculiarly adapted to a light dragoon." Nor should mathematics be neglected. "From the contempt of figures, numberless inconveniences arise. I mention, as one of the most trivial, a false return which officers will continually sign if they trust the figure part to a sergeant . . . One great advantage which attends an application to this science is that it strongly exercises the mind, and common reading becomes a relaxation after it."

Above all the officers must study horsemastership. "How frequently may we see, even in old and celebrated regiments (at least in parties which have not

been looked over by a field officer or a riding master), bits ill-fitted, accoutrements slovenly put on, twisted stirrups, saddles out of their place, &c., while
the officer at their head, exactly equipped and a good rider, is wholly un-
conscious of anything amiss." To avoid this, "let every officer make himself
thoroughly acquainted with every part of the accoutrements, consider the
parts they severally serve, and look critically over every man at the troops'
parade. I recommend officers sometimes to accoutre and bridle a horse themselves till they are thoroughly acquainted with the use of each strap and
buckle. I submit to the consideration of those who may possibly think such
an employment a degradation, whether a reproof from a field officer or, what
is perhaps worse, a criticism from a judicious spectator, would not give them
more pain . . . The other points necessary to constitute a horseman, in my
sense of the word, and not at all below the attention of a gentleman, are a
competent knowledge of farriery, and, what might be reckoned a branch of
it, feeding horses for health and business."

There is little in the Code of Instructions which would be remarkable to a
cavalry officer of the twentieth century, but in the middle of the eighteenth
century much of the advice was revolutionary. The concept of the soldier as
a "thinking being" and the insistence on the practical and theoretical education of the officer were far ahead of the time. Forty years later Sir John
Moore was hailed as an innovator for instilling the same sentiments into the
light infantry. It is clear that the Code was not the production of some dilettante officer raised to command by political favour, but of a professional who
had studied his trade and was determined to make his regiment a model to the
army.

Burgoyne's officers were not only expected to study their duties, they were
expected to attend to them. By his insistence on this point the colonel made
an enemy whose malice and literary facility has done much to harm his
reputation. One of his first troop commanders was Edward Walpole, who
became regimental major in 1763. He obtained a year's leave direct from the
King "upon a promise of attendance for an equal space of time". He had,
however, scarcely returned to the regiment when he induced Lord Townshend, then Lord Lieutenant of Ireland, to apply for him as an additional
aide-de-camp. Burgoyne had served under Townshend and knew him well.
Nevertheless, ambitious officers did not lightly refuse requests from senior
ministers. He accused Walpole of making "a sinecure of the post which
ought to be the most active in the army". He told the Lord Lieutenant that
he hoped Walpole would reconsider his application for the post but, if he did
not, "I have only to hope that he may speedily find under your Lordship's
patronage a rank more worthy of his attention, and that an opening may be
made in my regiment for a major whose views of future preferment will rest

upon a diligent discharge of a present trust." Such an uncompromising answer was far from the work of a time-serving officer, dependent on political considerations for his advancement. It did, however, earn Burgoyne the dislike of Horace Walpole, a man who never forgot a slight to a relation. The diarist's comments on Burgoyne have been quoted against him ever since.

Burgoyne's teaching and attention to detail soon resulted in the Sixteenth Light Dragoons becoming one of the outstandingly well-trained regiments in the British cavalry. It became one of the pleasures of George II, in the months before he died, to ride out and see them exercising. In 1760 they were warned for service in Germany but Pitt decided that, instead, they should form part of a force of eight thousand men for another of his favourite raids against the French coast. The operation was postponed until the following year and was eventually mounted against Belleisle, forty miles off St Nazaire. In the event, only two troops of the Sixteenth were ordered to accompany the expedition but Burgoyne, despite his wife's pleas, insisted on accompanying them as a volunteer. The raid was successful and the island fell at a cost to the British of seven hundred casualties. The part the Sixteenth played in this operation is obscure. The campaign consisted of scaling a cliff path and the siege of a fortress, neither of them functions for which light dragoons are particularly well suited, but the regiment must have seen some fighting since one of the troop commanders was killed in action.

In the following year Burgoyne got a real chance of distinguishing himself. In March 1762, the French and Spanish ambassadors in Lisbon presented an ultimatum to the King of Portugal. They demanded that he declare war on England. Trusting in the long standing Anglo-Portuguese alliance, the Portuguese rejected the demand and called on Britain for troops. To the Royal Navy the all-weather port of Lisbon was as important in 1762 as it was when Napoleon made similar demands to Portugal forty-six years later. An army of six battalions and Burgoyne's Light Dragoons, 7,164 all ranks, was despatched with reasonable speed and reached Lisbon early in June.[22]

The military situation was far from promising. Three heavy columns of Spanish and French troops were invading Portugal. In the north one column had seized Traz os Montes and was threatening Oporto. In the centre, the border fortress of Almeida had fallen. The southern column, fourteen thousand men under Count de Aranda, was preparing to move on Lisbon down the Tagus. For the defence of Portugal there were, apart from the seven thousand British, sixty thousand Portuguese troops, newly raised, untrained, badly officered and, in some parts of the country, disaffected against their own government. Fortunately the Commander in Chief was a German officer of talent, Count Wilhelm of Schaumberg-Lippe-Bückeburg.

Count La Lippe (as he was known in Portugal) was a very remarkable man. His father had been the son of George I and the Duchess of Kendall, and he had started his military career in the British Life Guards with whom he had fought at Dettingen. He then transferred to the Imperial army and fought with both them and, later, the Prussians. After the Peace of Aix la Chapelle in 1747 he retired to his tiny sovereign state in Germany, where he established a military academy for the training of artillery and engineer officers. At the outbreak of the Seven Years War he served as commander of the Hanoverian artillery and was promoted to the command of all Prince Ferdinand of Brunswick's guns. Appointed to Portugal with the rank of Marshal in 1762, he found the native troops in a most unsatisfactory state. His opinion of the Portuguese artillery was made clear when he offered a prize to any officer who could, with a round shot, hit the central pole of his tent while he, the Marshal, was dining inside it.

According to Scharnhorst, who was later his pupil at Bückeburg, La Lippe was a military genius and he needed all his talents in his desperate situation. He recognised Burgoyne as one of the men who could help to extricate him. Promoting him Brigadier General, he gave him a force of three thousand men. Two-thirds of them were Portuguese and the remainder consisted of the Sixteenth Light Dragoons and six British grenadier companies. Burgoyne's orders were to check the southern Spanish columns before they could emerge into the plains of the Alentejo. He was given absolute discretion as to how he should act and promised La Lippe's discretion should his plans miscarry. "The count ordered him, if pushed, to secure his cavalry and retire only when it was no longer possible for him to stay; but he added that, whatever might happen, he would take the measure upon himself, and General Burgoyne had only to persevere and be confident of his [the count's] protection."

Burgoyne made his objective the main Spanish supply depot at Valencia de Alcantara, sixteen miles south of the Tagus and just inside the Spanish border. Valencia lies in a plain bounded on the west by the heights of Peta-ranha over which ran the road, such as it was, into Portugal. There were two other approaches to the town. To the north-east ran the road to Alcantara, De Arando's link with the Spanish centre column at Almeida; to the south there was a road to Albuquerque and Badajoz. Burgoyne planned to block all three roads and burst into the town from the west. "I was informed that the patrols were not regular, nor at a distance; that there were no advanced piquets, no barricadoes, and that the only guard was in the great square." This information was comforting but suspect. Somewhere around Valencia there was known to be a Spanish army of fourteen thousand men and the reputation of the Spanish army still stood high.

Dividing his men into three units, Burgoyne sent Portuguese troops, supported by detachments of the Sixteenth, to block the roads to Alcantara and Albuquerque. The British grenadiers were to march against the Petaranha gate and storm the town at first light, while the two Portuguese units demonstrated against the walls to divert the enemy's attention.

This was a bold plan but it was never put to the test. When Burgoyne and the grenadiers were still four miles from Valencia it became clear that dawn would break before the troops were in position. The Portuguese guides "had greatly deceived me with regard to the distance; they assured me at Petaranha I had an hour of darkness more that I wanted and pressed me to stay longer to avoid falling in with the patrols which, they said, retired a little before day." A quick decision was essential. It would be too late to get the Portuguese troops back to the cover of the hills before dawn broke and, once they were seen, all chance of surprise would be lost.

"I thought it therefore expedient to lay aside my first disposition and carry forward the light dragoons, who might possibly effect a surprise or, at worst stop up the avenues [of escape]. I accordingly went with that corps at three quarters speed without molestation and the advanced guard, consisting of forty men led by Lieutenant Lewis, finding the entrance clear, pushed into the town, sword in hand. The guard in the square were all killed before they could use their arms, and the ends of the streets were possessed with very little resistance. By the time the body of the regiment was formed in the square, a few desperate parties attempted an attack, but all perished or were taken. The only firing that remained was in single shots from windows, which did not continue long after the grenadiers came up . . . I detached the dragoons into the country to pick up all who escaped; they brought in a good many horses."

The prisoners included a Spanish general and his ADC, a colonel and his adjutant, two captains and seventeen subalterns. The Regiment of Seville was shattered and the depot of stores, arms and ammunition destroyed. De Aranda's advance was delayed by three months. The King of Portugal gave Burgoyne a diamond ring and Marshal La Lippe reported to the British government on "the remarkable valour, conduct and presence of mind of Brigadier Burgoyne . . . It is my duty to mention this officer as an excellent one and extremely worthy of his Majesty's remembrance."

Valencia de Alcantara made Burgoyne a public hero in England, a status that was reinforced when troops under his command won another creditable little victory at Vila Velha four months later. It also showed that he was a commander of talent and initiative, a point underlined by La Lippe who not only recommended him to London but consistently trusted him with independent commands. The Marshal was unlikely to have put his confidence in a man promoted for political and family reasons. While the campaign was in progress, Burgoyne was complaining bitterly to London that promotion was being given for political reasons to his own disadvantage. When a brevet of colonels was announced, he wrote to the Secretary at War that, "the government thinks proper to allow family weight and protection to take place [i.e. to decide who should be promoted] rather than military merit."

Valencia, however, decided the matter. He was made colonel in the army in a special brevet on 8th October and when, in March 1763, it was decided that the Sixteenth Light Dragoons was to be a permanent regiment on the peace establishment, he became colonel of the regiment.

CHAPTER 4

Honourable and Gallant Member

Before Burgoyne first led the Sixteenth Light Dragoons into action he had started a second career as a member of Parliament. In the general election of 1761 he was elected to the House of Commons as one of the members for Midhurst. The little town of Midhurst in Sussex was not quite a rotten borough. The franchise was in the hands of about a hundred burgage holders, men who held certain buildings and plots of land. Almost all the burgage holders were dependent for their tenure of employment on two men, the 7th Viscount Montagu and Sir William Peere Williams, Bart. Lord Montagu was a Catholic so that he could not use the seat for his own relations. He was also notoriously extravagant and, to make ends meet, leased the right to nominate one member for Midhurst to the Prime Minister in return for a pension of £1,000 a year. The government's candidate, who was duly elected, was a Mr William Hamilton, who resigned the seat after three years to take up a diplomatic appointment in Naples. He became famous as an antiquarian, a student of volcanoes and as the husband of Nelson's Emma. Sir William Williams bestowed his seat on Lieutenant Colonel John Burgoyne under whom Sir William was serving as a captain in the Sixteenth. Thus Burgoyne owed his introduction to Parliament neither to court favour nor to the patronage of the Stanley family, but to the generosity and admiration of one of his own officers.

It was not until the end of the Portuguese campaign that Burgoyne was able to take his seat. On one of his first attendances he received the thanks of the House, voted both to him and his regiment, for the victory at Valencia de Alcantara. Apart from this he seems to have taken his parliamentary duties lightly. He devoted himself to the care of his regiment, now known as the Queen's Regiment of Light Dragoons, and to social life. Both he and Lady Charlotte were favourites at Court, and Burgoyne also mixed with artists and actors, being a friend of both Reynolds and Garrick. He was a member of Brook's, where he indulged his hereditary love of gambling and made friends with Charles James Fox, and was a regular visitor to the Green Room at Drury Lane.

Although, unlike his father, Burgoyne was both skilled and fortunate at gambling, the young couple were habitually short of money. It is difficult to live a fashionable life on a pittance and, by the standards of the great territorial families and, even more by the standards of the Nabobs back from India, a pittance was all the Burgoynes had. Lady Charlotte now had an allowance from her family, probably of £400 a year. Burgoyne had nothing but his pay. As colonel of a dragoon regiment he received 35/- a day, less than £650 a year. To this was added the pay of one warrant man[1] for each of the four troops in the regiment—an additional £125 a year. The gross pay was subject to a number of deductions such as poundage, agency fee and a day's pay a year towards the upkeep of Chelsea Hospital. Burgoyne's net pay was certainly not more than £675 a year. In addition there was, as has been said, the colonel's financial interest in the clothing of his regiment. Some colonels, particularly those of infantry regiments stationed in remote overseas stations, could and did make a substantial private profit from the clothing account. For the colonel of a smart cavalry regiment stationed in England and constantly under the eye of the Royal Family it was far more probable that the colonel would have to supplement the government grant from his own pocket in order to keep the troops clothed to a standard of which the colonel could be proud.

Perhaps it was to economise that in the summer of 1766 the two Burgoynes set out on a long tour of Europe to visit the battlefields of the last war and to study the main armies of Europe. The colonel had with him a letter of introduction from William Pitt to Prince Ferdinand of Brunswick, the much admired commander of the Anglo-German army from 1757 to 1762. Pitt said that the letter was hardly necessary—"a letter which General Burgoyne[2] could little want to a Prince well informed of all actions of *éclat* throughout the whole theatre of the late extended war, and which is sure to be well received from the hand that is to deliver it." Flattery it might be to some degree but it was not the kind of compliment that Pitt would have paid to one of whom he had no high opinion. He added his hope that Burgoyne would, "agreeably to yourself, and usefully to your country, add to the rich stock of military treasures already your own, fresh matter of future contemplation and of future action."

Having visited Brunswick, the Burgoynes moved on to Berlin to see "the best of the Prussian army" and from there to Dresden which they used as a centre from which to visit the battlefields of Frederick the Great, "tracing the positions and marches of both armies during the different periods of the late war". They went to Prague and saw Kolin where Frederick had been so heavily defeated in 1759 but, after that, Burgoyne found that the Austrian Emperor had issued an order forbidding foreign officers attending the grand manoeuvres of his army. "To ask leave that had been refused to men of the first rank was in vain; but by a little intrigue, a good deal of perseverance, and perhaps more assurance than I ought to boast of, I have succeeded to be present *incognito* at the practice of the principal manoeuvres."

The fruit of this tour was a memorandum on the three main continental armies which was submitted to Pitt, who in the meanwhile had become Earl of Chatham and had joined the cabinet as Lord Privy Seal. The most interesting parts of the memorandum are those dealing with the Prussian army, that being the force with the highest contemporary reputation and the one on which, thanks to the Duke of Cumberland, the British army had been largely modelled. "The first principle of the Prussian system is subordination and the maxim 'Not to reason but to obey'. The effects are attention, alertness, precision and every executive quality in the officers which, assisted by the constant exercise of the soldiers upon the soundest principles of tactics, enable the troops to practice with wonderful ease and exactness, manoeuvres that others hardly admit in theory."

Such a system of "Not to reason but to obey" lay diametrically opposed to the principles Burgoyne had laid down in the Code of Instructions for his own regiment and he set out to prove that the Prussian system was dictated by that country's poverty in resources and manpower. "The ranks are filled up, perhaps more than a third part, with strangers, deserters and enemies of various countries . . . The difficulties of recruiting are not to be described. Not only every species of decoy and cajolment, but sometimes violence, is employed to draw men from other countries. Hence the evil of desertion, which in spite of every precaution the genius of man can devise, is supposed to amount in time of peace to nearly the fifth of the army every year. In war it is much more considerable. The army is more harassed with precautionary guards against their own soldiers, than against the enemy . . . In an army thus composed it is wisdom and sound policy to sink and degrade all intellectual faculties, and to reduce the man as nearly as possible to mere machinery, and indeed, as nature has formed the bulk of the King of Prussia's subjects, that task is not very difficult. But it is impossible to close this observation without touching on the mistake of those who prefer this plan, when the disposition of their country offers the best groundwork of national character or publick spirit. The King of Prussia, deprived of such principles to work upon, turns his defects to advantage and substitutes a species of discipline where the mind has no concern; many of his disciples suppose his necessity to be his choice and destroy a great, solid, natural foundation to build upon one merely artificial."[3]

The Austrian army more nearly conformed to Burgoyne's ideas of training troops. "The officers have liberality, the soldiers national spirit . . . In the exercise of arms and the military step the Austrians differ but little from the Prussians; they are not yet arrived at the extraordinary steadiness of the latter under arms, but cannot fail of soon attaining it, with the advantage of seeing their ends compassed with good will and little severity . . . Zeal, emulation and honour . . . will out-go any diligence arising from dread of punishment or other slavish punishment."

In France he was distressed to see that, under the guidance of his old friend the Duc de Choiseul, the Prussian system was being introduced. Discipline had always been light in the French army in the belief that "the French character would bear the old principles of glory and duty to be wound up to a height that would answer the purposes of the strictest disciplinarians." Reactions had set in after the disasters of the Seven Years War. "The want of subordination and discipline has long been supposed the cause of all their misfortunes." In consequence, "the more violent measure is adopted in France, and the Prussian severity of command together with the free use of the stick, is without preparation established among men of impatient spirit habituated to all the prejudices of punctilious honor, and even in the lowest class regarding a blow as an irreparable disgrace . . . Among the common soldiers it is received with repugnance that causes at present an incredible desertion."

Chatham's acknowledgment of this memorandum can leave no doubt that his already high opinion of Burgoyne's military talent had been raised. "Allow me to offer, in one hasty line, more real acknowledgments than the longest letter could contain; and to assure you that I count the minutes while indispensible business deprives me of the pleasure of seeing you. If Wednesday morning next at eleven should suit your convenience, I shall be extremely happy in the honour of seeing you."

Sir William Williams had been killed in action at Belleisle and Burgoyne's seat at Midhurst was no longer available to him at the General Election of 1768. Instead he was invited to stand at Preston in the Stanley interest.

Preston in those days was no more than a substantial market town which was a minor centre for the cottage weaving industry. It was chiefly memorable for being the first town in England at which Prince Charles Edward was cheered on his march to Derby during the Forty Five rebellion. This was largely because there was a substantial Roman Catholic element among the population, there being three Catholic chapels in the constituency. Preston had returned two members to the Commons since the time of the Plantagenets, and in 1661 a parliamentary decision had declared that the franchise resided in "all the inhabitants". Over the years this had come to be taken as meaning that only the inhabitants of those properties which existed in 1661 had the right to vote. This gave an electorate of some 450 who returned a series of old-fashioned Tory members who were probably more genuinely tainted with Jacobitism than the bulk of mid-eighteenth century Tories.

While the Earls of Derby were the pre-eminent family in Lancashire their parliamentary interest was small compared with other great English families. In fact, like the rest of northern England, the representation of Lancashire was small. There were two seats for the county (one of which was usually held by a Stanley) and two each for the boroughs of Clitheroe, Lancaster, Liverpool, Newton, Preston and Wigan. Three of these boroughs were strongly under the influence of other families;[4] Liverpool, where the mercantile influence was paramount, was impossible to dominate; Lancaster, with an electorate of two thousand, would be a very expensive proposition. It seemed that only Preston with its distorted franchise was suitable for conversion into a Stanley family borough. The Earl, therefore, put forward two candidates, Sir Henry Hoghton Bt.,[5] a local landowner, and his own charming and popular son-in-law, Colonel John Burgoyne who had the added attraction that he was a military hero. Both stood under Whig colours.

Against them the Corporation nominated Sir Peter Standish and Sir Frank Leicester, and before the end of the previous year had brought into the town "lawless bands of colliers from the neighbourhood of Chorley" to intimidate those who might vote for the Stanley candidates. The town rang with cries remembered from the Forty Five—"Down with the Rump!" "White Cockades!" "Prince Charles!" "No King George!" "King James!" Prudent householders barricaded their doors, windows were smashed and some houses were demolished. Stanley supporters were beaten in the streets. In retaliation, or self defence, Burgoyne and Hoghton brought in "armed blackguards from Longridge and Ribchester". The mayor was put under the pump in Fishergate and when one of his neighbours remonstrated with the mob, he too was thrown under the pump. Since he was an elderly man and it was a cold February, he died of the experience.

As was usual with eighteenth century mobs, some of the violence turned against the Catholics. St Mary's chapel in Friargate was sacked and that at Cottam seriously damaged. The mob then set out for the remaining chapel at New House but on their way they were detained near Hollowforth Mill by a Protestant friend of the priest who regaled them with bread, cheese and ale, eventually persuading them to go home.

Voting started on 21st March and continued for two weeks. Voters on both sides needed an armed escort as they went to the poll and publicly declared their vote. The hired bully boys of both sides fought constant skirmishes. All Lancashire was scoured by Whig supporters for those who could claim to be freemen of the town but were living elsewhere. One such was a traveller selling dyed hair, a native of Preston but living in Bolton. His name was Richard Arkwright and he had come to Preston in the hope of raising some capital with which to launch the manufacture of a water frame that was to revolutionise the spinning industry. He was to become a knight, a high sheriff and a very rich man, but in March 1768 he was in "so tattered a plight" that a subscription was raised to buy him a suit of clothes lest the Returning Officer should turn him away as a vagrant.

On 2nd April the mayor, who was also Returning Officer and manager of the Tory party machine, announced the result:

Sir Peter Leicester	289
Sir Frank Standish	276
Colonel John Burgoyne	259
Sir Henry Hoghton	239

and that consequently Leicester and Standish were elected.

Immediately there was uproar. According to the Whigs Burgoyne headed the poll with 589 votes and Hoghton was second with 588. They maintained that Leicester and Standish had only 290 and 277 respectively.

Both sides agreed that some pauper voters were ineligible, but the Whigs claimed that the mayor had rejected 328 votes for Hoghton and 330 for Burgoyne, although he had disallowed only one each for their opponents. He had also refused to admit the votes of twice as many non-resident freemen for his opponents as he had for his own party. Moreover, he had admitted the votes, for Leicester and Standish, of twenty-eight papists, while he had disqualified men who voted for their opponents on the grounds that they had been promised out-door relief at the alms houses. One man was disallowed because "he hath laid many wagers that Colonel Burgoyne will be chose". Others he disqualified because they were such dubious residents as "soldiers, militiamen and strolling players".

There was another outbreak of violence. It was said that the Corporation delivered bludgeons to the Town Hall and deprived the town of street lighting so that their hired colliers could roam the streets unobserved. They set aside money to prosecute the opposing thugs and laid an information which resulted in Burgoyne being hauled before the courts, accused of sanctioning "brutal violence". He admitted having gone about Preston with a pair of loaded pistols in his pockets but claimed that they, like the "armed blackguards", were for "protection and defence". It was not until May 1769 in the Court of King's Bench that, according to the Gentleman's Magazine, "Mr Justice Yate, after a most nervous and pathetic speech on the turpitude of riots at elections", fined Burgoyne £1,000. Four of his supporters were fined £100 each and given three months imprisonment while three rioters, "on account of their low circumstances", were sentenced to six months.

Before this the Stanley party was taking steps to have the election result reversed on the grounds that the corporation had illegally restricted the franchise. On 10th November 1768, Burgoyne and Hoghton petitioned the Commons to be declared elected since the Returning Officer had "conducted the poll with the most apparent partiality to the interests of Sir Peter Leicester and Sir Frank Standish, baronets, the other candidates; rejecting, without any good reason assigned, a very great majority of the persons entitled to vote by the constitution of the borough, the last Resolution of the House [1661] and the statutes making such resolution final." On 29th November 1768 the Commons ruled that "the words" all the *inhabitants* "did not mean only the in-burgesses are inhabitants of the said place but all the inhabitants at large".[6]

Burgoyne and Hoghton took their seats in the House early in 1769 and later in the year the King made Burgoyne Governor of Fort William, a sinecure worth £300 a year, which was vacant because of the death of General Henry Kingsley, a veteran of Dettingen and Minden. It was one of about two dozen similar governorships in Britain, ranging from Windsor Castle (£1,120.17.1d) to Scarborough Castle (£15.4.2d), which had no further military significance but which were used to reward distinguished officers. Under George II these posts had frequently been used as part of the political patronage of the government. There were many who believed Burgoyne had been given Fort William as the price of his support for the ministry in the Commons. In fact it was just at this time that George III was doing his best to wrest the military patronage away from the politicians and the strong probability is that Burgoyne was made governor because the King liked him as a person, admired his record as a soldier and knew him to be short of money.

At almost the same time Burgoyne attracted the attention of Junius, the scabrous anonymous letter writer who was then at the height of his notoriety. Junius attacked the Duke of Grafton, then Prime Minister, for having sold the patent for collecting the customs at Exeter for £3,500[7] "to one Mr Hines." The money, Junius claimed, was paid to "Colonel Burgoyne to reward him, I presume for the decency of his deportment at Preston; or to reimburse him, perhaps, for the fine of one thousand pounds which, for that very deportment, the Court of King's Bench thought proper to set on him . . . No man is more tender in his reputation [than Burgoyne]. He is not only nice, but perfectly sore in everything that touches his honour. If any man, for example, were to accuse him of taking his stand at a gaming table and watching, with the soberest attention, for a fair opportunity of engaging a drunken young nobleman at piquet, he would undoubtedly consider it an infamous aspersion upon his character and resent it as a man of honour.— Acquitting him therefore of drawing a regular and splendid subsistence from such unworthy practices, wither in his own house or elsewhere, let me ask your Grace, for what military merits you have been pleased to reward him with a military governorship? He has a regiment of dragoons which one would imagine was at least the equivalent for any services *he* ever performed. Besides he is but a young officer, considering his preferment, and except in his activity at Preston, not very conspicuous in his profession."

In anonymous letters a man is not on oath and there seems to be no reason to take Junius' accusations seriously. The Duke of Grafton may have sold the custom patent, it was neither illegal nor unusual to do so. It seems unlikely that he paid that or any other money to Burgoyne to pay his fine. The Earl of Derby had fought the election at Preston not to support the government but to secure the borough to his own interest. The fine would be one of his election expenses and he was more than able to pay it. As to the insinuation about Burgoyne's card playing, it was too much even for Horace Walpole to swallow. "Junius," he wrote, "was thought to be unjust as [Burgoyne] was never thought to do more than play very well." Moreover, had there been any suspicion that Burgoyne's play was anything but strictly fair, it is un-likely that the most experienced card players of the day would have con-tinued to welcome his presence at the tables at Brook's and elsewhere.

Until 1777 Burgoyne's activities in the House of Commons were very much in the tradition of the independent members. He had been elected under the Whig colours but the Whig party was, by 1769, so fragmented that the label meant little. He aimed to exercise his judgment on each question as it arose but with a general intention to support the King's ministers where he found this possible. "My principles of acting in public lay in a small compass. To assist government in my general line of conduct; but that in great national points, and where the vote of a House of Parliament might lead to important consequences, detrimental or disgraceful in my conviction to the interest of the state, I would ever hold myself at liberty to maintain my own opinion."

Certainly he was no slavish supporter of government. In 1770 the Spaniards seized the small British settlement in the Falkland Islands and, for a time, war with Spain seemed inevitable. Characteristically, North determined to handle the incident in a very low key. He persuaded the Spaniards to blame the seizure on their governor of Buenos Aires and to restore the settlement without touching the complicated and explosive matter of the sovereignty of the islands. In London a bellicose minority, led by the Earl of Chatham, claimed that the agreement was "worse than war" and an affront to the national honour. North, however, had judged the national mood rightly. The necessary naval precautions had already added a shilling to the land tax and the country gentlemen were most reluctant to pay for a war over a remote and infertile island. Burgoyne voted with the minority against the agreement and the King remarked that, "the seeing of Colonel Burgoyne's name on the side of the minority appears so extraordinary that I almost imagine it is a mistake." On another military matter, a bungled expedition against the Caribs of St Vincent, he voted against the government again.

In 1774 the government was defeated on a motion to make perpetual Grenville's Act of 1770 for settling disputed elections. Burgoyne spoke and voted against the ministry. On this occasion Walpole wrote that, "General Burgoyne, a classic scholar, who had more reading than parts, made a set and florid declamation." Hansard, however, reported that he made "a spirited speech". In the lobby while the voting was taking place Burgoyne found himself with such opposition stalwarts as Barré, Burke and Dunning, together with Lord George Germain and both Admiral and General Howe. Charles James Fox acted as teller for the government and Generals Clinton and Conway supported the ministers.

Many historians have sought to prove that Burgoyne was the obedient "tool" of the so-called Court party by quoting a phrase used by the King in 1772. Writing to Lord North he said that North's "attention in correcting the impression I had that Colonel Burgoyne and Lieutenant Colonel Harcourt[8] were absent yesterday is very handsome to those gentlemen; for I should certainly have thought myself obliged to have named a new governor [of Fort William] in the room of the former, and to have removed the other from my Bed-chamber."

The occasion of this letter was one of the votes of the Royal Marriages Bill which restricted the right of members of the Royal Family to marry under the age of twenty-six without the King's consent. Since, in the King's view, this was a matter dealing exclusively with his own family, he believed that Parliament should treat it as a formality. The opposition saw it as an opportunity to denounce ministers' subservience to the Crown. This the King felt to be unforgivable interference with his private affairs and he would have been justly affronted if members of his own Household and those, like Burgoyne, whom he believed to be his personal friends, voted against the Bill. It is interesting to note that Charles Fox resigned from the ministry in protest against the Royal Marriages Act although he had introduced it into the Commons himself.

The greatest sensation Burgoyne made in the Commons before the American war was his intervention on the affairs of the East India Company

In his speech to Parliament in January 1772, the King had said that Indian affairs required the "most vigilant and active attention" and added that if "either for supplying defects or remedying abuses, you shall find it necessary to provide any new laws, you may depend on my ready concurrence."

Most members agreed that the abuses of the East India Company were flagrant and when, two months after the King's speech, North's government had brought in no legislation for remedying them, Burgoyne moved for a Select Committee to consider them. This was agreed without a division although Edmund Burke spoke warmly against the motion, perhaps because he had a brother who was unsuccessfully trying to make a fortune in the Company's service. The Committee, under Burgoyne's chairmanship, sat during the parliamentary recess but it had not completed its deliberations when Lord North, in November, proposed a second, secret, committee on the same subject. Part of the reason for this move was that Burgoyne's committee had been chosen by ballot and included Robert Clive, who could hardly be said to be disinterested.

Although distressed by the creation of North's secret committee, Burgoyne put a good face on his disappointment and supported North's motion. "Could a hundred committees be established they could hardly be equal to the task of investigating the various crimes and misdemeanours, the multiplied evils that lurk in that corrupted body. Why then should I oppose this committee? I will not oppose it; though it seems strange to pass over the enormities of the east, and to institute a minute inquiry into the petty larcenies of Leadenhall."9

In May 1773, Burgoyne opened an attack on the Company and on Clive in particular. He proposed three motions. The first asserted that all conquests in India resulting from Clive's victory at Plassey in 1759 should belong to the Crown. The next laid down that, "to appropriate acquisitions made under the influence of military force, or by treaty, &c., is illegal." The third raised the question of who had benefited from the vast sums paid by native rulers for their protection.

There was a long debate cutting across the usual party lines. The Attorney General and the Solicitor General spoke warmly against each other. Fox supported Burgoyne. Burke defended Clive and the Company. The House was crowded and became intolerably hot from the great numbers of candles which lit it. "The young members," said Walpole, "thought it would melt their rouge and wither their nosegays." They went out to dinner "and returned flushed with wine, growing impatient as the interesting part of the debate was over, they roared for the question". It was eleven o'clock at night before Burgoyne's motions were put to the vote. The first two were carried, the third postponed. "In so tumultuous a fashion was the sovereignty of three

Imperial provinces transferred from the Company to the Crown."

The second motion was a clear censure on Clive, and on 19th May, Burgoyne attacked him directly, accusing him of having acquired a fortune of £234,000, "and that in so doing the said Robert, Lord Clive, abused the powers with which he was entrusted, to the evil example of the servants of the public." There was another acrimonious debate. Fox said that Clive "was the origin of all plunder, the source of all robbery", while Burke, according to the Attorney General, "showered a bright confusion of images" on Clive's defence. Lord North "wavered from censure to encomium", and Clive defended himself with the classic phrase, "Sir, I stand astonished at my own moderation." Again the two law officers took opposite sides and Lord George Germain helped greatly in Clive's defence by drawing "a picture of the doubts Lord Clive must have fluctuated between if, at the outset of the battle of Plassey, he had the Attorney General on the one hand, and the Solicitor General on the other, prompting him to conduct directly opposite."

Wedderburn, the Solicitor General, Clive's chief advocate, took the attack into the enemy's camp. He reminded the House of Junius' attack on Burgoyne and suggested that before Burgoyne started preaching reform, he should mend his own way of life. He added that if Clive had enriched himself by military force, Burgoyne appeared to have carried Preston by the same means. Considering that a writ for libel had been issued against Junius, if he could be identified, it was a highly improper comment for a law officer to make. Walpole, who detested Wedderburn, who was a Scot, even more than Burgoyne, was shocked. "The Court, Lord Mansfield in courts of judicature, every man almost had pronounced the writings of Junius libels. The Attorney General first, the Solicitor General next, are the prosecutors of libels. Here was the aspersions of that writer against the honour of an officer, an officer that had distinguished himself and that was countenanced by the Crown, as matter for a parliamentary exchange against a member of parliament."

Burgoyne replied directly to Wedderburn. "I am now personally marked, and rejoice in the opportunity. I have long groaned in secret for an occasion of venting myself against these scandalous assertions; and if that wretch Junius is lurking here in any corner of this House, I now tell him to his face he is an assassin, a liar and a coward."

At four o'clock in the morning the vote was taken. Clive was vindicated by 153 to 95, and Wedderburn followed up his triumph by putting forward a motion that, "Robert, Lord Clive had rendered great and meritorious service to this country." This was agreed without a division. The feeling of the House was that although Clive was undoubtedly rapacious he was also a hero and had broken the back of French influence in India.

The failure of his attack on Clive was a disappointment to Burgoyne. The most wounding side was that he had been encouraged in the project by Lord North and, although North himself had voted with Burgoyne, most of the ministers and their supporters had voted for Clive. Burgoyne felt that he had been put in a false position and this was particularly humiliating because North was not only a friend but a relation by marriage.[10] For the next two years, "though I bore respect to Lord North's character, no two persons not in direct enmity could live at a greater distance."

In consequence, 1773 and 1774 were quiet years for Burgoyne. He had been promoted Major General by seniority on 25th May 1772, the day on which Thomas Gage, William Howe and Henry Clinton, all his seniors, received the same step. He thus became "the last and humblest on the list of generals", but it brought no increase in pay since there was no employment for him "on the staff". His social life became quieter as Lady Charlotte's health was beginning to deteriorate. He had always been drawn to play-writing and now he took to writing professionally for the stage. When his nephew by marriage, who later became the 12th Earl of Derby, married the daughter of the Duke of Hamilton in 1774, Burgoyne wrote a play for amateur production on the occasion of the wedding. Tidied up by his friend David Garrick the same play, *The Maid of the Oaks*, was produced at Drury Lane in November of that year, with Mrs Abingdon in the lead. Although by modern standards it was not a memorable play, it kept its place in the repertoire, at Drury Lane and in the provinces, for many years and, despite what Horace Walpole said,[11] it achieved a measure of success within a few weeks of the day when Sheridan's *The Rivals* flopped on its first night at the same theatre.

Meanwhile the troubles with the American colonies were growling in the background. Burgoyne took the view of the great majority of his fellow backbenchers. While prepared to agree to all reasonable concessions, there was a limit beyond which he would not go. Appeasement was useless if it led only to fresh demands. When it was proposed, in 1774, to abolish the duty on tea, he spoke late in the debate. "I look upon America to be our spoilt child, which we have already spoiled by too much indulgence. We are desired to conciliate measures by the Americans; I look upon this measure to have a totally different effect; I think it a misuse of time to go into committee [on this proposal], and that even the enquiry, the news of which will soon reach America, will tend to nothing but to raise heats, and not appease, but irritate and disturb the more. It is said, if you remove this duty, you will remove all grievances in America; but I am apprehensive it is the right of taxation they contend about; it is the independent state of that country upon [?from] the legislature of this which is contended for; but I am ready to resist that proposition, and to contend at any future time, against such independence."

It was a well worn theme and on this occasion Burgoyne had left his speech too late. His fellow members agreed with him but wanted to go to bed. "The House seemed very noisy and did not attend. He therefore sat down, concluding that he wished America convinced by persuasion rather than the sword."

PART III

Rebellion

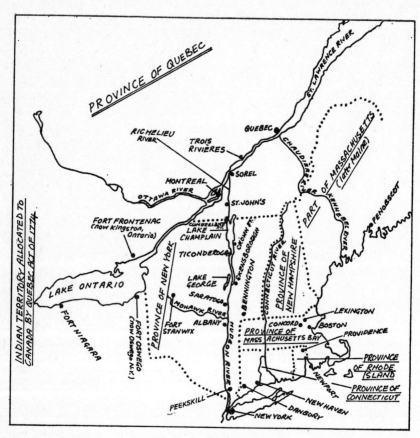

2. The Campaigns of 1775–1776

CHAPTER 5

"A Professional Tragedy"

On 4th September 1774, the Continental Congress held its first meeting in Philadelphia and a week later, hearing the reports of growing disorders in the colonies, the King wrote, "The dye is now cast, the colonies must either submit or triumph; I do not wish to come to severer measures but we must not retreat; by coolness and an unremitted pursuit of the measures that we have adopted I trust that they will come to submit."

The King undoubtedly spoke for the majority of his subjects (who became even more united when they heard of the Congress), but the means of enforcing "the measures we have adopted" were patently insufficient. In Boston there were only four understrength battalions, about 1,500 muskets, and a company of artillery. This little force had no transport and no horses to draw the guns. Parliament, on 29th November, voted to increase the Boston garrison to ten thousand men but a vote of the House of Commons does not create soldiers. All that could be done was to concentrate the whole force in the colonies in Boston and to add to it two battalions from Canada where the governor was confident that they would not be needed. By the spring of 1775 there were eleven battalions in Boston, amounting to less than five thousand rank and file. A few more units were being scraped together and despatched across the Atlantic. No great efforts were being made to enlarge the army. On 15th February, the Secretary at War moved in the Commons that "£67,706 7s 1d be granted for the service of the year 1775 to enable his Majesty to augment his land service with 4,383 men, officers and non-commissioned officers included."

In Boston, holding the offices of Governor of the province of Massachusetts Bay and Commander in Chief in North America was Major General (local Lieutenant General) Thomas Gage, whose family was chiefly memorable for having introduced the greengage into England. He was believed to be a sound man for conciliating the colonials, having married a lady from New Jersey, but he was not the government's first choice for the post. It had been offered to Lieutenant General the Hon. Robert Monckton, who had been second in command to Wolfe at Quebec. Monckton however, had been pre-empted by the East India Company who had offered him the more lucrative post of Commander in Chief, India, which, in fact, he never took up.

Gage was a competent but pedestrian soldier. He had good reason for pedestrianism. He was one of the few men who had been present at both the major British disasters in America—Monongahela river in 1755 and Ticonderoga three years later. George III, who liked him, referred to him as "an honest determined man", but Lord George Germain lamented "that General Gage, with all his good qualitys, finds himself in a situation of too great importance for his talents. The conduct of such a war requires more than common abilities, the distance from the seat of government leaves much to the discretion and resources of the general, and I doubt whether Mr Gage will venture to take a single step beyond the letter of his instructions, and whether the troops will have the opinion of him as to march with confidence of success under his command."

As early as November 1774 it had been suggested that Gage should be superseded. "It was proposed to send out Sir Jeffrey Amherst and two major generals. Lord North approved the proposition and so did Lord Dartmouth [Secretary of State for America], only he had difficulties on account of the harshness to General Gage, who was to be continued in his government [of Massachusetts] and second in command. Lord North showed it to the King, who started at it, and asked who could have thought of doing so unjust and cruel a thing to General Gage."

Gage's fluctuating estimates of the mood of the Americans had already made it difficult for the government to form a just view of the situation in Boston. A larger than usual change in his advice now overcame the King's reluctance to supersede him. In February he had assured the King that the colonists "will be lyons while we are lambs but if we take the resolute part they will undoubtedly prove very weak." In mid-November the King learned that, in a private letter, Gage had advocated revoking the penalties against Boston and Massachusetts. "His idea of suspending the acts seems to me the most absurd that can be suggested . . . This must suggest to the colonies a fear that alone prompts them to their present violence. I do not mean by this that I am averse to new measures; but that I am for supporting those already undertaken." The King thereupon withdrew his objection to offering the command to Amherst.

Sir Jeffrey Amherst was the most senior of the successful generals surviving from the Seven Years war. He had taken Louisburg and he had commanded in the final act of the acquisition of Canada, the campaign against

Montreal. His reputation stood deservedly high. He was a great military organiser and he had a talent for cooperating with the colonials. He had married an American and had been governor of Virginia until, in 1768, he had quarrelled with the Duke of Grafton's government. According to his close friend Lord George Germain, his demands on that occasion "went to a peerage, which was not complied with, and he then gave up his regiments."[1] In 1774 he was Lieutenant General (and effective head) of the Ordnance and Governor of Guernsey. The government made every effort to persuade him to take the American command. "They offered him a peerage and everything else he could ask . . . and for a week they thought he had consented, but his wife dissuaded him, and he gave answer that he could not bring himself to command against the Americans, to whom he had been so much obliged."

Instead it was decided to send three major generals junior to Gage. The King considered a list of eleven possibles for what he considered "not a very desirable commission." It is not clear why it was decided to send three. One was to act as second in command, one was to command in New York (which as it happened was evacuated before any of the three arrived). The third had no obvious role, as the small force in Boston could scarcely need this large reinforcement in the higher command, having an adequate number of competent brigadiers already on the strength.

The eventual choice fell on three members of the House of Commons, none of them regular supporters of the government, William Howe, Henry Clinton and John Burgoyne. With his usual acerbity, Horace Walpole summed them up in a paragraph. "Howe was one of those brave and silent brothers, and was reckoned sensible, though so silent that nobody knew whether he was or not. Burgoyne had offered himself for this service; he was a vain and ambitious man, with a half understanding that was worse than none; Clinton had not that fault, for he had no sense at all."

William Howe was the youngest of the three distinguished sons of a viscount in the Irish peerage. A parliamentary seat for Nottingham was hereditary in the family and William had held it since 1758. Wolfe had considered his eldest brother, George, the 3rd Viscount, the most promising officer in the army and he had greatly contributed to the original training of British light infantry. Had he lived he might have been a great general. Unfortunately he had been killed in a skirmish near Ticonderoga in 1758. The colonists had erected a statue to his memory in Boston. The title had passed to the second brother, Richard, a talented naval officer who sat in the Commons for the Admiralty borough of Dartmouth, although he was far from being a tame supporter of the government. He was taciturn and reputedly incomprehensible when speaking in the House. As an Admiral he was more than competent and was, in later years, to go down in history as the victor of the Glorious First of June.

William, the youngest, was admired by the King, the army and the public. He had made his name in a single night when he led Wolfe's Forlorn Hope up the Heights of Abraham. This single glorious exploit established his reputation beyond reach of doubt. For the rest of his military career, he had commanded a battalion at the capture of Louisburg, and a brigade (which did no fighting) at the taking of Montreal. He had been present at the capture of Belleisle and, as Adjutant General, at the seizure of Havanna in 1762. As a commander his capabilities were untried, but he had a dashing reputation. In fact, the aura which had surrounded his beloved and brilliant eldest brother had been transferred to him and, although he was a competent regimental officer, he was credited with a talent for generalship which he did not possess. He was irresolute, idle by nature and concealed his indecision behind a facade of silence. Walpole wrote that he "never wastes a monosyllable", but to his friends he was given to lengthy and ill-tempered grumbling.

The second major general, Henry Clinton, suffered from an overwhelming diffidence. Almost the whole of his active service had been as an aide-de-camp in Germany. He was known to be brave but his powers of leadership and his grasp of tactics were untried. Being a cousin of the Duke of Newcastle, he sat in the Commons for Boroughbridge and, later, for Newark, both seats controlled by the Newcastle family. His father had been a "querulous, fussy and ineffective" naval officer,[2] who had been governor of New York where Henry had lived as a boy, and his first commission had been as an ensign in a locally raised independent company. While serving with it he had had a humiliating escape from a French ambush. Later he transferred to the Coldstream Guards.

As it turned out, Clinton proved to be a sound tactician, but one who was never able to convince either his superiors or his subordinates of the soundness of his ideas. To make matters worse he was constantly under the impression that he was being ill-used by his colleagues, political, military and naval. This showed itself in his "recklessness in pursuing a grievance". As Lord George Germain said of him later in the war, "Sir H. Clinton is of all men the most jealous, and when he has not the whole credit of a measure is apt to dislike the plan however well concerted." However, in 1775, he was on friendly terms with Howe and Burgoyne and wrote that, "I could not have named two people I should sooner wish to serve with."

Despite Walpole's assertion, Burgoyne was far from "offering himself for this service". He had good reasons for staying in England. Lady Charlotte was far from well and his play *The Maid of the Oaks* was in the repertoire at Drury Lane. Nor was he anxious to go to Boston as fourth in command, the more so since Howe and Clinton, although his seniors in the Army List, were respectively seven and eight years younger than he. He liked and respected them both but he would hardly have been human if he had not reflected that, unlike himself, neither of them had held independent and victorious command in the field.

His first intimation that he might be sent to America came from Charles Jenkinson.[3] "We were coming in the crowd together out of the House of Commons after the debate on the affairs of America in the latter end of January [1775]. He wished I was in that country with a look and emphasis that conveyed more than ordinary conversation. It struck me that he meant to sound my inclinations. I answered that 'every soldier must go where he is ordered;' but that I believed that, in the present state of things, *that* service would not be a very desirable one."

He was sent for by the Secretary at War on 2nd February. For a few moments Lord Barrington made light conversation and then said abruptly that, "he hoped and did not doubt that everything in America would mend when I and the other two generals for whom he was to make out letters of service should arrive there . . . I desired to know whether he was directed by the King to deliver to me finally his commands; that if this service was in any degree optional, I had some professional reasons to decline it, but many more arising from such private feelings as most affect the human heart; critical family situations probably ensuing, in which my presence might be of great concern to my fortune; unambitious pleasures; friendships and affections; in all which absence and distance would make a breach that no emolument in the power of the government to bestow (and I had no claim to any but the regular stipend of my situation) would compensate. That if, on the contrary, his Majesty had done me the honour to think of me as particularly necessary to his service upon this occasion, and had sent me his orders as such, I should act in conformity to the principle which I had ever held indispensible with a soldier when called forth upon a duty of service, to forgo every consideration of private interest or happiness, in obedience to that call." Barrington replied that, "his Majesty had expressed himself decisively in regard to Generals Howe, Clinton and myself." The Secretary "did not spare compliments: it is a language in which he is always ready", and Burgoyne "requested him to assure his Majesty of my ready obedience to his commands."

Soon afterwards Burgoyne had the first of several interviews with Lord North. Although the two men were connected by marriage, relations were not close between them. "I had thought myself, some years ago, treated by him with very undeserved slight, and had occasionally expressed my resentment. Civil messages had sometimes passed between us through friends; but no indication of attention towards me, that showed like cordiality, had ever taken place on his part."

In these interviews North put forward the suggestion that Burgoyne should act as a confidential channel of communication between the cabinet and the army in America. North, who had serious doubts about the wisdom or practicability of settling the colonies by force, needed some frank source of information on the other side of the Atlantic, a source which he could trust and which would come to him unfiltered by protocol and self-justification. Burgoyne, a kinsman who was unlikely to hold an independent command in which he would have to justify his actions, would be ideal for this purpose. "He assured me of . . . the satisfaction he should have in the fullest communication of our mutual sentiments." Burgoyne countered by asking for the command at New York, where he might have some opportunity of settling the whole American dispute by negotiation. At worst he asked for some "other department where my zeal might be of more use and extent than the bare superintendence of a small brigade. His lordship acquiesced entirely in all my reasoning, but was very cautious of committing himself in any engagment further than to lay all I had said before the King."

As it happened, the King agreed with Burgoyne's desire to go to New York since, "I think [he] would best manage any negociations." Unfortunately Howe, when accepting service, had stipulated for the New York command. He was as reluctant to serve under Gage as Clinton and Burgoyne were to serve under Gage and Howe. Moreover he had rashly promised his Nottingham constituents that he would decline service in America and this gave him a fairly plausible excuse for exacting a price before agreeing to serve.

Burgoyne's task in Boston, therefore, must be to act as a confidential correspondent to the cabinet and to infuse some spirit into General Gage. As the King wrote, "if he remains in Boston he may be able to suggest what falls in conversation to the Commander in Chief, which may prove of great utility." It would not have escaped the King's notice that Burgoyne and Gage had been contemporaries at school. To ensure that London was fully informed of events in Boston before the next campaigning season, Burgoyne was to report in person at the end of the year. The King "very much approved of his request of coming home during the time the troops cannot be employed the next winter, as it will be of importance to his private affairs, and he will be able to bring a very full account of the minds and dispositions of the people in that part of the globe. . . . I desire you will not mention this to any one, and I will keep as exact a silence on this subject." Unfortunately Lord North took this last injunction too literally and omitted to pass to Burgoyne the King's eager agreement to his taking leave as soon as the campaigning season was over.

Burgoyne also called on Lord Dartmouth, the Secretary of State for

America, in whom he observed "a good deal of caution in committing an opinion on nice subjects", and on Lord George Germain, who was to succeed Dartmouth later in 1775. "He had more information, more enlarged sentiments and more spirits than any of the Ministers. He acknowledged that he was in all consultations upon American measures; that indeed his warmth had led him almost to offer himself to Lord North . . . He told me he had for a long time goaded every part of the administration upon the neglect of New York; that he knew not where they could find a more proper person than myself to send there; that the proper place for General Howe was with the main body of the army, where his name as well as his abilities would be instrumental to restore discipline and confidence."

Yet another call was on Thomas Hutchinson, who had been Governor of Massachusetts until superseded by Gage. Hutchinson noted in his diary that when they breakfasted together, Burgoyne "spoke freely of the present state of administration: the want of one vigorous direction: the indecision in all councils; the aptness to procrastination: and tho' he expected to sail in 8 days, doubted whether any instructions [had been prepared for them], and rather feared [they] should go without any."

The three generals got the nearest they were to get to receiving instructions on 3rd April when they were summoned to dinner at Lord Dartmouth's. "There were present", wrote Burgoyne, "all the cabinet, and moreover Lords Sandwich [First Lord of the Admiralty], and Barrington [Secretary at War], General Harvey [Adjutant General], Governor Hutchinson and Mr Secretary Pownall [Under Secretary to the American Department]; and to the whole was added (I could never guess for what purpose) the Earl of Hardwicke.[4] I did not conceive much expectation of business upon the sight of so numerous and motley a company, and except for a short conversation between Lord Suffolk [Secretary of State for the Northern Department], General Howe and myself, who sat near each other at table, and which Lord Suffolk expressed a desire to extend upon some other occasion, we talked of every subject but America."

The frigate *Cerberus* with Howe, Clinton and Burgoyne on board reached Boston on 25th May. They had expected to find a tense situation but one in which it would be possible to negotiate. Even if Boston proved obdurate, they all had hopes of being able to reach a reasonable settlement at New York. They found the garrison of New York drawn in to Boston and that town under siege. As Clinton wrote, "On our arrival we found, to our great astonishment and concern, that hostilities had been already begun and that the King's troops were in consequence confined within a circle of scarcely two miles diametre, as the insurgents had seized every avenue into the surrounding countryside, whereby all supplies of fresh provisions by that course were cut off from the garrison."

On 19th April, while *Cerberus* was at sea, General Gage had attempted to seize the magazine of military stores at Concord. He was right to do so and it may be that he left the operation too late. His mistake was to under-estimate the possible opposition. From Boston to Lexington is almost twenty miles, and he sent out only the flank companies of his garrison and some marines, about five hundred muskets. He made no arrangements to support them. On Lexington Common, twelve miles on their route, the advance guard found militia men drawn up across the road. The troops were fired upon and replied with volleys. Eight Americans were killed and more wounded. They then continued their advance to Concord where, after brushing aside some minor opposition, they destroyed the small remnant of the stores which the Americans had not succeeded in removing. Their retreat was a hideous experience. They were continually harassed with small arms fire and suffered heavy casualties. Discipline began to break down and had some Americans not scalped the dead and wounded, thus making surrender appear as dangerous as continuing the march, it is probable that the force would have disintegrated.

Belatedly Gage sent out a brigade under Lord Percy which joined them when they returned to Lexington, and the combined force fought its way back to Boston having suffered 270 casualties, including 19 officers. It was, wrote Lieutenant Lord Rawdon (later to be known as General Lord Moira, Marquess of Hastings), "a very foolish affair. Our men were even un-provided with sufficient ammunition, and the two pieces of cannon sent out with Lord Percy were only supplied with four and twenty rounds when they had to fight every yard of their way for almost as many miles."

As soon as Percy's force was back in Boston, the town was blockaded by the rebels. Gage was still unwilling to take harsh measures. He believed the trouble was caused by a small, unrepresentative minority of trouble makers. In consequence, "as many of the inhabitants as chose to quit the town were permitted to remove all their valuable effects, and what was very extra-ordinary, each man was permitted to carry out his arms with him. In this manner many thousand stand of arms were carried out, though every officer that saw it knew well that they were to be used against us." The morale of the troops slumped and there was a universal loss of confidence in Gage.

Gage was, of course, in a very difficult position. He knew there was a substantial number of rebels within the town and that, if he was attacked, he would have to detach troops to secure the streets. Nor could he drive the blockading forces away. Being on the peace establishment, his small force was totally without transport. It could not undertake more than a raid. As

Burgoyne pointed out, "we are totally deficient as to bread-waggons, bât-horses, artillery horses and many other articles necessary for an army to move to a distance—but chiefly money with which the military chest is unprovided."

Some things however would have been possible and Gage failed to do them. Boston is the worst military position imaginable. The town stands on a peninsula jutting out into the harbour. It is commanded on the north by another peninsula, Charlestown Heights, and on the south by yet another, Dorchester Heights. Boston would be untenable and the harbour unusable if these two positions were seized, fortified and armed with heavy cannon by the rebels. The general made no attempt to secure either of them although neither of them was held by the rebels. It is hardly surprising, therefore, that when the three major generals arrived they found "army and town unrecovered from the consternation into which they had been thrown by the ill-success of April 19th, and from the general revolt that followed."

It was not until a month had passed that the combined arguments of Howe, Clinton and Burgoyne persuaded Gage to sanction an operation to seize Dorchester Heights. It was to take place on the morning of 18th June, and Clinton was to command the attacking force.

The attack never took place. On the night of 16th/17th June, the rebels occupied Charlestown Heights. Advised by the brilliant engineer, Richard Gridley, they contrived to build, during the hours of darkness, a substantial earthwork on Breed's Hill, the nearer of the two heights. It was a measure of the demoralisation of the British troops that the sentries in Boston "had heard the rebels at work all night without making any other report of it than mentioning it in conversation in the morning. The first knowledge the general had of it was by hearing one of the ships firing at the workmen and going to see what had occasioned the firing."

Gage's situation was now desperate. Unless the Charlestown Heights were taken that day the redoubt could be made impregnable. It commanded Boston at a range of 1,500 yards and could make navigation in the harbour very difficult. Moreover, "as the shore where it was judged most proper to land was very flat, the landing could not be made with proper facility after the ebb of the tide was much run off. It was, therefore, necessary that no delay should be made in our preparations, since it would be high water at 2 o'clock in the afternoon." To mount the operation in the time available was a feat of improvisation which reflects the greatest credit on the military and naval commanders responsible.

Gage and Howe have frequently been pilloried for making a frontal attack on the rebel position. They had no alternative except to put their troops across the shortest sea-route. Howe, commanding the assault, was subject to the same limitations as control all planners of opposed landings. He had to make his landing where he could build up his strength fastest. He believed that the rebels had six thousand men on the heights and he could not afford to have his first landing force overwhelmed before he could reinforce it. The size of this first landing force depended on the number of boats available. "The troops we could land at one embarcation, in our number and species of boats (not one of our accustomed flat boats among them) was not more than 1,100 rank and file."

It would have been preferable to make the landing from the Mystick river on Charlestown Neck so that the rebels on the heights would have been cut off and forced to surrender. The risk involved would have been wholly unjustifiable. The rowing time for each "lift" would have been more than doubled and 1,100 isolated men could have been overwhelmed before help could reach them. Operations had to be completed by nightfall and every second was precious. At the Council of War which Gage held to give orders for the attack, Clinton proposed that five hundred men should be landed on the Neck while the main attack went straight across the narrows. This was properly dismissed as unsound. It would be offering two small hostages to fortune, five hundred men at the Neck and six hundred at Morton's Point, where Howe aimed to land. Both forces could have been destroyed before they could be reinforced.

Burgoyne's part in the ensuing action was a passive one. He and Clinton were stationed with a heavy battery on Copp's Hill. When Howe's left gave way, Clinton "desired General Burgoyne to save me harmless to General Gage for going without his orders, and went over to join Howe." Burgoyne took no part. "Except two cannonballs that went a hundred yards over our heads, we were not in any part of the direction of the enemy's fire." In a letter to his nephew, Lord Stanley, he wrote, "To consider this action as a soldier, it comprised, though in a small compass, almost every branch of military duty and curiosity. Troops landed in the face of an enemy; a march sustained by a powerful cannonade from moving field artillery, fixed batteries, floating batteries and the broadsides of ships at anchor, all operating separately and well disposed; a deployment from the march to form for the attack; a vigorous defence; a storm with bayonets; a fine and large town [Charlestown] set on fire with shells. Whole streets of houses, ships upon the stocks, a number of churches, all sending up volumes of smoke and flames, or falling together in ruin, were capital objects. It was great, it was high spirited, and while the animated impression remains, let us quit it. I will not engage your sensibility and my own in contemplation of humanity upon the subject; but will close en militaire by lamenting your brother Thomas was not arrived, because in a long life of service he may not have an opportunity of seeing any professional tragedy like it."

"A professional tragedy" was an admirable description of the battle of Bunker Hill. Howe, a brave man but a cautious commander, was forced to commit his men to the kind of operation for which an eighteenth century army was least suitable. It was comparable to storming a fortress without previous bombardment. Howe's plentiful artillery could not be deployed so as to be effective. Lord Rawdon, who was attacking with the grenadiers of the Fifth Foot, wrote that, "the men-of-war in the harbour could not elevate their guns sufficiently to bear upon [the redoubt], for which reason twenty four pounders were ordered from the artillery park to play upon it [from Copp's Hill]. They struck it several times, but being at a great distance and the work of an extraordinary thickness and solidity, they could make no impression upon it."

Howe's only effective weapon was the bayonet. This meant that his men had to make the long, exposed march up to the ramparts in close formation, constantly checking the dressing so that, when they reached the enemy, they could make the final attack in a solid, effective body. Not all the troops were sufficiently well-trained for this desperate task. Rawdon's grenadiers, although the company was reduced to eleven men, kept their discipline and coherence but he wrote that, "Our confidence in our troops is much lessened. Some did, indeed, behave with remarkable courage, but others behaved remarkably ill. We have a great want of discipline [i.e. training] among both officers and men." Burgoyne echoed this view. "Discipline, not to say courage, was wanting. In the critical moment of carrying the redoubt, the officers of some corps were almost alone."

Through no fault of his own, Burgoyne was only an observer at the battle but he had every chance to draw conclusions from what he had seen. His first was that the rebels had been widely under-estimated as soldiers. In the French wars many of the militia had behaved badly, but "those who have been well led did on many occasions behave well." The rebels on Breed's Hill had, he saw, put up "a vigorous defence". He realised that the rebels would be averse to risking pitched battles. "It is not to be expected that the rebel Americans will risk a general combat, or even stand at all, except behind entrenchments as at Boston. Accustomed to felling timber and grubbing up trees, they are very ready at earthworks and palisading, they will cover and entrench themselves, whenever they are for a short time left unmolested, with surprising alacrity." He saw the attempt to recapture large tracts of America as a long series of attacks on fortified positions from which the enemy would have to be "dislodged either by cannon or by a resolute attack of light infantry". If the British were to succeed they must have more light infantry, "greater numbers than one company per regiment", and large quantities of artillery for battering purposes. Only with these requisites could the infantry be spared the crippling casualties they had suffered at Bunker Hill. As Clinton remarked, "A few more such victories would soon put an end to British domination in America."

2,500 British troops had been engaged at Bunker Hill. 1,100 of them were casualties. It was clear to all those present that they had a full-scale war on their hands and that it was not one that could be won quickly. A week after the battle Howe wrote that, "we cannot (as the general tells us) muster now more than 3,400 rank and file for duty, including the Marines and the three last regiments from Ireland [which arrived after the battle] . . . I very much doubt whether we shall get much further this campaign."

Gage relapsed into inactivity. He ordered an attack on the Dorchester Heights but cancelled it after the troops had been embarked. The troops lost all confidence in him. They knew him to be unenterprising and they believed him to be indifferent to their discomforts and hardships. Captain Charles Stuart of the Thirty Fifth wrote five weeks after Bunker Hill, "We have bad fluxes among the men from the salt provisions, which renders the fifth part of them useless; nay, so careful is the general to save expence, that tho' fresh meat is sold every day at a shilling a pound, he will not have the hospitals provided with it. [Only] the hatred the troops have for the rebels lulls the dislike they hold for General Gage who, by the by, seems the most unhappy man existing."

Gage had much to be unhappy about. He had too few troops, no transport, no orders from London, pitifully little money. His naval colleague was incompetent and unco-operative. "The rebel privateers cruize at the mouth of the harbour. They have taken an ordnance store ship, which had on board a thirteen inch mortar, a great quantity of shells and two thousand small arms. A ship laden with blankets and stockings has fallen into their hands. In the mean time we have the fleet lying inactive in harbour . . . Admiral Gage deserves to be made an example of much more than Byng did." The navy was so inactive that, to bring in a supply of slaughter-cattle, Gage armed and sent out a number of transports with military gunners.

Burgoyne loathed his time in Boston. As fourth in command of a stationary army he had, as he had foreseen, only "the inspection of a small brigade—to see that the soldiers boiled their kettles regularly." He painstakingly fulfilled his duty of keeping Lord North informed of the state of affairs in the army. While making it clear that, in his view, Gage was "not equal to his situation", it was a situation to which no general could be equal. "Our situation here is extremely disagreeable—without an army fit to undertake any business of consequence against the rebels opposed to us. They are strongly entrenched and very numerous in every part in which they are assailable, and we could not muster above 3,600 men for an attack on their army, after leaving a proper number for the defence of Boston. Added to this—were they drove from their camp, we could not establish ourselves six miles from Boston; our numbers not admitting of our preserving a communication with that place at so small a distance as I have mentioned."

He did his best to convince the government that the war could not be won on the cheap. "If the continent is to be subdued by arms, . . . you have no probable recourse of bringing the war to a speedy conclusion with any force that Great Britain can supply. A large army of such foreign troops as might be hired, to begin their campaign up the Hudson river; another army composed of old disciplined troops and partly of Canadians to act from Canada; a large levy of Indians, and a supply of arms to the blacks to awe the southern provinces, conjointly with regulars; and a numerous fleet to sweep the whole coast, might possibly do the business." If this was impracticable it would be as well to concede the rebels claims immediately. "Any intermediate measure between these disagreeable extremes . . . will be productive of much fruitless expense, loss of blood and a series of disappointments."

Howe, Clinton and Burgoyne agreed that the evacuation of Boston was the prerequisite for any effective offensive action. In early August they "presumed to offer their advice to General Gage. That he would order the most diligent preparations for the removal of the army to New York and evacuate Boston entirely, unless an additional force should arrive from Europe with orders that should direct the plan of operations otherwise." Burgoyne would have gone further. He foresaw that authorisation would not arrive until the season was too far advanced to undertake an attack on New York before the following spring. Gage, while not dissenting from his subordinates, took no action.

While Burgoyne waited for permission to go on leave to England, permission which North indolently omitted to forward, he received a letter, sent under a white flag, from the rebel lines. This came from Major General Charles Lee, a competent soldier but a thoroughly disagreeable man, who had served under Burgoyne in Portugal. Being, he said, convinced of "the wickedness of the [British] court and cabinet", he had embraced the rebel cause. His letter to Burgoyne was a brazen attempt to detach him from his duty but, with Gage's consent, Burgoyne tried to arrange a meeting with him.

"The great object I proposed myself in my answer was to obtain an interview; and had I succeeded I would have cut him short in his paltry jargon with which the infatuation of the vulgar is supported, and would have pressed upon him, to conviction if possible, the sentiments of the nation at large in support of the government . . . I would then have endeavoured to touch his pride, his interest and his ambition. I know the ruling passion of Lee's mind to be avarice . . . He would have started at a direct bribe, might have caught at an overture of changing his party to gratify his interest, provided a salve were suggested for his integrity. It is not impossible that the example of General Monck[5] might have presented itself to his imagination, and though not with the same powers, he might have flattered himself, with the same intentions, to restore the state."

The project came to nothing. Lee affronted Burgoyne by publishing his letters in the *New York Gazette* and the negotiations were broken off. In the following year Lee was captured by, ironically enough, the Sixteenth Light Dragoons. Washington later sent him before a court martial for insubordination.

To while away the weary weeks, Burgoyne returned to his other profession, the theatre. He wrote and produced a play with music, *The Blockade of Boston*. Lord Rawdon wrote, "We are to have plays this winter in Fanteuil Hall. I am enrolled as an actor; not that I love sporting in public but I do not think it right to refuse on this occasion. General Burgoyne is our Garrick: our ladies are few, but I daresay we shall produce some good actresses. A meeting house was proposed as a theatre, but we feared your censure at home, and were afraid it might have furnished Lord Chatham with the old joke of turning the Lord's House into a den of thieves. The money collected by these performances is to be a fund for the benefit of the wives and children of those who fall in action."

The Blockade of Boston had a memorable opening. "At the moment when a crowded house was impatient for the show, the rebels opened a battery of heavy cannon against the town; the audience, who thought the discharge of artillery which they heard to be a prelude to the play, gave the warlike sounds every mark of the approbation and when one of the performers entered on the stage in a great hurry to tell them that the siege was begun in earnest, they considered him as performing his part in the piece and received him with loud applause."

Despite these alarms, the siege had not begun in earnest and the days continued to drag by without incident. General Gage was recalled to London, ostensibly for consultations, and Howe succeeded to the command. The garrison was delighted. Charles Stuart commented that, "the hatred of Gage is general among the men and the joy they express at his departure equal to it." As Burgoyne had foreseen, the government's authorisation to evacuate Boston arrived too late in the year to be put into execution before the winter. Months of dreary inactivity loomed ahead.

Burgoyne was spared the worst of it. His leave to return to England, signed by Lord Dartmouth early in November, reached him in time to enable him to embark on HMS *Boyne* on 5th December.

CHAPTER 6

"Unactivity and Want of Spirit"

Dartmouth's letter authorising Burgoyne's leave was one of the last he wrote as Secretary of State for the American Department. On 10th November 1775, he handed over the seals to Lord George Germain and it was with him that Burgoyne had to deal when he reached London.

Lord George is one of the most enigmatic characters in English history and he was to play a crucial part in Burgoyne's career. He had been born George Sackville in 1716 and was the third and favourite son of the 7th Earl of Dorset, who was to be created 1st Duke of Dorset when George was four. He was sent to Westminster, but left in 1731, two years before Burgoyne went there, to join his father, who had been made Lord Lieutenant of Ireland. In Dublin he attended Trinity College which, in the opinion of Lord Chesterfield, was "indisputably better" at that date than Oxford or Cambridge. He took a Master's Degree in 1734 but, according to Nicholas Wraxall who knew him well in later life and admired him, "his education had not altogether corresponded with his extraction, and he owed far more to nature than to cultivation . . . He possessed little information derived from books, nor had he improved his mind by study in the course of subsequent years."

His Dublin studies may have suffered from the fact that he was simultaneously acting as his father's private secretary and also acquired a cornetcy in the Seventh Horse. He had inherited military talent from his mother's family[1] and in 1741 he fought as a lieutenant colonel at Dettingen with so much distinction that he was made ADC to George II, who was present. In 1743 he commanded the Twenty Eighth Foot at the glorious defeat at Fontenoy, where he was shot through the chest in the middle of the French camp. He recovered in time to take part in the suppression of the Forty Five when the Duke of Cumberland wrote that he had "a disposition to his trade that I do not always find in those of higher [social] rank." Meanwhile he had been MP for Dover since 1741 and established a reputation in the House

of Commons as high as that he held in the army. In 1746 he was made Colonel
of the Twentieth Foot, in which he earned the high opinion of the regimental major, James Wolfe, who remained his friend until his death at Quebec.

By 1757 it was clear that Lord George was likely to go to the top of his
profession. He was a lieutenant general, Colonel of the Queen's Bays and
Lieutenant General of the Ordnance. The King admired him and he was the
close friend of the Commander in Chief, Lord Ligonier, whom he was
widely expected to succeed. With all this he was an able parliamentarian and
happily married. "In his person, which rose to nearly six feet, he was mus-
cular and capable of enduring much bodily as well as mental fatigue. Though
his features were strongly pronounced and saturnine, yet considered as a
whole, their effect was by no means displeasing." Yet underneath all this
glittering facade there was an inner uncertainty. He was a shy man and tended
to appear abrupt to those he did not know well. Perceval Stockdale, who
served under him, wrote that, "there was a reserve and haughtiness in his
manner which depressed and darkened all that was agreeable and engaging
in him." Wraxall said that, "on first acquaintance his manner and air impressed those who approached him with an idea of a proud reserve; but no
man in private society unbent himself more." Lord Shelburne, a hostile
witness, said that there was in him "a mixture of quickness and a sort of
melancholy in his look which runs through all the Sackville family".

His reserved manner, his apparent haughtiness and his outstanding talents
earned him many enemies and detractors. He was much criticised, without
any apparent reason, for the failure of the raid on St Malo. The King withdrew some of his friendliness when Lord George was reported to be associa-
ting with the Prince of Wales. This did not prevent him being made second
in command of the British troops in Germany, for in those days military
appointments were decided by William Pitt, and Pitt was Sackville's friend.
Before the end of 1758 he had succeeded to the command of the contingent
—six regiments of British cavalry, six battalions of infantry and three batteries of field guns.

Then came 1st August 1759 and the battle of Minden. No day has ever
brought more glory to the British infantry and artillery, but when the allied
Commander in Chief, Prince Ferdinand of Brunswick, ordered Sackville to
bring the cavalry forward, nothing happened. The French army was routed
but escaped total destruction. The Prince repeated the orders several times
but the charge which should have consummated the victory never eventuated.

The King relieved him of his command and, at his own request, Sackville was brought before a court martial. On 5th April 1760 the court pronounced their verdict, "that Lord George Sackville is guilty of having disobeyed the orders of Prince Ferdinand of Brunswick . . . and it is the

further opinion of this court that the said Lord George Sackville is, and he is hereby adjudged, unfit to serve his Majesty in any military capacity whatever." This sentence was read at the head of every regiment and garrison of the British army. There were many who thought he was lucky to have escaped with his life. It was only three years since Admiral Byng had been shot on his own quarterdeck for, allegedly, showing insufficient resolution in attempting to relieve Minorca. The King was said to be angry that Sackville had escaped the death penalty, and dismissed him from the Privy Council.[2]

No satisfactory explanation has ever been put forward for Lord George's behaviour at Minden. There were allegations, mostly outside the court, of cowardice. This seems wholly out of character as, both before and after Minden, he showed himself a notably brave man. He was known to be on bad terms with Prince Ferdinand but it is both unlikely and uncharacteristic that he would risk his career and his life to work off a petty spite. On the contrary, he was reputed to be avaricious of personal glory and it is most unlikely that he would have deliberately have let slip a chance of leading a charge which would have gone down in history as a classic of cavalry action. His defence was that he brought the cavalry forward as quickly as was compatible with keeping them in formation and with deploying them in the necessary order. He also claimed that he was hampered by contradictory orders delivered by over-excited aides. There was much truth in this defence, but the fact remained that the cavalry arrived too late and a great opportunity was lost.

Throughout the trial Sackville conducted himself with calm confidence. Horace Walpole wrote that, "Nothing was timid, nothing humble, in his behaviour. His replies were quick and spirited." Some of the prosecution witnesses made no attempt to disguise their malice against him. One of them, Colonel Sloper, avowed that the order to advance "alarmed Lord George to a very great degree", a statement which the court refused to believe. It seems probable that some pressure was put on both court and witnesses to secure a conviction and it is noticeable that many of the prosecution witnesses were promoted after the trial, while those who supported the prisoner were persecuted, his most effective defender being ordered to sell his commission. Lord George himself never wavered in the belief that he was innocent and determined to re-establish himself in public life.

It was a long, hard climb back and, whatever one's view of Sackville's character, it is impossible not to admire the courage and pertinacity with which he tackled it. Immediately after the court martial he was ostracised. Walpole claimed that there were "only three men in England" (including Walpole himself) "who dared to speak or sit by Lord George in public places." The King refused to receive him at court, but this had the compensation that the Prince of Wales, ever anxious to annoy his grandfather, whom he was soon to succeed, welcomed him to Leicester House. He continued to sit in the House of Commons[3] and if few of his fellow-members would associate with him they could not stop him speaking. Gradually he became an accepted part of the parliamentary scene, and in 1765 the unlikely alliance of George III and Lord Rockingham made him Vice Treasurer for Ireland and restored him to the Privy Council. When his former friend Pitt returned to office in the following year he was removed from the Irish post, but at least the principle had been established that he could hold civil office under the Crown. His struggle for re-establishment was assisted by a very happy home life and by the death of Lady Betty Germain in 1770. At the wish of her late husband she left him a great estate and £20,000 on condition that he changed his name to Germain.

Lord George had taken a close interest in American affairs for many years before they simmered over. In 1765 he had written, "Everybody is distressed about America. The spirit that rages there is beyond conception. God only knows how it will end, for as yet I have heard no human reasoning that promises a happy issue to it." He set out to study colonial problems and by 1774 the retired governor of Massachusetts wrote that, "He has great knowledge of American affairs."

As the crisis in America grew nearer, North's government increasingly turned to Lord George for advice. In the election of 1774 North, who was now Lord Warden of the Cinque Ports as well as Prime Minister, offered to have him returned for his old seat at Hythe. He preferred to stay in the family borough of East Grinstead. To have accepted Hythe "would have called at least for personal attention from me to his lordship. As it is, I must comfort myself with knowing that I begin this parliament absolutely at liberty to take part which shall seem to me the most advisable." The part he chose was that supported by the overwhelming majority of his fellow independent members —that there was a limit to appeasement and that future policy must be firm and consistent. Earlier in 1774 he had told the House of Commons that, "there is no use entering into the calamities that had been brought on America—*it had been owing to the different conduct of different ministers.* The wisdom of parliament was now requisite. It would not be right to let the Americans steal a constitution they had no right to. The mischiefs were owing to the repeal of the Stamp Act and want of uniformity in the proceedings of parliament." He was widely applauded.

When Burgoyne breakfasted with Governor Hutchinson before sailing for Boston in 1775 he had spoken of "the want of one vigorous direction". This thought was echoed throughout the nation and it was equally widely agreed that it was of no use to look to Lord North for vigorous direction. By his own admission, "upon military matters I speak ignorantly, and therefore without effect." His talent for managing Parliament was still essential but someone must be found to play Pitt to North's Newcastle. Pitt, of course, was still alive and there were a few who wished to turn to him again, but his statements on America, even when comprehensible, were unacceptable to the majority of Parliament. The Earl of Chatham was only the broken shadow of William Pitt. To reinstate him in 1775 would have been comparable to recalling David Lloyd George in 1940.

Since there was no commanding figure in the cabinet and the Secretary for America, Lord Dartmouth, did not believe in the use of force, it became apparent that only one man seemed capable of directing a distant and difficult war. Lord George Germain had shown himself determined, courageous, consistent and capable. He had been on the way to becoming a great general when a single incident had broken his career. Fifteen years after Minden there were many who wondered whether the verdict of his court martial had been just. In Parliament his views echoed those of the majority. "As there is not common sense in protracting a war of this sort, I should be for exerting the utmost force of this kingdom to finish the rebellion in one campaign." No one saw any chance of this conception being brought to reality under North and Dartmouth. If there was anyone who could settle the American troubles competently it was Germain.

Late in 1775, North offered him the American Secretaryship and with it the executive direction of the war. Germain was reluctant. All too clearly he saw the pitfalls ahead. The whole squalid business of Minden would be raked over again and again. His less inhibited opponents would delight in throwing it up in his face. He must start his task with a heavy handicap. To a close friend he wrote, "I fear you will find me in Lord Dartmouth's office as Secretary of State for America. I have try'd and cannot avoid it. Pity me, encourage me and I will do my best."

His appointment was widely welcomed, not least in the Secretary of State's office where an unaccustomed atmosphere of purpose and efficiency began to make itself felt. One of the clerks recalled, "there was at once an end to all circumlocutory reports and inefficient forms, that had only impeded business, and substituted ambiguity for precision . . . He studied no choice phrases, no superfluous words, nor ever suffered the clearness of his conceptions to be clouded by the obscurity of his expressions, for the simplest and most unequivocal that could be made use of for explaining his opinions or dictating his instructions. In the meanwhile he was so momentarily punctual to his time, so religiously observant of his engagements, that we, who served under him in the office, felt the sweets of exchange we had so lately made in the person of our chief."

Even without the taunts of Minden, which he bore uncomplainingly and which he left unanswered, he had troubles enough for any less courageous man. It was proposed that Admiral Howe should be made Commander in Chief of the fleet in American waters. Germain and the Admiral had not been on speaking terms since St Malo in 1757 and yet Howe had the best qualifications for the post. Germain exerted himself to heal this breach. For a time his relations with both the admiral and his brother, now in command at Boston, were established on a friendly basis.[4]

The military situation on the far side of the Atlantic could scarcely be more unpromising. The army's only striking force, small as it was, was mewed up in Boston. The navy was failing to control the rebel coastline. An unexpected rebel attack into Canada had taken Montreal. When the last ship left the St Lawrence before it was sealed with ice, Quebec seemed certain to fall. There was a strong rumour in England, which turned out to be untrue, that the rebels had seized Halifax, the only fleet base left on the American continent.

Burgoyne had been on friendly terms with Lord George for some time. When he called on him before going to Boston, he had found him "very open in his conversation and I thought his sentiments just and firm. He assured me very warmly of his esteem. I found [him] communicative, a sort of behaviour he has shown me on all occasions." Burgoyne was delighted when Germain was appointed to the Secretaryship. "I partake with all the well wishers of the cause of the Constitution in this important contest that I have met with in satisfaction of seeing the affairs of America in the able hands of Lord George Germain; and when I consider the resolution with which he is supported from the Throne, I derive great confidence in the prospect of the next campaign." On his side Germain had a high opinion of Burgoyne's military talents and it had probably been he who had proposed his name for employment in America in 1775.

In the three months in which Burgoyne was in England he had several long conversations with the King, Lord North and Lord George. He made clear the joint view of Howe, Clinton and himself that Boston was untenable and that the sooner the army moved to New York the better. The government had adopted this view before his arrival but far too late to enable the move to be carried out before winter set in. He made no secret of his dissatisfaction with his supernumerary situation in the army in America and made it clear that he would prefer not to continue service in that continent. In this view he was reinforced by a series of family bereavements. On 22nd February, his father-in-law, Lord Derby, died after a long illness. Two days later Lady Derby also died. These losses "a good deal affected Lady Charlotte's weak state of spirits". Scarcely two weeks later, "by the mistake of a servant in the delivery of a note, she received suddenly and unprepared, the shock of Lady Margaret Stanley's death and of the probability that Lady Mary would not survive a week."[5] Burgoyne feared, justly, for his wife's life and was anxious to stay with her. The King and Lord George were determined that he should go to Canada to help the governor retrieve a desperate situation. Reluctantly he agreed. He set out for Portsmouth at the end of March. He was never to see Lady Charlotte again.

It was not to be expected that everyone would take a charitable view of Burgoyne's visit to England. Horace Walpole recorded that, "General Burgoyne had left Boston, not much to his credit nor to the satisfaction of the Court . . . On his arrival [he] had been very communicative of complaints, even to Charles Fox and the Opposition, [and] had the latter any activity they would have questioned him in Parliament before the Court had time to buy off his affected dissatisfaction. But before there was a single question started in the House of Commons, Burgoyne's rank and pay were raised, fifteen men added to each company of his regiment (all to his profit) and four cornetcies given him to sell . . . After these favours nobody more reserved than General Burgoyne on any mention of America in parliament."

There was scarcely a word of truth in this diatribe. The court could scarcely be dissatisfied with Burgoyne's return since the King had authorised and encouraged it before he had ever sailed to America. Nor was his promotion (and consequent rise in pay) authorised until he had been in England more than two months and had appeared in the Commons on several occasions. On 1st March, he was notified that, together with Henry Clinton and Lord Percy, he was to be promoted to the local rank of Lieutenant General in North America only. All these promotions were backdated but only so that the three men should have seniority over Lieutenant General Knyphausen, who had sailed with the Hessian troops to join Howe.

It is true that fifteen men were added to each troop of the Sixteenth Light Dragoons but this was the normal procedure when a regiment was warned for active service.[6] The same increase was made in the Seventeenth Light Dragoons whose colonel was not a member of Parliament and had no "interest", having started his military career as a kettle drummer. Nor would the increase be "all to his profit". At a time when recruiting was very difficult, the cost of raising men might well exceed the government grant for the purpose since every regiment in the army was competing for recruits. As for the "four cornetcies given to him to sell", it was the fixed rule of the army that new vacancies on the establishment could not be sold.[7]

Ten days before he knew of his promotion Burgoyne had warmly supported the government in the House of Commons. In the course of a debate, Colonel Barré asserted "that the troops, form an aversion to the service, misbehaved on Bunker's Hill on the 17th of June last." Burgoyne "rose in wrath and contradicted the last hon. member in the flattest manner. He allowed that the troops gave way a little at one time, because they were flanked by the fire out of the houses at Charles Town; but they soon rallied and advanced; and no men on earth ever behaved with more spirit, firmness and perseverance, till they forced the enemy out of their entrenchment." Writing immediately after the battle, in a confidential letter, he had been more critical of the troops. Even then he had stressed that he did not mean "to convey any suspicion of backwardness in the cause of government among the soldiery". He had contended that some "defective corps" were undertrained. It was not a point he was prepared to make when rebutting a sweeping charge made by a former officer for factious ends.

On 30th March, Burgoyne went to Portsmouth to sail for Canada in HMS *Blonde*. The First Lord of the Admiralty had advised him that Captain Philemon Pownoll "will receive you with pleasure. It seems he is rich and you need not fear putting him to expense."

Canada had only been a British possession for a dozen years when the American rebellion broke out. During most of that time it had been ruled by Guy Carleton who had been successively Acting Governor and Governor of Quebec since 1766. Carleton had been on Wolfe's staff and had earned that general's high opinion, but, as a modern Canadian historian has written, "Though he possessed many admirable qualities, it is more and more apparent that his nature had an ugly twist. When crossed he displayed a treacherous temper, and when cornered he would cut his way out unrestrained by any scruple." He had a sharp tongue which made him many enemies, among them George II, whom he had offended by a slighting reference to Hanover, and Sir Jeffrey Amherst, the most distinguished living British soldier.[8]

Carleton's work in the resettlement of Canada had been admirable. He was largely responsible for the Quebec Act of 1774, an enlightened and largely successful attempt to settle a new problem for British colonial policy. The conquest of Canada had, for the first time, given Britain a colony with a predominantly European, but non-British, population, the French settlers. The Act established a nominated Legislative Council on which French Canadians would serve. It specifically did away with the legal bars which, in the rest of the King's dominions, prevented Roman Catholics from holding office under the Crown. Priests were given the right to collect tithes from the Catholic inhabitants of their parishes, although the Crown reserved the right to collect the tithes from the non-Catholic minority for the support of Anglican clergy. At the request of the inhabitants, French law was retained in civil cases although trial by jury was introduced for criminal offences.

There was passionate opposition to the bill at Westminster, the opposition making great capital out of the concessions to Catholics. They maintained that the proposals were unconstitutional and undemocratic. Power, they contended, should be placed in the hands of the Protestants, mostly merchants, who had moved into Canada since the peace of 1763. When questioned at the bar of the House of Commons, Carleton pointed out that "the Protestants in Canada are under 400; about 360; but the French inhabitants, who are all Catholics, amount to 150,000."

Similar protests arose from the American colonies, the louder since most of the merchants in Canada had moved north across the border in the wake of the British army. The real cause, however, of American opposition was that the Act restored the western boundaries of Quebec to those that had existed under French rule. This extended Canada to include the triangle between the Mississippi and Ohio rivers, the area which now contains the states of Ohio, Michigan, Illinois, Indiana and Wisconsin. On the face of it, this was a logical arrangement since the land, as far as it was settled, was settled by French Canadians. In practice, it blocked American expansion to the west. In particular, it blighted the financial hopes of the Vandalia Company, a group of speculators among whom was Colonel George Washington.

Having seen the Quebec Act through Parliament, Carleton returned to Quebec in September 1744, believing that it would ensure the loyalty of the Canadian people. He was over-optimistic. He secured the loyalty of the *seigneurs* and the priests, but the ordinary *habitants* showed little interest and wanted only to be left in peace. Any gratitude they might have felt to the governor was balanced by a flood of propaganda leaflets which poured north from New England, although this largely defeated its own purposes by revealing a consistently anti-papist tone. Meanwhile the Anglo-American merchants loathed Carleton and moved steadily closer to open disloyalty.

Nevertheless Carleton continued to show the greatest optimism. He wrote to London, "All ranks among . . . his Majesty's Canadian subjects . . . vied with each other in testifying their gratitude and respect, and the desire they have by every mark of duty and submission to prove themselves not unworthy of the treatment they have met with." So confident was he that he readily agreed to Gage's request to send to Boston two of the five battalions in Canada. He asserted that there would be no difficulty in raising in their place a Canadian regiment "which, in time of need, might be augmented to two, three or more battalions."

At dawn on 10th May 1775, three weeks after the action at Lexington, a rebel force struck at Fort Ticonderoga. They consisted of a group of banditti from the Hampshire Grants who for years had been terrorising the peaceful population of northern New York. They were commanded by Ethan Allen and they had with them, as a volunteer, Benedict Arnold.

The garrison consisted of a weak company of Cameronians, forty-eight of all ranks, and was quite unprepared. The sentry saw the assailants and tried to give the alarm. His musket, the priming charge soaked with dew, failed to fire and the garrison were captured in their beds. As soon as Allen's men had recovered from the effects of the fortress's store of rum, they moved eighteen miles north and took Crown Point, where there was a collection of stores in charge of a sergeant and eighteen men who surrendered without resistance.

On 13th November, rebel troops entered Montreal in triumph. They would have done so earlier had not Major Charles Preston defended St John's with great tenacity for fifty days. When that fort fell, more than half the regular troops in Canada became prisoners of war. Simultaneously Benedict Arnold, with another rebel force of 1,500 men, was making an incredible march through the mountains and forests of Maine to appear before Quebec on 8th November. Two hundred men died of hardship on the march and three hundred, including a colonel, deserted. Nevertheless the remainder greatly outnumbered the garrison of Quebec, which consisted of sixty regulars and a local regiment, the Royal Highland Emigrants,[9] which was being raised and had enlisted 192 men.

Everything now depended on the Governor. His resources were small. His regular strength consisted of detachments amounting to less than a battalion.[10] The *habitants*, whose enthusiasm for British rule could not be expected to extend to backing the losing side, were beginning to view the *Bastonnois* with limited favour. Some of them went so far as to enlist in the rebel ranks.

In this situation Carleton showed at his best. Realising that Montreal was indefensible, he embarked his available regulars, a hundred and twenty of them, and set out to sail down the St Lawrence to Quebec, which he recognised as the key to the situation. Near Sorel he found his way blocked by what purported to be a heavy battery of rebel guns. He moved into a small boat, captained by a French Canadian, and slipped through the barrier at night dressed as a Canadian sailor. Transferring again to a naval vessel, he reached Quebec on 19th November.

The city was in charge of Hector Cramahé, his lieutenant governor, who had written that, "there is too much reason to apprehend the affair will soon be over." He had much reason for his despondency. His garrison totalled 1,126 men of whom 780 consisted of newly raised militia, part English, part French, and 150 more were sailors, artificers and newly arrived recruits. What Cramahé failed to appreciate was that the rebels were scarcely better off than the garrison. Although Richard Montgomery, a brilliant officer, had brought to Quebec some of the rebel troops who had seized Montreal, the

American force was suffering so severely from sickness that Montgomery and Arnold together could scarcely raise one thousand effectives. They had brought breaching cannon and mortars from Montreal but they could not attempt a formal siege as the ground was too frozen to dig trenches. Their only chance of taking Quebec was by a *coup de main*, pouring a small but overwhelming force against some lightly held part of the defences, which were far more extensive than the British could hope to man.

Carleton's first task was to restore the morale of the defenders. This he set about immediately, starting by putting outside the walls all those who had pro-rebel sympathies, mostly merchants whose hopes of an American victory had been much encouraged by Cramahé's insipid leadership. The rebel assault came on New Year's Eve. They were unfortunate that Montgomery was killed in the first clash and Arnold was wounded soon afterwards. There was hard fighting, but Carleton's leadership and example had given the garrison confidence. When 1776 dawned the city was safe. The rebels had suffered almost five hundred casualties, of whom 389 were captured. Carleton, who had lost only twenty, had a chance to counter-attack and might have destroyed the demoralised American remnant. He preferred to remain within the fortifications and the rebels kept up the semblance of a siege through the winter and spring.

The governor had done great service to Britain and to Canada. His defence of Quebec was the only really creditable victory won by the British in 1775. It is possible to understand, but easy to regret his inactivity in the early months of 1776. If he had acted boldly before the rebels were reinforced he might at least have captured Benedict Arnold, who continued to command the Americans from his bed until, after damaging the same leg again, he was superseded in March. He was not a likeable character but he was an outstanding leader of men in battle and few men caused more trouble to the King's troops before he decided to change sides.

On 6th May 1776, the garrison of Quebec was overjoyed to see the frigate *Surprise* sail up the St Lawrence. The rebels, although now 1,900 strong with a thousand fit for duty, wisely decamped westwards.

The convoy with which Burgoyne was due to sail from Portsmouth was delayed by the late arrival of a ship carrying hospital stores. It was not until 2nd April that he went on board HMS *Blonde*, which was dressed overall and had the yards manned in his honour. He was surprised to see one figure on the yard-arm standing on his head. That, Captain Pownell reassured him, was Midshipman Pellew who was always liable to such pranks. The voyage took scarcely five weeks, but it was too slow for Burgoyne. Since some of the transports were bad sailors, the whole convoy was forced to wait for them, and

Burgoyne applied to the convoy commander for *Blonde* to be allowed to push on alone. Permission was refused. Burgoyne believed that he could have reached Quebec in time to sail past the city and cut off the rebel retreat.

When the convoy straggled into Quebec, Carleton was already in pursuit with his handful of regulars. On the first ship to arrive and continue up the river was Major Edward Williams, an artillery officer. "About 50 miles above Quebec we met General Carleton coming down the river. He sent on board and directed me to go to Trois Rivières where we anchored the 3rd [June]. The troops that were on board many of the ships that could not get up the river were ordered to disembark and march up the land; and as the ships with some regiments had separated, some of them were 60 leagues astern of the others, therefore they got up to Trois Rivières by one, two or three companies of a corps. We continued increasing by the 8th instant, I believe, to the amount of two thousand, Col. Fraser[11] being the senior officer.'

Simon Fraser, commanding the Twenty Fourth Foot, was an excellent officer, and a close friend of Burgoyne's. He was a light infantry specialist and was particularly alert at Trois Rivières at 3.30 on the morning of 7th June. Major Williams was "much suprised to hear Col. Fraser hail me and beg for God's sake I would send what artillery on shore I possibly could, assuring me the rebels were within a mile of the town, to the amount of two or three thousand. I could scarce believe it; however, as I had 2 six pounders on deck with 80 rounds of case and grape shot, I had them on shore in less then twenty minutes."

The rebels, unaware of the strength Fraser had built up at Trois Rivières, were attempting a counter-attack under Brigadier General Thompson. Fortunately for Fraser the attack was delayed because a requisitioned Canadian guide deliberately led the assailants into a swamp. When the assault was delivered it was decisively repulsed, largely because the rebels were unprepared for the grape shot from Williams' two guns, which were reinforced by three more 6 pounders during the fighting.[12] Colonel St Leger took over the command of the British and seeing that the Americans were on the run, sent the flank companies in pursuit with two guns. "We kept the rebels marching through a marsh of 13 miles long in a parallel line with us and thro' the woods. They wanted to get on the main road but our guns kept them always in cover." By nightfall two hundred rebel prisoners had been taken, including General Thompson.

Next day Carleton and Burgoyne came up to Trois Rivières and the governor immediately recalled the advance guard to that place," for what reason," wrote Major Williams, "I know not". There was widespread discontent among the troops at Carleton's caution, and this was nothing new among the men who had served under him throughout the winter. A month earlier, Allan Maclean, who commanded the Highland Emigrants, had written, "I hope we have had experience sufficient to convince us that our unactivity and want of spirit was what greatly contributed to the distresses to which this province has been reduced."

It was not until four days later that the governor allowed the army to resume the pursuit up the river.[13] They reached Sorel, where the Richelieu river, flowing down from Lake Champlain and Ticonderoga, joins the St Lawrence, on the next day to find the rebels had evacuated the new earth-work they had constructed there. Here Carleton divided his army. He took four thousand up river to recapture Montreal and then swing south to reach the Richelieu overland. The other four thousand men were entrusted to Burgoyne, who was to pursue the defenders of Sorel up the same river. His orders positively forbade him to attack until Carleton's column regained touch with his right. Under the circumstances it was hardly surprising that both American forces escaped safely to the south.

There was now an essential pause. The British could not continue the pursuit southward until they had established naval superiority on Lake Champlain. According to Major Williams, writing on 23rd June, Carleton said that, "we shall not be able to move for three weeks; but I say six at least." Both had seriously underestimated the difficulties.

The previous day Burgoyne had written to Lord George. He spoke highly of "the spirit and enthusiasm of the troops" who had "cheerfully undertaken" forced marches in the hope of catching the enemy. The Canadians "appear overjoyed at the British success" and he gave it as his opinion that, though there were said to be some hidden traitors, Canada, with careful management, would become "a quiet and tractable province". He reported that Carleton appeared "very satisfied with all the arrangements made by the government", except on one point, "the disagreement between the general and Colonel Christie."

Gabriel Christie was an experienced soldier who had settled in Canada after the Seven Years War. Although an excellent administrator, Christie, like Carleton, was a difficult man to deal with, and the two had been on bad terms for some years, not least because Christie, as a Canadian resident, had signed a petition against the Quebec Act.[14] He had been in Britain when the fighting broke out and returned to Canada with a commission as Quarter-master General of the army in Canada. This infuriated Carleton who had already, with the agreement of Lord Dartmouth when he had been in office, appointed his brother Thomas to the post, having previously failed to obtain for him the post of Surveyor General for Canada.

When Lord George had given Christie his commission, he did not know that Dartmouth had already approved Carleton's choice of a QMG and, in any case, the increase of the army by eight thousand men would have justified the appointment of a far more experienced staff officer than Major Thomas Carleton. The governor, however, decided to take Christie's appointment as a personal affront. He refused to acknowledge his commission and treated him with great discourtesy. Burgoyne wrote to Lord George that, "it is to be hoped, for the sake of the general cordiality so essential for conducting the service with spirit, that the two may be separated." Germain agreed to remove Christie but, before his agreement could reach Canada, Carleton had settled down to conducting a private war with the Secretary of State.

It is far from clear why Carleton took such a dislike to Lord George. They had never served together and there is no evidence that they had ever had more than casual social dealings with each other. It was not until Quebec had been relieved in early May that the governor could have known that Germain had taken over the seals. Apart from the appointment of Christie, there was nothing in Germain's letters to him that could cause him to take offence. Carleton, however, wrote a series of letters of increasing insolence to the Secretary of State, beginning by blaming him for some civil appointments which Lord Dartmouth had made. Lord George replied to these outbursts with studied moderation. Naturally he developed a dislike and distrust of Carleton but it was not until December 1776 that the King remarked "a great prejudice perhaps not unaccompanied by rancour . . . against Governor Carleton" in Lord George, but even then the Secretary of State continued to treat Carleton with civility if not warmth. The details of the squabble are unedifying and largely irrelevant to this story.[15] What is important is that it put Burgoyne, as Carleton's second in command, in a very difficult situation which he handled with tact and moderation, keeping on good terms with both men.

While Carleton was waging literary hostilities against the American Department, there was great activity at both ends of Lake Champlain. British and Americans were busy building fleets with which to dominate the lake. The rebels had an initial advantage as they possessed the *Royal Savage*, a 14 gun schooner, captured the previous year. Against this they had great difficulty in finding shipwrights, carpenters and sailors in the area round Ticonderoga. The British could call on plenty of craftsmen from the fleet and the troop transports in the St Lawrence, but they had vast problems in getting their larger vessels up the ten mile stretch of rapids on the Richelieu, north of St John's, where the lake navigation began. Schooners had to be dismantled, taken forward in sections and reassembled on the lake.

Their most impressive achievement was the work of Lieutenant John Schanck RN, who built and transported to St John's a frigate in miniature,

HMS *Inflexible*, a ship of over 300 tons, armed with eighteen 12 pounders. She "was originally put on the stocks at Quebec; her floors were all laid, and some timbers were put in; the whole, namely the floors, keel, stem and stern, were then taken down and carried up the St Lawrence to Chambly, and from thence to St John's. Her keel was laid for the second time on the morning of the 2nd September and by sunset, not only were the above mentioned parts laid, but a considerable quantity of fresh timber was, in the course of the day, cut out and formed into futtocks, top-timbers, beams, planks, &c. On the 30th September, being twenty-eight days from the time the keel was laid, the *Inflexible* was launched; and on the evening of the 1st October actually sailed, completely manned, victualled and equiped for service. In ten days afterwards this vessel was engaged with the enemy."

While the artificers were building the fleet at St John's, Burgoyne was commanding the covering force to the south, holding a position astride the lake. Although the main bodies of the opposing armies lay more than seventy miles apart, there was continuous skirmishing between patrols in which, thanks largely to the support of the Canadian Indians, the British had the advantage. In the rear there was administrative chaos. The Commissary General, Nathaniel Day, was a former cornet of the 16th Light Dragoons and a lifelong friend of Burgoyne's but, like all other commissariat officers, he was wholly inexperienced and quite incapable of managing the complicated task he was called upon to perform. His task was made no easier by Carleton who "either lost or mislaid" all the bills of lading for the transport ships.

It was not until 7th October that the fleet was ready to sail and the light troops under Simon Fraser marched down the shores of the lake to Pont du Fer with orders to keep abreast of the fleet. Two days later Carleton embarked and the heavy ships started south. The main body of the army, with Burgoyne in command, marched along the shore in the rear.

The two fleets were evenly matched in fire power. The British had 94 guns with a combined weight of broadside of 1,101 lbs. The rebels had 102 guns throwing 921 lbs. In any considerable breeze the advantage would lie with the British, who had three heavy ships, the *Inflexible* with eighteen 12 pounders and two schooners with eighteen and fourteen guns respectively. They also had the *Thunderer*, a *radeau* or floating battery mounting six 24 pounders but this proved impossible to manoeuvre. The rebels had only two schooners (one with fourteen and one with eight guns) and two cutters (ten and eight guns). In still weather the Americans would have the advantage, since they had three row-galleys each mounting at least ten guns including two 24 pounders. The rest of the rebel fleet consisted of gondolas, large flat-bottomed boats armed with one 12 and two 9 pounders. The British had one captured gondola and a large number of gun-boats mounting single 24 pounders. The British were better supplied with crews, drawing on the Royal Navy for sailors and on the Royal and Hanau Artilleries for gunners. The rebels, however, enjoyed the undivided and inspiring leadership of Benedict Arnold. On the British side the nominal command was in the hands of Captain Thomas Pringle RN, a very competent officer, but Carleton insisted on embarking with him and persistently interfered with his arrangements.

It was probably because of this divided command that the battle on 11th October was bungled. There was a "splendid and auspicious" following wind as the fleet sailed south, but Carleton was convinced that Arnold was lying close to the southern end of Grand Island and no systematic search was made further north. In fact the rebel ships were between Valcour Island and the western shore of the lake. As a result, the British fleet overshot their enemy and had to beat back against the wind to attack.

When darkness fell the rebels had lost their heaviest ship, the schooner *Royal Savage*, and one gondola. On the British side, one gunboat was sunk, "for a cannon ball from the enemy's guns going through her powder magazine, it blew up", but two of the heavy ships were very severely handled. To make matters worse, Arnold managed to sail his ships southward during the night, despite a line of gunboats drawn across his course. Had the wind not changed he would have escaped to Ticonderoga. As it was, the British caught up with him at Split Rock Fort, fifteen miles north of Crown Point. One row-galley was sunk, the remaining schooner and one cutter escaped, and the rest of the fleet was burned to save it from capture. The crews made their way south overland. British supremacy on Lake Champlain was assured.

There the campaign of 1776 ended. The advance guard occupied Crown Point on 19th October, but although Ticonderoga, the key to further movement south, was only eighteen miles further on, Carleton declined even to reconnoitre the place. Certainly it was too late in the year to attempt a formal siege and he, Burgoyne or Phillips, the senior artillery officer, were all convinced that it could not be taken by a *coup de main*. Burgoyne and Phillips, however, believed that it would be worth trying the effect of passing troops round the fortress and cutting its communications with the south. This, in their opinion (and, as it happened, in the opinion of George Washington), might well have the effect of frightening the garrison into abandoning the place. Their morale was known to be low, for the rebel northern army had had a disastrous campaign in Canada and their fleet had been destroyed. The British would have risked nothing by making the attempt and the results might be very rewarding. Carleton would have none of it. He withdrew the whole army to winter quarters in Canada. The southernmost outpost was at

An Engraving of Burgoyne dating from 1780.

A cartoon of General Burgoyne published in 1789 after his disgrace, showing him as a Colonel in Light Dragoon uniform with petition in hand. (*National Army Museum*)

Two portraits of
James Wolfe: a
sketch of him as a
young man (*National
Portrait Gallery*), and
a likeness from the
time of the expedition
against Quebec.
(*National Army
Museum*)

A painting of the
death of General
Wolfe. (*National
Army Museum*)

New York City on
fire, 19 September
1776. The fire
destroyed a third of
the city.

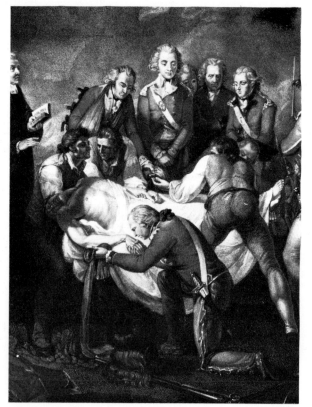

An engraving of the
burial of General
Fraser (*National
Army Museum*)

An engraving of Burgoyne addressing the Indians in 1777.

The British enter New York in 1776 thr●

ed streets (*National Army Museum*)

General Sir William Howe. (*National Army Museum*)

Colonel Bouquet. (*National Army Museum*)

General Sir Henry Clinton. (*National Army Museum*)

Île de Noix at the northern end of Lake Champlain.

While the army had waited at St John's, Burgoyne had heard that his beloved Charlotte had died in England on 7th June. As soon as there was no prospect of further fighting, he asked Carleton for leave to return to England to settle his wife's affairs and to recoup his own impaired health. The Governor agreed with alacrity. Having quarrelled irrevocably with Lord George, Carleton badly needed some intermediary to represent to the government in London the needs of the Canadian army. Burgoyne, who was liked and trusted by both Secretary of State and Governor, was the ideal emissary.

A letter followed him on his journey. It was from General Phillips who had been left to supervise the retreat of the army. He summed up the despair which the army felt at Carleton's caution. "I stand alone," he wrote, "unable to bear up against the sloth and changes of this atmosphere. You will scarce suppose that there is neither reconnoitring post nor scout sent forward, but as the whim of a drunken Indian prevails. I have endeavoured in vain to form a small detachment to feel the pulse of the enemy; the answer is that it is wrong to teach these people *war*. I must be of opinion that, notwithstanding the success on the lake, we end this campaign ill. It was upon the positive declaration that a post was to be established *here* [Crown Point] that I proposed sending the troops back into winter quarters for the power of more easily supplying the corps here; for I do protest that otherwise I think the army should have moved forward and a trial made at Ticonderoga. Had we failed in a feint, we could have retired, and I think there were good chances of success . . . I was never of opinion to attack the entrenchments seriously, but I am and ever shall be of opinion that every art of war should be practiced against these people . . . I am tardy in saying all this as it has been our joint opinion, and it has been a flattering, most flattering, most satisfactory reflection to me that we have agreed, I think, almost in every proposal and plan for this campaign . . . The army seems distressed and hurt at the languor which governs every movement."

It was not only the army which was distressed and hurt by Carleton's apparent languor. It was a bitter disappointment to Howe, now established in New York, and to Germain in London. The news of the relief of Quebec was received in England with delight by all but the most extreme "patriots".[16] It had arrived, according to Horace Walpole, in "a very unintelligible, ostentatious letter from General Carleton, in which it appeared that, having received 200 recruits by the *Isis*, he sallied out, and found the Provincials [i.e. the Americans] preparing to raise the siege on the sight of the *Isis* and other ships. Carleton said the Provincials had immediately fled and left their cannon and stores . . . This seems to speak the Provincials a rabble without military discipline, and much alarmed the friends of liberty."

Ministers decided that the event should be marked as a major triumph. At a cabinet meeting, "the opinion of seven of the persons present were that General Carleton deserved encouragement and reward, and that even if some parts of his conduct were doubtful, good policy required them. Notice should be taken of him now. The Red Ribband was thought a very proper mark of his Majesty's approbation. Lady Mary [Carleton], who sets out in a fortnight, may carry it to him." Lord George thought the award premature. "My wish was that such a mark of favour should have been deferred till the province of Canada should have been reclaimed. I then imagined it would have done the general more honour." The King, however, sided with the majority and Lady Maria sailed for Canada with her husband's insignia of the Order of the Bath.

Further news from Canada kept up hopes of great success. Writing to Burgoyne in August, Lord George, said, "The success you have met with is the more pleasing as Canada has been regained with the loss of so few men . . . I am glad you commanded the column which drove the rebels from Sorel to the lakes. Everyone does justice to your conduct upon that occasion. The King expressed himself upon that subject in a manner that gives one great pleasure, as it did you so much honour."

News of the naval victory at Valcour Island reached London on 8th November, days ahead of Carleton's despatch. Edward Gibbon wrote, "News from the Lakes. A naval combat in which the Provincials were repulsed with considerable loss. They burned and abandoned Crown Point. Carleton is besieging Ticonderoga."

The government took a less optimistic view. The officer who brought Carleton's despatch reported that the governor "is wholly uninformed of the state of Ticonderoga, or of the rebel army, which some reports make no more than 5,000 and others 25,000." Lord North received an "obscurely penned" letter from Carleton, acknowledging the Red Ribband but saying that, "much more is not to be expected on that side during the remainder of the campaign." It was, therefore, without surprise but with deep disappointment that the government heard from Canada that Ticonderoga was not to be attacked. The abandonment of Crown Point was, on the other hand, a very unwelcome piece of news, particularly since Carleton failed to make clear the very real difficulties which its retention would entail. Lord George reported the news to the King with a pointed absence of comment.

PART IV

Masterstroke

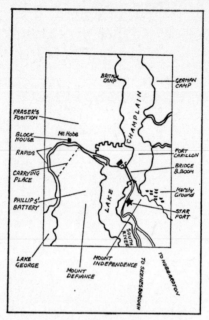

3. Ticonderoga, July 1777

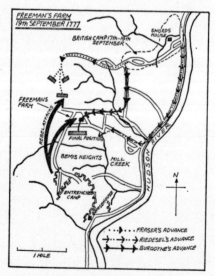

4. Freeman's Farm, 19th September 1777

CHAPTER 7

"To finish the Rebellion in One Campaign"

Burgoyne reached Portsmouth on 9th December 1776 and took the coach to London. His welcome was not as warm as it had been the previous year. There were those who felt his wife's death and his own poor health were not sufficient reason for taking annual leave from the theatre of war. Some of the disappointment felt over Carleton's tame withdrawal from Crown Point attached itself to his second in command. Horace Walpole, with his usual malice, wrote, "General Burgoyne is again arrived from Quebec as he had done the last year. He now pretended grief at his wife's death, which was laughed at. Some thought he had quarrelled with Carleton. He brought the news that Carleton had caused his army to recross the lakes, had abandoned Crown Point, and had not attempted Ticonderoga, where Major Gates was with 12,000 men."

Lady Charlotte's kinsman, Hans Stanley, MP for Southampton, wrote that he was "sorry to say, but not surprised, that there is a very great clamour against Burgoyne, particularly in the army. This may perhaps have in part arisen from the jealousy attending his return to a profession he had quitted, and the extraordinary favour he has since met with. I am afraid Burgoyne, in whom I supposed the highest ambition and ardour to distinguish himself, has thrown away an opportunity he will not find again, for I do not conceive it possible that Carleton should be relied upon again for the operations of another campaign, and he would certainly have succeeded him if he had been recalled."

On 10th December, Burgoyne went to call on Lord George Germain at his office in Pall Mall and to deliver Carleton's requisition for reinforcements and equipment for the next campaign. Germain was surprised, and possibly a little cold, at the general's unexpected return, but he was in no doubt that it was valuable to learn at first hand of the situation in Canada.

It has been alleged that on this occasion Burgoyne went out of his way to denigrate Carleton to the minister in the hope of taking over his command.

Certainly he would have said that he disapproved of falling back to Canada without making any attempt to secure Ticonderoga. This, however, was a point which he would have discussed with the governor and on which they had openly disagreed. Carleton must have expected him to express this opinion to Germain.

It is inherently improbable that Burgoyne attacked Carleton. Despite his acting rank, he was too junior a major general to be a strong candidate for the governorship of Canada, even if he had coveted the post, which is unlikely. If he hoped to command any field force sent south from Canada, he was most unlikely to succeed without the confidence and cordial assistance of the governor. It would have been directly contrary to his interest to intrigue against Carleton. It is more probable that he had to exert himself to defend a man with whom he had been at pains to build up good relations.

Certainly Lord George needed no urging against Carleton who had already sent him a number of insubordinate letters and who had bitterly disappointed the whole government by the meagre results of his campaign. Germain had also received a damning, and probably exaggerated, catalogue of Carleton's faults from Colonel Christie, the displaced Quartermaster General. "Confusion and embarassment appeared everywhere under a commander absorbed within himself, giving answers to few and saying little, who follows a scheme or plan absolutely incomprehensible. The merit or demerit is his own because the great assistance he might have drawn from his second in command and other spirited officers of merit I have reason to think he despised and was his own projector. Many days often passed without any orders and even what was intended not circulated as they ought. His immoderate ambition led him on board the fleet to command it; this *gêné*'d those whose province it was, [so] all was confusion . . . His not proceeding to look at Ticonderoga, within 15 miles of him, is beyond all human comprehension . . . I shall not venture further than saying my real belief that he is totally unfit for such a command."

Moreover, Lord George must have mentioned to Burgoyne early in their interview that he had been chosen for the field command in Canada as early as August 1776. In that month Germain had written Carleton a letter "which was entrusted to one of [Carleton's] aide-de-camps. After having been three times in the Gulph of St Lawrence, he had the mortification to find it impossible to make his passage to Quebec, and therefore returned to England with my dispatch." After congratulating Carleton on his successes, Germain had expressed the hope that, "before this letter reaches you, you will by your spirit and activity have cleared the frontiers of Canada of all rebel forces and will have taken proper measures for keeping possession of the lakes [lakes Champlain and George]. His Majesty commands me to acquaint you that there still remains another part of your duty to be undertaken, which will require all your abilities and the strictest application, the restoring peace and the establishment of good order and legal government in Canada. It is an object of the greatest importance to this country, the difficulties attending it are immense; but his Majesty depends upon your zeal and experience in carrying it out. His Majesty, ever anxious for the happiness of his subjects, commands me to inform you that no time should be lost in beginning so important a work, and that you do therefore return to Quebec, detaching Lieutenant General Burgoyne or such other officer as you shall think most proper with that part of your force as can be spared from the immediate defence of your province, to carry on such operations as shall be most conducive to the success of the army acting on the side of New York; that you will direct the officer so detached to communicate with and put himself, as soon as possible, under the command of General Howe; you will order such artillery as you shall judge necessary to proceed with this detachment; and as a great quantity of heavy cannon and military stores were sent, upon the supposition that Quebec might be in the hands of the rebels, you will, upon requisition from General Howe, supply him with such cannon and stores as shall not be wanted for the defence of Canada."

Thus, as soon as he reached England, Burgoyne would have realised that he was likely to return to Canada as the designated commander of the force to march south and join the main army under Howe.

There is little doubt that Germain would have been glad to recall Carleton from Canada, especially after his apparently spiritless behaviour at Crown Point, but he knew that the King would not agree to such a move. "Perhaps," wrote the King, "Carleton may be too cold and not so active as might be wished which makes it advisable to have the part of the Canadian army which must attempt to join General Howe led by a more enterprizing commander; but should the proposal be to recall Carleton from his government or censure his conduct, that would be too cruel and the exigency cannot authorize it."

Burgoyne was the obvious candidate for the role of that "more enterprizing commander". He knew the route as far as Crown Point; he knew the troops and their officers; he had shown he could work closely with the difficult Carleton. Though Walpole supposed that, "the King scarcely spoke to [Burgoyne], and he was forced to ask for an audience", it was only four days after he set foot in England that the King wrote, "Burgoyne may command the corps to be sent from Canada to Albany."

At his first interview with Germain, Burgoyne would have been told the news from southern army. Boston had been evacuated in mid-March and the troops, only nine thousand strong, had been shipped to Halifax. After a long pause the army, reinforced to 25,000 rank and file, had sailed against New York. By the end of August they were firmly established on Long Island after a battle in which Howe had shown great tactical skill. The rebels, under Putnam, had been out-generalled and out-fought. They had fled in disorder, but Howe had not made full use of his victory. The enemy had not been destroyed as they might have been and twenty thousand rebels lived to fight another day. September had seen the British crossing to Manhattan Island and the occupation of New York City, together with an inconclusive action on Haarlem Heights.

The latest information, which reached London at the beginning of December, was that the only remaining rebel position on Manhattan was Fort Washington. Despite the lack of a decisive victory, the situation around New York seemed to be satisfactory. The army had been well received by the inhabitants, especially on Long Island. On the rebel side, the militia showed signs of disintegration. There was every reason to suppose that, by the end of the campaigning season, Howe would have secured a base from which to execute the stroke which was to end the rebellion in 1777.

Burgoyne stayed in London until the end of the year. On 17th December, he appeared on the hustings in Covent Garden to speak in support of his friend Captain Lord Petersham. Petersham, who was commanding the light company of the Twenty Ninth in Canada, had not returned to England for the by-election for Westminster, the most democratic constituency in England. After short speeches by Burgoyne and Mr Foley, he was elected unopposed, the whole affair being over in fifteen minutes. It was a clear indication that the people of England were behind the government's American policy.

A few days after Christmas, Burgoyne had a private interview with the King "in his closet". He asked leave to go to Bath[1] to take the waters and added "that as the arrangements for the next campaign might possibly come under his royal contemplation before my return, I humbly laid myself at his Majesty's feet for such active employment as he might think me worthy of."

Meanwhile more good news was on its way across the Atlantic. Fort Washington was taken on 16th November, completing the conquest of Manhattan. In this action the rebels lost three thousand men killed, wounded and captured, and 146 cannon, together with large stores of small arms and ammunition. The British lost less than five hundred men but once again the main rebel army managed to escape. Howe, on this occasion, undertook an energetic pursuit, following the Americans across the Hudson. He had intended only to occupy the coastal strip between Newark and Perth Amboy, but the rebels made so little resistance that he allowed Lord Cornwallis, who commanded the advance guard, to push the pursuit to the Delaware river. Advanced posts were established at Burlington and Trenton, within easy striking distance of the seat of the Congress at Philadelphia. This was a wide dispersion of his army, but the rebels' army did not seem to be formidable and Howe was anxious to secure the widest possible foraging ground for the winter.

While this pursuit was in progress, Howe wrote a letter to Lord George which outlined his plans for the campaign of 1777. He proposed to divide his army into three corps:

"1st. An offensive army of 10,000 rank and file to act on the side of Rhode Island by taking possession of Providence, penetrating from thence into the country toward Boston and, if possible, to reduce that town. Two thousand men to be left for the defence of Rhode Island, and for making small incursions, under the protection of the shipping, upon the coast of Connecticut. This army to be commanded by Lieut. Gen. Clinton.

'2nd. An offensive army in the province of New York to move up the North [Hudson] river to Albany, to consist of not less than 10,000 men and 5,000 for New York and adjacent posts.

'3rd. A defensive army of 8,000 men to cover Jersey, and to keep the southern [rebel] army in check by giving a jealousy to Philadelphia, which I would propose to attack, as well as Virginia, provided the success of the other operations will admit of an adequate force to be sent against that province.'

This plan, with its twin offensives to Boston and Albany while a strong force kept Washington in check to the southward, was sound in theory. The overriding objection was that Howe's army would have to be reinforced to 35,000 rank and file. This was impossible even though, by the statistics in London, its strength at the end of the year was 27,000. Howe, moreover, counted his effectives at only twenty thousand and said that "to complete this plan not less than ten ships of the line will be absolutely requisite, and a reinforcement to the amount of 15,000 rank and file", beside a substantial additional supply of artillery.

Howe's letter also mentioned that Clinton was about to sail from New York with six thousand men to secure Rhode Island. Germain, therefore, wrote only an interim reply to the proposals. "As your next letters (of which I am in daily expectation) will probably throw new light on the subject, his Majesty thinks it proper to withold his royal sentiments until he shall have an opportunity of taking into consideration the whole state of this momentous affair." He also told Howe that he could not expect more than 7,800 reinforcements.[2]

The proposal for an offensive against Boston made a strong appeal to the British government, army and people, all of whom smarted under the humiliation the troops had suffered there in the summer and winter of 1775.

The advance to Albany in cooperation with an army from Canada was of far more consequence. It was the accepted British strategy for winning the war. The belief was that if New England could be cut off from the Middle Colonies by seizing and holding the line of the Hudson, the rebellion would wither and die.

This conception has been ridiculed. Even Sir John Fortescue, whose judgments are never to be dismissed lightly, wrote that, "it would require from thirty to fifty thousand men." This, of course, would leave the British without a striking force.

The facts are otherwise. In 1777, with France still neutral, the Royal Navy was available to do the major part of the work of holding the line of the Hudson. The key stretch of the river was the 150 miles from New York to Albany. For more than a hundred of these miles the river was wide and deep enough to be patrolled by ships with a draught of between twenty and fourteen feet—a task for frigates and sloops. For the last 46 miles, between Livingstone's Manor and Albany itself, the river was shallower, but it could still be patrolled by gunboats and these, supported by a relatively small number of troops employed as mobile columns and as the garrisons of small fortified strongpoints, could control the river. The reaches above Albany would require only the lightest guard. There was little settlement in that area and no east–west communication.

It would, of course, be impossible to prevent small parties from slipping across the river at night but there could be no major troop movements across the line. Quite as important was the fact that New England was largely dependent on the Middle Colonies for food. With the rebels thus divided and the most unyielding of them straitened for food, Britain would have a real chance to crush the rebellion in detail. It would rob the Americans of their main strategic waterway while, at the same time, solving much of the British army's most intractable problem, the shortage of land transport. Up to the end of 1777 it seemed both promising and practicable.[3] Certainly no other plan held out such a prospect of subduing the colonies.

Lord Dartmouth had suggested this strategy to Gage four days before the battle of Bunker Hill. One day earlier, Howe had outlined it in a letter from Boston. He had repeated it in September 1775, in May of the following year and in August 1776. On that occasion, when his New York campaign had not gone as fast as he had hoped, he wrote from Staten Island that, "the extent of my expectations [for this campaign] are bounded by the possession of New York and Rhode Island and a junction with the northern army."

There could be no reasonable doubt in London that Howe was committed to the Hudson river strategy and all plans were made on the assumption that this was to be the main operation of 1777.

On 23rd February, a ship arrived with two more despatches from Howe. The later of the two reported that Washington had succeeded in destroying three Hessian battalions at Trenton on Christmas Day and had greatly reduced the extent of the British hold on New Jersey. The earlier letter offered a revised plan for the campaign of 1777. Howe now proposed to defer "the offensive plan towards Boston [since] the opinion of people being much changed in Pennsylvania, and their minds in general, from the late progress of the army, disposed to peace, in which sentiment they would be confirmed by our getting possession of Philadelphia. I am from this consideration fully persuaded the principal army should act offensively on that side where the enemy's chief strength will certainly be collected." Believing "on a rough calculation that the extent of our strength at the opening of the campaign will not exceed 19,000 men", Howe proposed leaving two thousand on Rhode Island, four thousand in and around New York, three thousand on the Hudson river and taking ten thousand men to Philadelphia.

In this modified plan Howe made no direct reference to his second "offensive army", the one which was to go up the Hudson to Albany. The proposal to operate towards Boston was specifically abandoned. The force to be left in and around New York was not large. It was, on the other hand apparent that Howe intended moving against Philadelphia "at the opening of the campaign". This suggested that he would move in April or early May. When the letter was written Howe's outposts on the Delaware were within forty miles of Philadelphia. Even after the reverse at Trenton the distance to Philadelphia, by land or sea, was not long. There was nothing impossible in switching troops from Pennsylvania to the Hudson to act with the troops already in New York and with the promised reinforcements. There seemed no reason why the Hudson river strategy should not be implemented. Germain, and everybody else in authority in London, never doubted that Howe still held a junction with the Canadian army on the Hudson to be the pre-eminent operation for the year. Howe, indeed, had confirmed this belief by writing, in the same letter, "We must not look for the northern [i.e. Canadian] army to reach Albany before the middle of September." The implication was clear. That by mid-September he would be on the Hudson to cooperate with the northern army.

By the time this letter reached London it was known that Henry Clinton was on his way home. This set Germain a further problem and he commented acidly that, "Burgoyne will not be sorry to see that he is not the only general, second in command, who takes the liberty [of coming home] without the King's leave." Clinton, who actually reached London on 28th February, had a grudge against ministers and against Germain in particular. In July 1776 he had undertaken an abortive expedition against Charleston,

South Carolina, and his despatch on the event had been edited in London. The editing, which covered up a quarrel between himself and his escorting admiral, was wholly justified but Clinton considered that the result showed him in an unfavourable light and, according to some reports, he was determined to challenge Germain to a duel. The offer of the Canadian command to his junior, Burgoyne, might well inflame Clinton further. The government was reluctant to give Clinton the command in the north. Apart from his quarrel with Admiral Parker, he had failed to establish a working relationship with Howe who had written, "If General Clinton, being senior to General Burgoyne, should go to Canada as the prior command, I hope General Burgoyne will join this army." This was a clear indication that Howe wished to dispose of Clinton. On the other hand, Clinton, with his inability to stay on good terms with his colleagues, his "recklessness in pursuing a grievance", was the last man to cooperate happily with Carleton and if Clinton quarrelled with the governor, the expedition to Albany might be postponed indefinitely. Reluctantly, the cabinet decided that he must be offered the command.

It seems clear that, on receipt of Howe's revised proposals, Lord George asked Burgoyne, the general with the most recent knowledge of Canada, to write a paper suggesting the best way in which the northern army could cooperate with Howe on the Hudson river. This is the most natural explanation of how Burgoyne came to submit his much misunderstood memorandum of 28th February 1777, entitled *Thoughts for Conducting the War from the Side of Canada*.[4] It must be noticed that the four days in which Burgoyne wrote the paper were precisely the days on which he was least likely to be given the command of the Canadian army. On 24th February, the day on which he would have started the paper, the King wrote to Lord North, "Lord George Germain will tomorrow propose General Clinton for Canada and Burgoyne to join Howe. I thoroughly approve of this." Even if Burgoyne did not know of this arrangement he certainly knew that Clinton was on his way home. He cannot have failed to realise that government could have no alternative to offering the command to Clinton as the senior officer.

The crucial sentence in the *Thoughts*, when speaking of the advance to Albany, is, "These ideas are formed upon the supposition that it is the sole purpose of the Canada army to effect a junction with General Howe, or after co-operating so far as to get the possession of Albany and open the communication to New York, to remain upon the Hudson's river, and thereby enable that general to act with his whole army to the southward." In other words, either Albany was to be seized in cooperation with Howe or some other move should be decided upon for the Canadian army. The alternatives suggested by Burgoyne were a drive down the Connecticut river to act in concert with the garrison of Rhode Island or the shipping of all disposable troops from Canada to strengthen Howe's force at New York.

Burgoyne assumed, as did Lord George and the King, that the march to Albany was only practicable if Howe's army cooperated. There was no need for any major formation of Howe's army to go physically to Albany. Howe's task was to seize the Highlands, the place where the Hudson flows through a gap in the hills around Peekskill. Once this strong position was held it would be largely a naval task to open up the communication by river between New York and Albany. Neither Burgoyne nor Germain had any illusions about supplying even a small army at Albany from Canada through the winter. It was fair to assume that Howe, who had wintered in Canada in 1759/60, would be equally aware that if troops at Albany were not fed from New York they would starve.

Burgoyne assumed that the first stage of getting to Albany must be the taking of Ticonderoga where, "I will suppose the enemy in great force; the different works there are capable of admitting twelve thousand men." Once Ticonderoga was captured it should be made into a firm base, "the place of arms", for the onward march. South of that fortress he expected the Americans to use delaying tactics rather than risk pitched battles. He anticipated that they would throw up temporary fortifications of earth and the abundant timber on "strong ground in different places". This was a legacy of Bunker Hill. Nothing had impressed the British so much as the speed with which the rebels had thrown up a substantial earthwork in a single night. To overcome these fortifications the army would have to carry with it "a weight of artillery". This, of course, would slow down the march and help the rebels' delaying tactics "by felling trees, breaking bridges and other obvious impediments, though he should not have the power or spirit finally to resist" the army's progress. Burgoyne's proposal to take a sizeable field train with the army was in line with the suggestions of Governor Carleton and by Major General Phillips, the senior gunner officer with the army in Canada. It also confirmed with Germain's order of the previous year for Carleton to send heavy artillery overland to Howe.

Beyond Ticonderoga, Burgoyne recommended the route up Lake George so as to economise on land transport. He had, nevertheless, to point out that the rebels would have "a considerable naval strength" on that lake. This might be counteracted "by throwing savages and light troops around it, to oblige them to quit it without waiting for the [British] naval preparations". Transporting substantial warships, like the *Inflexible*, across the portage from Ticonderoga to Lake George was bound to be a lengthy business however well it was managed.

The alternative to crossing the lake was "the road by South Bay and

Skenesborough . . . but considerable difficulties might be expected as the narrow parts of the river may be easily choaked up and rendered impassable, and at best there will be a necessity for a great deal of land carriage, which can only be supplied from Canada." It would be difficult and tedious to take this route and Burgoyne did not underestimate the problems involved. Nevertheless, he considered them preferable to the delays inseparable from establishing a fleet on Lake George. "Lest all these attempts [i.e. frightening the rebels away by Indians and light troops or taking the road by Skenesborough] should unavoidably fail, and it becomes necessary to attack the enemy by water on Lake George, the army at the outset should be provided with carriages, implements and artificers for conveying armed vessels from Ticonderoga to the lake."

As for the force required, "I humbly conceive the operating army (I mean exclusive of the troops left for the defence of Canada) ought not to consist of less than eight thousand regulars, rank and file, the artillery required in the memorandum of General Carleton, a corps of watermen, two thousand Canadians, including hatchetmen and other workmen, and a thousand or more savages." In addition, there was to be a subsidiary expedition from "Lake Ontario and Oswego to the Mohawk river which, as a diversion to facilitate every proposed operation, would be highly desirable, provided the army should be reinforced sufficiently to afford it."

It was essential that the "operating army" must be set in motion early enough to be certain of reaching Albany before the weather closed in for the winter. This could only be done with the active cooperation of the governor, who was likely to raise objections to anything proposed by Lord George. The *Thoughts*, therefore, had to serve a double function. They had to be an information paper to Germain on which he could base his orders to Carleton but at the same time they had to be an *aide-memoire* to Clinton as the commander-designate who had no first hand knowledge of Canada.[5] Burgoyne, therefore, made his recommendations very detailed. In particular he recommended which of the troops in Canada should accompany the expedition and which should be left in garrison in the province. Apart from various detachments, the main British units to be left behind should be the Thirty First Foot because, "when I saw it last it was not equally in order with the other regiments for services of activity", the Twenty Ninth because "it is not at present brigaded", and the Royal Highland Emigrants "because I very much apprehend desertion from such parts of it as are composed of Americans should they come near the enemy. In Canada, whatsoever may be their disposition, it is not so easy to effect it." He recommended the total of the Canadian garrison to be three thousand rank and file.

There are also in the *Thoughts* three paragraphs which Burgoyne would hardly have inserted if he were expecting to have the command himself, but which could be important if the notoriously difficult Clinton should go to Canada. The purpose of the paragraphs is to eliminate friction between the governor and the field commander by defining explicitly their responsibilities.

"A business thus complicated in arrangement, in some cases unusual in practice, and in others perhaps difficult can only be carried on to the desired effect by the peremptory powers, warm zeal and consonant opinion of the governor; and though the former are not to be doubted, a failure in the latter, vindicated or seeming to be vindicated by the plausible obstructions that will not fail to be suggested by others, will be sufficient to crush such exertions as an officer of sanguine temperament, entrusted with the future conduct of the campaign and whose personal interest and fame consequently depend upon a timely outset, would be led to make.

"The assembly of savages and Canadians will also depend entirely upon the governor.

"Upon these considerations, it is presumed that the general officer employed to proceed with the army will be held out of reach of any possible blame till he is clear of the province of Canada and furnished with the proposed supplies."

Writers of the "give-a-dog-a-bad-name-and-hang-it" school have pounced on these paragraphs as evidence of an attempt by Burgoyne to exculpate himself for any possible failure by blaming Carleton in advance. This is absurd. Whatever risks a commander might face in upper New York, he had no serious dangers to fear while still in Canada and, in any case, the King and Lord George would have seen through such a bare-faced attempt to shift the blame for future ill-success. If, however, it was inserted to reassure a somewhat "tetchy" friend, the passage becomes understandable and, indeed, sensible.

In case Howe should decide to "act with his whole force to the southward" *throughout the campaigning season*, Burgoyne suggested that, after taking Ticonderoga, the bastion of Canadian defence, the northern army might march over the mountains to the eastward and establish itself on the Connecticut river. He did not underestimate the difficulties of such a move. "The extent of the country from Ticonderoga to the inhabited country upon that river opposite Charles Town is about sixty miles, and though to convey artillery and provisions so far would be attended with difficulties, perhaps more than those above suggested upon a progress to Skenesborough, should the object appear worthy, it is hoped resources might be found." If this plan was adopted he proposed that all that should be attempted should be to "fortify one or two strong redoubts opposite to Charles Town" and a chain of subsidiary posts to guard the mountain road back to Ticonderoga. If

Howe's operations to the southward were such that the great bulk of the rebel army was drawn in that direction, it might be possible for the army from Canada and the garrison of Rhode Island to carry out on the Connecticut the kind of concerted operation that was being planned on the Hudson. In this case, "it is not too sanguine an expectation that all the New England provinces will be reduced by their operations." It must be noted that this last "sanguine expectation" was conditional on New England being denuded even of its militia, an unlikely event. The limited operation of seizing a key town on the Connecticut might well have been a practicable proposition. The most reliable topographical source available to the British, Montressor's map published in 1759, showed a practicable track across the mountains and a later map[6] shows three.

As a last resource, in case the strength of the army in Canada had been unexpectedly eroded during the winter and "the force is not sufficient for proceeding on the above ideas [i.e. operations on either the Hudson or Connecticut rivers] with a fair prospect of success, the alternative remains of embarking the army at Quebec, in order to effect a junction with Howe . . . And though the army, upon examination of the numbers from the returns here, and the reinforcements designed, should appear adequate, it is humbly submitted as a security against the possibility of its remaining inactive, whether it might not be expedient to entrust the latitude of embarking the army by sea, provided any accidents during the winter and unknown here, should have diminished the numbers considerably."

Burgoyne's own view was that this last course "ought not to be thought of but upon a positive conviction of its necessity . . . I do not conceive any expedition from the sea can be so formidable to the enemy, or so effectual to close the war as an invasion from Canada."

In the Royal Archives there is an unsigned memorandum commenting on Burgoyne's *Thoughts*. It is probably written by Sir Jeffrey Amherst, who had fought his way at the head of an army from Albany to Montreal by way of Ticonderoga seventeen years earlier. The commentator, whoever he was, agreed that "the outlines are founded on a proper foundation" but doubted whether the number of troops stipulated by Burgoyne could be made available. Calculating the total number of soldiers in Canada to be 11,443, "as drawbacks always happen by sickness &c., I doubt whether above 7,000 of these can be spared over Lake Champlain. Your Majesty's Ministers (who have, of course, the best intelligence of the inclinations of the people in Canada) can better judge as to what numbers shou'd be left in that country. Certainly no hazard shou'd be run as to having any disturbance there. The numbers which are to be left shou'd be particularly ordered. The fixing the stations [of the garrison] shou'd be left to the governor. The particular corps which are named may be as proper as any."

The commentator stressed two other points. "I have ever been of opinion that it has been a mistaken idea of humanity in not employing the Indians. I am afraid it will be proved so, as if they are not for your Majesty's service, they will act as enemies. For this reason, I submit whether such instructions should not be sent to the respective commanders as will putt them out of doubt, as to what measures should be taken.

'Strong instructions also to General Carleton to assist (with as many Canadians as he can) the general who advances with the main army." It is clear from this that Burgoyne was not the only man who believed it necessary to spell out Carleton's responsibilities for the expedition.

The two alternative schemes proposed by Burgoyne were rejected. "As Sir W. Howe seems to think that he can't act in the Massachusetts from Rhode Island, it may be advisable to [take the] force down to Albany and join [Howe] at that place . . . The idea of carrying the army by sea to Sir W. Howe would certainly require leaving a much larger part in Canada. I greatly dislike the idea." The commentator's only doubt about Burgoyne's main proposal was whether the diversion on the Mohawk could be made strong enough.

This memorandum, together with the *Thoughts*, was submitted to the King who agreed with the commentator, writing a note in his own hand which incorporated much of the commentator's wording. Germain, thereupon, began to put the plan into execution. The drafting of orders for Carleton was put in hand and, on 3rd March, Germain wrote to Howe authorising his plan for the attack on Philadelphia. "I am now commanded to acquaint you that the King entirely approves of your proposed deviation from the plan you formerly suggested, being of opinion that the reasons which induced you to recommend this change are solid and decisive." At the same time he told the general that he would be getting only about three thousand reinforcements and drew his attention to the advantages that would accrue from "a warm diversion upon the coasts of Massachusets Bay and New Hampshire, [which] will not only impede the levies of the Continental army, but tend much to the security of our trade."

In this letter Lord George meant exactly what he said. Basing himself on Howe's letter of 20th December, he was giving approval for the substitution of an attack on Philadelphia for the proposal for an "offensive army of 10,000 rank and file to act on the side of Rhode Island, penetrating from thence into the country towards Boston and, if possible, to reduce that town". He did not mention the long planned double attack, from north and south, on Albany because it never crossed his mind that Howe did not intend to carry it out. In any case the position would be made clear when, in a few days time, the orders for the operations of the Canadian army were issued.

On the day this letter to Howe was sent, Clinton decided that he would not accept the command of the Canadian army. He allowed his pique over the edited despatch to be assuaged with a knighthood and agreed to return to New York as second in command to Howe. The choice of a leader for the northern army in the joint advance to Albany finally reverted to John Burgoyne.

CHAPTER 8

"Directed to Make a Junction"

Lord George's orders to Governor Carleton were completed on 26th March and entrusted to Burgoyne, who set out immediately for Plymouth to board the "fast sailing, copper bottomed ship of twenty guns", *Ariadne*. It was important that both he and the orders reach Canada as soon as the melting of the ice made it possible to sail up to Quebec. For some days, the wind made it impossible for the *Ariadne* to sail. On 2nd April, Lord George was writing irritably, "I am sorry Burgoyne cannot avail himself of this fine wind . . . I didn't know two winds were necessary at Plymouth before they could put to sea there."

Nevertheless, the *Ariadne* made a quick and fortunate passage and Lieutenant Hadden of the Artillery wrote in his diary, "The 6th of May Gen'l Burgoyne arrived at Quebec from England; it is remarkable that, that very day twelve months the garrison was relieved, and that no ships ever arrived sooner, the passage up the river be'g obstructed with ice." At Quebec the orders for the expedition were handed over to Carleton.

Lord George's letter began by reiterating the contents of his undelivered letter of 22nd August 1776. Then, with more forthrightness than tact, the Secretary of State expressed his "mortification" at learning that "upon your repassing Lake Champlain [in the previous year], a very considerable number of the insurgents, finding their presence no longer necessary near Ticonderoga, immediately marched from thence and joined the rebel forces in the provinces of New York and Jersey. That unexpected reinforcement was more particularly unfortunate for us as it enabled the rebels to break in with some degree of success upon parts of the winter quarters that were taken up by the army under the command of Sir William Howe."

Although one can sympathise with Lord George in wishing to retaliate in kind for some of the unprovoked abuse heaped on him by Carleton, it was stupid of him to start a letter which the governor was bound to find unpalatable by blaming him for the *débâcle* at Trenton. He went on to instruct

Carleton to retain only "about 3,000 men under your command for the defence and duties of [Canada] and employ the remainder of your army upon two expeditions—the one under Lieutenant General Burgoyne, who is to force his way to Albany, and the other under the command of Lieut. Colonel St Leger, who is to make a diversion on the Mohawk river. As this plan can not advantageously be executed without the assistance of Canadians and Indians, his Majesty strongly recommends it to your care to furnish both expeditions with good and sufficient bodies of those men. And I am happy in knowing that your influence amongst them is so great that there can be no reason to apprehend you will find it difficult to fulfil his Majesty's expectations."

Germain accepted the advice of the unknown commentator and did not "fix the stations" of the troops to be left in Canada but he offended Carleton as much as if he had done so by pointing out the "several garrisons and posts which probably it may be necessary for you to take, viz: Quebec, Chaudiére, the disaffected of Point Levi, Montreal and posts between that town and Oswegatche, Trois Rivieres, St John's, Isle aux Noix, La Prairie, Vegere and some towns upon the southern shore of St Lawrence, opposite to the town of Montreal, with posts of communication to St. John's". It should be noted that Germain did not instruct Carleton to garrison these places but only said that they were the ones which "probably it may be necessary" to garrison. He did so to demonstrate that "this allotment for Canada had not been made without properly weighing the several duties which are likely to be required." Carleton received this suggestion with the worst of grace and insisted on regarding the suggestions as mandatory. At a later, and crucial, stage of the campaign he claimed that Germain "not only orders those [troops] I am to send and those I am to keep, but points out where the latter are to be posted, and you must observe the Isle aux Noix is the most advanced on [the south]." The wording of Germain's letter does not stand this interpretation.

Although Lord George told Carleton that he would be left with only three thousand rank and file, as Burgoyne had suggested, the units and detachments which were detailed to remain in Canada actually left him with a garrison of 3,770. This increase was found at the expense of the expeditionary forces. Burgoyne had proposed that the army to go to Albany "ought not to consist of less than eight thousand regulars, rank and file." The force allocated to him numbered only 7,173,[1] while St Leger's diversion was to be given only 675 including 133 American Loyalists.

The kernel of Germain's letter was the orders which Carleton was to give to the commander of the expeditionary force. "It is his Majesty's pleasure that you put under the command of Lieutenant General Burgoyne:—

"The grenadiers and light infantry [companies] (except the Eighth

Regiment) and 24th Regiment as the Advanced Corps under Brigadier
General Fraser   1,568
  "*First Brigade*: Battalion companies of the 9th, 21st and 47th regiments,
deducting 50 from each corps to remain in Canada.   1,194
  "*Second Brigade*: Battalion companies of the 20th, 53rd and 62nd regi-
ments deducting 50 from each corps as above   1,194
  "All the German troops, except the Hanau Chasseurs and a detachment
of 650.   3,217
  "The artillery, except such parts as shall be necessary for the defence of
Canada

                                                                     7,173

Together with as many Canadians and Indians as may be thought necessary
for this service, and after having furnished him in the fullest and completest
manner with artillery stores, provisions and every other article necessary
for his expedition and secured to him every assistance which it is in your power
to afford and procure, you are to give him orders to pass Lake Champlain
and thence by the most vigorous exertion of his force, to proceed with all
expedition to Albany, and put himself under the command of Sir William
Howe.
  "From the King's knowledge of the great preparation made by you last
year to secure the command of the lakes, and the attention to this part of the
service during the winter, his Majesty is led to expect that everything will be
ready for General Burgoyne's passing the lake by the time you and he shall
have adjusted the plan of the expedition."
  There were similar instructions to Colonel St Leger, who was allotted 200
British regulars, the Hanau chasseurs (342 strong) and a small Loyalist unit,
and told to "proceed to and down the Mohawk river to Albany and put himself under the command of Sir William Howe."
  Germain ended his letter by writing, "I shall write to Sir William Howe
from hence by the first packet; but you will endeavour to give him the earliest intelligence of this measure and also direct Lieutenant General Burgoyne
and Lieutenant Colonel St Leger to neglect no opportunity of doing the
same, that they may receive instructions from Sir William Howe. You will
at the same time inform them that, until they shall have received orders from
Sir William Howe, it is his Majesty's pleasure that they shall act as exigencies
require, and in such manner as they shall judge most proper for making an
impression on the rebels and bringing them to obedience; but that in doing so
they must never lose view of their intended junction with Sir William Howe
as their principal object."

Burgoyne could have had little doubt as to the meaning of these orders. He was to take his little army to Albany and join the southern army under Howe. As soon as he arrived in Quebec he had written to his friend Simon Fraser, commanding the Advanced Corps, that, "the military operations, all directed to make a junction with Howe, are committed to me". He had, in addition, discussed the orders with Germain and must have known what had been in mind when he wrote them. It is indeed very difficult to read the orders in any way other than as a straightforward instruction to march to Albany as quickly as possible. It is true that there was a discretionary clause which allowed him, before he received orders from Howe, to "act as exigencies require", but even this was qualified by the injunction not to "lose view of the intended junction with Sir William Howe as the principal object".

Nor had Burgoyne any reason to doubt that Howe intended to march north to cooperate with him, proposing to arrive in the area in mid-September. Even if he had not known that the joint operation on the Hudson had been Howe's favourite strategy since he succeeded to the southern command in 1775, he knew it was to be prescribed to him in Germain's orders "by the first packet". As a final reassurance, he had dined on several occasions before leaving London with his friend Sir Henry Clinton, Howe's second in command, who was fully informed of the plan.

What Burgoyne could not know was that there was a weak point in the communication between Germain and Howe. Germain did not write specific orders to Howe to undertake the march to Albany. He had intended to send Howe a copy of the orders to Carleton and Burgoyne with a covering letter pointing out Howe's part in the operation. He had never doubted Howe's intention to march north in the late summer. What actually happened is told by Germain's Under Secretary, William Knox. When Burgoyne's orders were complete and Knox "had them to compare and make up, Lord [George] came down to the office on his way to Stoneland,[2] when I observed to him that there was no letter to Howe to acquaint him with the plan or what was expected of him in consequence of it. His lordship started and D'Oyley[3] stared, but said he would in a few moments write a few lines. 'So' said his lordship, 'my poor horses must stand in the street all the time and I shan't be on my time anywhere.' D'Oyley then said he had better go, and he would write himself to Howe and inclose copies of Burgoyne's instructions which he would want to know; and with this his lordship was satisfied, as it enabled him to keep his time, for he could never bear delay or disappointment; and D'Oyley sat down and writ a letter to Howe, but he neither shew'd it to me or gave a copy of it for the office, and if Howe had not acknowledged the receipt of it, with a copy of the Instructions to Burgoyne, we could not have proved that he ever saw them."[4]

D'Oyley, as Deputy Secretary at War and the man who, according to Knox, "had the entire conduct of the military business", was a perfectly proper person to send both orders and information to Howe and it is difficult to blame Lord George for entrusting this task to him. It is impossible to acquit D'Oyley, a senior and responsible civil servant, of treating his duty too lightly. It seems that he contented himself with sending Howe a formal covering letter merely stating that he enclosed a copy of the Secretary of State's letter to Governor Carleton and making no reference to the obligations which Burgoyne's expedition imposed on Howe.

There is a clear implication that, like Germain and Burgoyne, D'Oyley had no doubt that, after taking Philadelphia, Howe intended to move up the Hudson to cooperate with Burgoyne. He therefore saw no necessity to give additional orders. In any case, assuming that Howe read the letter to Carleton, he could have no doubt that Burgoyne would be approaching Albany in August or September with definite instructions to put himself under his, Howe's, command. If the order for Howe to cooperate with Burgoyne was not specifically issued, it was implied in the clearest form. Howe was an exceptionally idle man but he seemed far from stupid. It was not to be imagined that he would leave a corps of his army to starve at Albany during the winter. Having endured a Canadian winter, he would know that there was no chance of supplying seven thousand men at Albany from Montreal once the snow came. Equally a force of that size could not live off the land round Albany. If Burgoyne's army was to eat during the winter the bulk of his rations must come up the Hudson and only Howe could ensure that they should do so.

When D'Oyley's letter reached him in early July, Howe contented himself with a bare acknowledgment.

Carleton's immediate reaction to the orders from London was one of unrestrained fury. He already loathed Lord George and was in the habit of blaming him for supposed slights for which he could not be responsible. Now he wrote three letters of mounting insolence in each of which he accused Germain of undermining his authority in Canada. "Your lordship was announced minister and distributor of all favours, it was then rumoured your lordship's intentions were to remove me from this command the first opportunity[;] in the mean time that you would render it as irksome to me as possible by every kind of slight, disregard and censure, ocasion and events might render plausible." He ended by resigning his governorship.[5] It is possible that Carleton's wrath would have been somewhat assuaged if Lord North had not forgotten to send the offer of a substantial pension on the Irish establishment which had been agreed as a palliative.

Carleton's outburst was received in London with shocked surprise. The King, who liked the governor, commented, "Carleton was highly wrong in permitting his pen to convey such asperities to a Secretary of State." Lord George, however, replied with studied moderation, pointing out that the decision to appoint Burgoyne was not his own act but "was particularly directed by the King, after his Majesty had taken into consideration every information which could be furnished from the Secretary's office, or from the report of General Burgoyne, so that all my business was in putting his Majesty's commands into the form as a dispatch; but I must add that there was not a part of it that I did not think most wisely calculated for the public service."

He explained at some length the reasons why it was impossible for Carleton to command the expeditionary force. Leaving aside Carleton's ability as a general, a point which Germain was careful to avoid,[6] the difficulty was that Carleton was senior in the Army List to Howe and could not be asked to serve under him. In addition Howe and his brother the admiral had been appointed commissioners to negotiate peace with the rebels. It would have been impossible to appoint Carleton as a commissioner since it would be impracticable for him to act in that capacity from Quebec. Moreover the Howe family was still highly regarded in the colonies while Carleton was detested as the originator of the hated Quebec Act. "His Majesty has uniformly declared his intention that as he has appointed two Commanders in Chief by commission under the Great Sea for different provinces, that they should not interfere with each other. Had that not been his Majesty's pleasure, it would have been impossible you could have commanded the army in which Sir William Howe served from the time it was judged necessary to appoint only my Lord [Howe] and Sir William Howe his Majesty's Commissioners."

Burgoyne had returned to Canada in some trepidation about the reception he might receive from Carleton. On landing he wrote, "My situation is critical and delicate." To his credit, Carleton, despite his rancour against Lord George, received Burgoyne with kindness and exerted himself to complete the army for action. "Sir Guy Carleton has received me and the orders I have brought in a manner that, in my opinion, does infinite honour to his private and public character. That he should have wished for the lead in active and important military operations is very natural. That he thinks he has some cause for resentment for the general tenor of treatment he has received from some of the ministers is discernable; but neither his disappointment nor his personal feelings operate against his duty; and I am convinced he means to forward the King's measures, entrusted to my hands, with all the zeal he could have employed had they rested in his own."

In only one branch was Carleton backward in giving all possible help. The expedition was going to need a vast number of horses to draw the large train of artillery and to move the supplies overland between the lakes and the Hudson. The original hope had been that, until horses could be procured in the province of New York, enough could be raised in Canada by the *corvée*, the feudal obligation of the French *habitants* which had not been abolished when Canada became a British possession. Carleton became increasingly reluctant to requisition by this method the number of horses required, thinking, no doubt, of the setback to Canadian agriculture and the ill-feeling among horse owners which must result. Early in June he seems to have decided definitely against the use of the *corvée* for this purpose. This meant that horses must be hired or purchased and he was reluctant to approve the adoption of either course, which must expose him to the criticism of the all-powerful Treasury whose automatic reaction would be that it would have been cheaper to use the *corvée*. It was not until the second week in June, when an overwhelming case was presented to him by Burgoyne and Phillips, that he authorised negotiations for the hire of 1,400 horses (1,000 for the supply waggons and 400 for the artillery). Even then he left it to Burgoyne to sign the contract.

While the administrative arrangements were being concerted at Montreal, the expeditionary force was collecting on the Richelieu river at Chamblé and St John's. The backbone of the force was four brigades of infantry of the line, two brigades of British and two of Germans. Five of the six British battalions were in very good shape. Each of them was commanded by an officer of more than twenty years service including active service in the Seven Years War. The sixth battalion was suspect. This was the Forty Seventh Foot, the regiment of which Carleton was colonel. It had been present at Bunker Hill and had not distinguished itself.

The Germans were a mixed lot. All but a single battalion from Hesse Hanau were Brunswickers. Brunswick troops, possibly unfairly, had a poor reputation in Britain. When their hire was proposed, the King had written to Lord North, "The Duke's [of Brunswick] troops shewed so much want of courage in the late war that I think Carleton . . . ought to have the Hessians." In fact, the quality of the Germans varied greatly. Their officers were skilled professionals but brought up in a school of war quite different from that in which they were now to fight. The men in the ranks were divided between those who, like their officers, were well trained professionals and the sweepings of the Brunswick and other German gaols, included to make up the numbers. A proportion of both categories were men who had already deserted from other armies and who were attracted by the comparatively good terms offered by the British.

The cream of the army was the Advanced Corps which consisted of the grenadier and light companies[8] of all the British regiments with the army, together with the flank companies of three British regiments left behind in Canada. These were organised into battalions of grenadiers and light infantry. Brigaded with them was the Twenty Fourth Foot, the best regiment in Canada, whose lieutenant colonel, Simon Fraser, commanded the whole Advanced Corps. He had been training the corps for a year and it was extremely efficient. One officer wrote that, "such a body could not be raised in a twelvemonth, search England through."

There was also a German *élite* corps consisting of a grenadier battalion, formed by taking the grenadier company from each of the Brunswick regiments (leaving them with five battalion companies) and a light infantry battalion which had been raised specially. This had five companies, one of which was armed with rifles. The Brunswick contingent was completed with a small regiment of dismounted dragoons. The dragoons counted as infantry and were included in the figure of 7,173 rank and file as the total figure for the army.

Burgoyne's artillery contingent, for reasons which have been explained earlier, was very large. It consisted of thirty-five guns, six howitzers and six mortars.[9] Most of this, including all the heavy guns (24 and 12 pounders) formed the Artillery Park, the siege train. The lighter guns (6 and 3 pounders) were divided into three field batteries. One of these was attached to the Advanced Corps, one to the British "wing" of the army and one, from Hesse Hanau, to the German "wing". One of the problems created by this great weight of artillery was that there were not enough artillerymen to serve the pieces. This deficiency was made good by pressing into service a detachment of 154 men, drafts for Howe's army sent to Canada in error. In the battery attached to the Advanced Corps forty infantrymen were seconded from the ranks to undertake the less skilled work with the guns.

His engineering strength was very limited, consisting of two lieutenants and a second lieutenant.[10]

Apart from the regulars in the army there were three bodies of auxiliaries recruited in Canada. Most important were the Indians, whose task was to act as the eyes of the army in the forests which lay ahead. The employment of "savages" was the cause of much heart-searching. Many men, including Carleton, believed it less proper to use them against American rebels than it had been against French enemies. The overriding argument for their employment was that they were most unlikely to stay neutral in the war. If they did not fight for the British they would fight with the rebels. Montgomery had recruited a small body of Indians during his invasion of Canada in 1775 and it was known that the Congress had sent commissioners among the tribes in an endeavour to bring them over to the rebel side. Burgoyne had proposed that "one thousand or more savages" should accompany the army. On arrival in Canada he was assured that, "a good body of Indians are ready to move upon the first call." In practice he never had more than "between three and four hundred. It was very difficult to collect what their number was exactly."

Even more disappointing was the number of Canadian volunteers. Burgoyne had hoped for two thousand of them "including hatchetmen and other workmen". He found on reaching Quebec that "the only corps yet instituted, or that I am informed can at present be instituted are three independent companies of 100 men each, officered by the *seigneurs* of the country, who are well chosen; but they have not been able to engage many volunteers. The men are chiefly drafted from the militia . . . Those I have seen afford no promise of use of arms—aukward, ignorant, disinclined to the service and spiritless." In the event, only 148 Canadian soldiers marched into New York province.

There were also the cadres of two regiments of Loyalists, amounting at the start of the campaign to 83 rank and file. These however steadily increased as the army penetrated into New York. At the highest point there were 682 Loyalists in the ranks and despite heavy losses there were still four hundred with the army when the campaign finished.

A small body of regulars acted with the auxiliaries. This was the Corps of Marksmen, one hundred strong, commanded by Captain Alexander Fraser, Thirty First Foot, nephew to Brigadier Fraser. Burgoyne had instituted this corps in the previous year by selecting one man from every company of the ten British regiments serving in Canada. The order raising them stipulated that the men "should be chosen for their strength, activity and being expert at firing ball: each man to be furnished with an excellent firelock, the lock in good order and the hammer well steeled. The soldier should, by his frequent experience, find out the quantity of powder with which his firelock fires the justest at the greatest distance and his cartridges should be made by that measure.[11] Tomahawks to be part of the appointments of this company." This little corps achieved a very high level of efficiency and, as things turned out, was of greater use to the army than the Indians.

There was a shortage of senior officers with the army. All six brigades were commanded by the senior lieutenant colonels with the local rank of brigadier. The only British major general was William Phillips, aged forty-six. He was stout and easy-going although he had a sharp temper. What made him so unusual was that he was one of the rare major generals in the Royal Artillery to be young enough to go on active service. Since promotion in that corps went entirely by seniority, officers were usually worn out with years before they achieved a lieutenant colonelcy. Phillips had been lucky in his youth. As a first lieutenant he had been appointed to the command of a company of miners formed for duty at Minorca in 1756. When Minorca was lost, the company of miners was converted into a company of artillery and Phillips was given rank to continue in command. This irregular step was taken "greatly to the indignation of the officers" of the Royal Artillery since it gave him accelerated promotion over the heads of several lieutenants and all the captain-lieutenants of the corps.

If he got his captaincy by good fortune, Phillips achieved his next promotion by undoubted merit. At the battle of Minden he commanded the three batteries of British artillery present. With extraordinary skill, speed and courage he brought them up to cover the exposed right flank of the British infantry in their epic advance. This earned him a reward of 1,000 crowns from Prince Ferdinand and a brevet promotion which set his feet on the ladder of automatic promotion to general's rank. While in Germany he made friends with Henry Clinton, whose confidant he became. Clinton introduced him to his cousin the Duke of Newcastle who put him into Parliament for his seat at Boroughbridge, making him one of the very few serving artillerymen ever to have sat in the House of Commons before 1914. He is also to be remembered as the founder of the Royal Artillery band.

Phillips only accompanied the army because Burgoyne insisted that he should. It was contrary to precedent for artillerymen to command infantry or cavalry. Carleton had given him a brigade in 1776, only to bring down on his head a rebuke from the Secretary at War. "Officers of artillery do not roll in duty with officers of the line, therefore the command to General Phillips as major general is not to be considered as a precedent." The King had ruled that Phillips should stay in Canada as second in command to Carleton, but Burgoyne was not to be deterred. Justifying himself on the grounds of "absolute necessity", he wrote to London that, "The staff being composed without any British major general and Brigadier Fraser being posted where he is of the most infinite use, at the head of the Advanced Corps, the service would suffer in the most material degree if the talents of General Phillips were not suffered to extend beyond the limits of the artillery."

This insistence was amply justified. Phillips not only commanded the artillery of the expedition but also the right, or British, wing beside acting as chief of staff to Burgoyne. He showed himself an able administrator and a brave and resourceful leader of men. He was, besides, much liked in the army. Lieutenant Anburey wrote that he was "much esteemed by the officers of the army; he gives them as little trouble as possible, but will have them perform their duty and seldom misses coming upon the parade in the morning."

The German wing was commanded by Major General Friederich Adolph Riedesel, Freiherr zu Eisenbach, aged thirty-nine. He was a Hessian by birth and, with a Hessian regiment, he had been stationed in England for two years, 1755–57, when he had acquired some knowledge of English. He had served as an ADC to Ferdinand of Brunswick at Minden and that prince had made him lieutenant colonel of the Brunswick Hussars. He was a good soldier who got on well with his British allies, particularly with Burgoyne and Phillips, although he had to conceal his admiration of the former after Frau General Riedesel joined the army half way through the campaign.

Before the expedition set out Burgoyne had two months in which to train his army. They had to be taught to abandon the European practice of fighting shoulder to shoulder in three deep line and instead to adopt a more flexible formation which would enable them to fight in close country. At the same time they could not be permitted too wide an extension as this would lose the volley effect which alone made muskets effective. The new battle drill came as a great shock to the Brunswickers. One of their officers wrote, "Here we have a special way of waging war which departs utterly from our system. Our infantry can only operate two deep and a man must have eighteen inches space on either side to be able to march in line through woods and brush. We cannot use cavalry at all, so our dragoons will have to rely on their own legs. Our colours bother us a lot, and no British regiment brought any with them."[12]

The gun-drill of the Hanau battery was tested against the British practice in live firing trials and the best points of each were combined into a common drill. Rules were laid down for the posting of sentries and piquets and for the immediate fortification of bivouacs and vital posts. Unnecessary ceremonial was to be dispensed with. "When the Lieutenant General visits an outpost, the men are not to stand to their arms or pay him any compliments." A system of signals was established for getting the army under arms in emergencies.

To cut down the number of encumbrances with the army, "His Excellency General Burgoyne directs that, without exception, no officer shall take with him any more baggage than he is in extreme need of. The officers are, therefore, ordered to deposit their baggage where it will be safe . . . By the express orders of General Burgoyne, no more than three women can be taken with each company."[13]

So that the orders were known and understood by all ranks "the rule to be invariably observed for the future by every regiment is to form each company in a circle at the evening roll calling; the officers of the companies are to remain within their respective circles till the whole of the orders of the day have been explained and read by one of them."

By the end of June, when the final preparations were complete, the army was in a high state of efficiency and readiness. The twentieth century critic, General J. F. C. Fuller, a man with little tolerance for old fashioned notions, wrote that, "This was no ordinary army. Burgoyne's army was modern in the extreme . . . [Burgoyne] never attempted to apply European tactics to forest and bush fighting but trained his army to commonsense tactics."

One point in the standing orders sounds far from modern. "The officers will take all proper opportunities, and especially at the beginning of the campaign, to inculcate in the men's minds a reliance on the bayonet. Men of half their bodily strength, and even cowards, may be their match in firing; but the onset of bayonets in the hands of the valiant is irresistable. The enemy, convinced of this truth, place their whole dependence in entrenchments and rifle pieces. It will be our glory and preservation to storm where possible."

Some authorities have taken this to mean that Burgoyne intended to pit brute strength against military skill. Nothing could be further from the truth. By dragging with him an unwieldy train of siege guns he had taken every precaution available to him against the menace which the rebel fortifications represented. Neither light infantry nor riflemen could overcome entrenched enemies. As James Wolfe had pointed out in his own Standing Orders, "It is of little purpose to fire at men who are covered with an entrenchment." Since Burgoyne's army was committed to offensive action, fortifications must be stormed and, once the artillery had done what it could, the bayonet was the only effective weapon.

When all was ready, Burgoyne issued a General Order in which he expressed "publickly the high opinion he entertains of the troops which his Majesty has been graciously pleased to entrust to his command; they could not have been selected more to his satisfaction." The army reciprocated his feelings. One officer wrote home, "As to our army, I can only say if good discipline joined to health and great spirits amongst the men, with their being led by General Burgoyne, who is universally esteemed and respected, can ensure success, it may be expected . . . The general combines to the dignity of his office and strict attention to military discipline, that consideration, humanity and mildness which must ever endear him to all who have the happiness to serve under him."

From the information available in Canada it seemed that the early stages of the advance would be strongly resisted. "A continuation of intelligence from different spies and deserters confirms the design of the enemy to dispute Ticonderoga vigorously. They are also building row-galleys at Fort George for the defence of [Lake George], &c., fortifying on the road to Skenesborough. It is consigned to the New England colonies to furnish supplies of

men and provisions to oppose the progress of my army, and they have undertaken the task upon condition of being exempt from supplying Mr Washington's main army. It is my design, while advancing to Ticonderoga, and during
the siege of that place, for a siege I apprehend it must be, to give all possible
jealousy on the side of Connecticut. If I can by manoeuvre lead the enemy
to suspect that, after the reduction of Ticonderoga, my views are pointed that
way, the Connecticut forces will be very cautious of leaving their own frontier, and I may gain a start that may much expedite and facilitate my progress
to Albany."

Two factors reported in this letter to Lord George had considerable effect
on Burgoyne's conduct of the campaign. The first, the news that there were
heavily armed row-galleys on Lake George, persuaded him to avoid the lake
until he had cut the defenders off from their base by a land move. The last
thing he was anxious to do was to spend weeks, if not months, transporting
heavy vessels across the mile and a quarter long portage at Ticonderoga and
then run the risk of losing a naval battle on Lake George.

The knowledge that the New England troops had undertaken to oppose
his advance had an even greater effect on his thinking. Although the cabinet
had ruled against his proposal for a thrust into the Connecticut valley, he
continued to be worried about the vulnerability of his eastern flank. On that
side lay the heartland of the rebellion and, as long as he depended on Canada
for supplies, his communications would become longer and more exposed
with every mile he advanced. He could not afford the men to leave a series of
garrisons along the road. It seemed to him essential that he must make a
series of feints and raids to the east to give "all possible jealousy" to the rebels
in that direction. A week after he landed at Quebec he wrote to Howe, "I
wish a latitude had been left me for a diversion towards Connecticut, but
such an idea is out of the question by my orders being precise to force the
junction [with Howe], it is only mentioned to introduce the idea still resting
in my mind, viz. to give the change to the enemy if I could, and by every
feint in my power to establish a suspicion that I am still pointed towards
Connecticut. But under the present precision of my orders I shall have no
view but that of joining you, nor think myself justified by any temptation to
delay the most expeditious means I can find to effect that junction."

This letter with its clear indication that Burgoyne intended to march his
army to Albany, reached Howe on 28th June. Eighteen days later, Carleton
received a letter despatched from New York on 5th April. Howe, who had of
course not yet received either his copy of Carleton's orders or Burgoyne's
letter from Quebec, was nevertheless expecting an army to advance south
from Canada. He wrote, "Having but little expectation that I shall be able
from want of sufficient strength in this army, to detach a corps in the

beginning of the campaign to act up Hudson's river consistent with the operations already determined upon, the force you Excellency may deem expedient to advance beyond your frontiers after taking Ticonderoga will, I fear, have little assistance from hence to facilitate their approach, as I shall probably be in Pensylvania when that corps is ready to advance, it will probably not be in my power to communicate with the officer commanding so soon as I could wish; he must therefore pursue such measures as may from circumstances be judged most conducive to the advancement of his Majesty's service, consistently with your orders for his conduct.

"The possession of Ticonderoga will naturally be the first object, and without presuming to point out to your Excellency the advantages that must arise by securing Albany and the adjacent country, I conclude they will engage the next attention; but omitting others, give me leave to suggest that this situation will open a free intercourse with the Indians, without which we are to expect little assistance from them on this side.

"The further progress of this corps depending so much upon the enmy's movements, cannot be foreseen at this distance of time; still I flatter myself, and have reason to expect, the friends of government in that part of the country will be found so numerous, and so very ready to give every aid and assistance in their power, that it will prove no difficult task to reduce the more rebellious parts of the province. In the mean while I shall endeavour to have a corps upon the lower part of the Hudson's river sufficient to open the communication for shipping thro' the Highlands at present obstructed by several forts erected by the rebels, which corps may afterwards act in favour of the northern army.

"Major Edmestone of the 48th Regiment having long been detained a prisoner at Albany, and having procured leave to come here to negotiate his exchange, I have sent him back with directions to inform Mr Shuyler[14] that if he permits him to go to Canada I shall release a major in exchange. He has information of too delicate a nature to commit to paper, and of the utmost importance in favour of the northern army advancing to Albany, which I trust he will find some means of communicating, even tho' he should not obtain leave to go to Canada in person.

"I beg your Excellency may be pleased to favour me with the earliest intelligence of your movements and flatter myself some method will be found of conveying it to New York."

Howe accompanied this letter with a copy of the one he had written to Lord George outlining his most recent modifications to his plans for the coming campaign. That letter will be dealt with more fully in a later chapter. At present it will be sufficient to note that he anticipated having to evacuate New Jersey and to make his attack on Philadelphia by sea rather than his previously implied plan of attacking across the Delaware river. There was little reference to the operations of Burgoyne's army except where he wrote that, "by the latter end of the campaign we shall be in possession of the provinces of New York, the Jersies and Pensylvania, tho' this must in some measure depend on the success of the northern army."

As soon as he heard that disaster had overcome Burgoyne's army, Howe was quick to assert that in this letter to Carleton "I positively mentioned that no direct assistance could be given by the southern army." If that was the message he intended to convey, he failed miserably. He made it clear that he would not be able to detach a corps towards Albany "*in the beginning of the campaign*" and that he would not be able to get into touch with Burgoyne "*as soon as I could wish*". This could be no surprise to Burgoyne who had seen in London Howe's letter of 20th December in which he said, "We must not expect the northern army to reach Albany before the middle of September." Mid-September was near the end of the campaigning season in northern New York and Burgoyne, who expected to have to conduct a lengthy formal siege at Ticonderoga, would not expect to co-operate with Howe's troops there any earlier in the year. By that time Howe was expected to have dealt with Philadelphia and switched some of his troops back to the Hudson. "In the mean while", Howe gave hopes of a corps of his troops securing the forts in the Highlands, the essential first step in opening the navigation of the Hudson up to Albany. Above all Howe made it clear that he wanted Burgoyne's corps to go to Albany.

One thing is quite certain. Neither Burgoyne nor Carleton believed that the army from Canada was meant to seize Albany unsupported. To do so must condemn Burgoyne and his men to destruction. Even if Burgoyne could contemplate such a desperate venture, Carleton would have forbidden it. If Burgoyne's army was destroyed, the frontier of Canada would again be open to a rebel invasion.

Burgoyne's orders were quite clear. He was "to proceed with all expedition to Albany, and put himself under the command of Sir William Howe". If Burgoyne and Carleton felt concerned about any ambiguities in Howe's letter, and there is no evidence that they did, they would realise that the letter had been written before Germain's copy of his orders to Canada, with presumably complementary orders to Howe, could have reached New York. When Howe received these papers his course would be clear.

PART V

Campaign

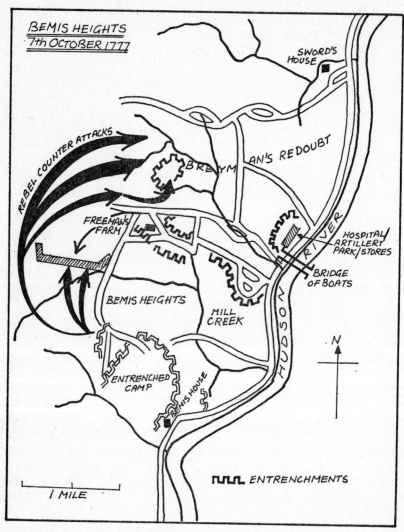

5. Bemis Heights, 7th October 1777

CHAPTER 9

"Critical and Conspicuous Services"

By 20th June the army had been assembled at Cumberland Point, a few miles north of Valcour Island where the rebel fleet had been brought to action in the previous year. Burgoyne had hoped that an earlier start could have been made but he had been thwarted by "the embarrassments I found, notwithstanding previous preparations and cordial assistance. Remote situations of the troops, currents, winds, roads, want of material for caulking the vessels, inactivity and desertion of the Canadian *corvée* were all against me . . . I have had to contend against wet weather that rendered the roads almost impracticable at the carrying places, and consequently the passage of the *bateaux* and [?gunboats was] exceedingly dilatory, beside a good deal of contrary wind. Indeed the combination of land and water movement, bad roads, inactivity and sometimes disobedience in the country, and a thousand other difficulties and accidents, unknown in any other service, disconcert all arrangements."

The following day he sailed down to the mouth of the Bouquet river, where he held a conference with the first group of Indians who had answered the call to join him. There were only four hundred of them but Burgoyne was assured that more would soon come in to fight against the colonials whom they certainly detested. From the start the Indians were discontented. In 1776 Carleton had put severe restraints on their traditional form of guerilla warfare. Burgoyne's speech on this occasion did little to reconcile them to the service. He pointed out that, "The King has many faithful subjects dispersed in the [rebellious] provinces" and that the army's task was "to chastise and not to destroy". He laid down rules "for your invariable observation during the campaign".

"I positively forbid bloodshed when you are not opposed in arms.

"Aged men, women, children and prisoners must be held sacred from the knife, even in time of actual conflict.

"You shall receive compensation for the prisoners you take, but you shall be called to account for scalps.

"In conformity and indulgence to your customs . . . you shall be allowed to take the scalps of the dead, when killed by your fire, and in fair opposition; but on no account, or pretence, or subtlety, or prevarication, are they to be taken from the wounded or even dying."

This was not a prescription for the kind of warfare they wanted to wage. Their leader was the Chevalier de la Corne Saint Luc, who seventeen years earlier had led them against the British and the colonials. No such restrictions had then been placed on their habitual methods. Although an old chief of the Iriquois dutifully replied that, "with one common assent we promise a constant obedience to all you have ordered and all you shall order", the braves suddenly found the prospect of the campaign less attractive, a feeling that was to grow when they discovered that the general intended to enforce his orders to them.

Their immediate resentment was somewhat lessened when "the general ordered for them some liquor and they had a war dance in which they throw themselves in various postures, every now and then making most hideous yells; as to their appearance, nothing more horrid can you paint in your imagination, being dressed in such an *outré* manner, some with the skins of bulls with the horns upon their heads, others with a great quantity of feathers, and many in a state of total nudity: there was one at whose modesty I could not help smiling, and who rather than be divested of any covering, had tied a blackbird before him. Joined to these strange dresses, and to the grotesque appearance, they paint their faces in various colours, with a view to inspire an additional horror."

On the same day as the Indian conference, Burgoyne issued a proclamation to the rebellious colonies. It threatened justice to those who had inflicted "arbitrary imprisonment, confiscation of property, persecution and torture unprecedented in the inquisitions of the Romish church [upon] the most quiet subjects, without the distinction of age or sex, for the sole crime, often only suspicion, of having adhered in principle to the government under which they were born." It offered encouragement to those "whose spirit and principle may induce them to partake in the glorious task of redeeming their countrymen", protection to "the domestic, the industrious, the infirm and even timid inhabitants provided they remain quietly in their homes".

This document was mercilessly satirised by the rebel propagandists. When it reached England, Walpole commented that it was "ridiculous bombast, penned with such threats of his arms as would expose him to ridicule to derision if he failed and would diminish the lustre of his success if he obtained any." It is, of course, difficult not to be pompous in a proclamation and Governor Hutchinson described it as "flowery, but upon the whole, well adapted". No one seems to have noticed that all the style and most of the wording had been plagiarised from Wolfe's proclamation to the people of Canada eighteen years earlier.

Meanwhile the great fleet sailed serenely southward down Lake Champlain. To the ships which had sailed in the previous year had been added a brig, a cutter and a gondola captured from the rebels, and there were now twenty-four gunboats. With them went some four hundred *bateaux* carrying troops or stores. Each of these was nearly forty foot long and more than six foot wide. Each "carries a load of seven or eight thousand pounds or twenty eight to thirty people." The *bateaux* had usually to be rowed but could move under sail with a following wind.[1]

"The army passed the lake by brigades, generally advancing from seventeen to twenty miles a day, and regulated in such a manner that the second brigade should fill the encampment of the first, and so on successively for each to fill the ground the other quitted . . . When we were at the widest part of the lake, it was remarkably fine and clear, not a breeze stirring, when the whole army appeared at one view in such perfect regularity as to form the most perfect and complete regatta you can possibly conceive. In front the Indians went in their birch canoes, containing twenty or thirty in each; then the Advanced Corps in a regular line with the gunboats; then followed the *Royal George* and *Inflexible*, towing large booms which are to be thrown across to points of land, with the other brigs and sloops following; after them the first brigade in a regular line; then the generals Burgoyne, Phillips and Riedesel in their pinnaces; next to them the second brigade, followed by the German brigades, and the rear brought up with the sutlers and followers of the army."

The followers of the army presented a problem, but an inescapable one. Army rations provided only bread, meat and spruce beer (or rum). Vegetables and other foods could only be obtained through private enterprise. Nothing would be obtainable by local purchase until, at the earliest, the army reached the Hudson river. Therefore twenty or thirty sutlers, with their staffs and stock in trade, had to be found room in the *bateaux*. To make matters worse, arrangements had to be made for a shuttle service of boats to operate between the army and St John's, to enable the sutlers to replenish their supplies.

Like so much in the military system, this arrangement had been calculated on the assumption that any war would be fought in the fertile parts of Europe where vegetables and liquor could be obtained with reasonable facility. This assumption, when applied to almost uninhabited tracts of North America, left the commander with difficulties that he would gladly have been spared, but it kept the cost to the taxpayer to a minimum and, since the sutlers had to pay for their transport, enabled the Treasury to make a small profit.

A similar problem was presented by women. Under no circumstances would the Treasury permit an allowance to be paid to soldiers' wives but, by a long standing custom, rations could be issued to six wives from every company and half rations to their children. Thus each of Burgoyne's seven British battalions was accompanied by sixty soldiers' wives. Taking into account the wives of men in the artillery and the detached light companies[2] the establishment for wives with the army would be about 450 with not less than twice as many children (and doubtless more to be born during the campaign).[3] Burgoyne managed to reduce this encumbrance by leaving three married men from each company among the detachment of fifty which each regiment had been ordered to leave in Canada. He could not cut down the number of women further without depriving the army of its non-commissioned officers, who had priority in having their wives on the company quota. There were, therefore, about 225 wives with their children who had to move with the army. They could not be left behind since they were only entitled to draw rations while actually accompanying their husbands. If they remained in Canada they would be dependent for subsistence on the charity of the people of the province. Naturally a number of officers' wives elected also to accompany the army.

Fraser's Advanced Corps reached Crown Point on 25th June. From this place southward the lake is only about a mile wide and, eighteen miles further on, lay the army's first objective, Fort Ticonderoga. From spies and deserters Burgoyne learned that it was "the design of the enemy to defend Ticonderoga vigorously." He also knew that the rebels had been busily engaged on strengthening the fortifications ever since they had seized it two years previously. Every indication was that a formal siege would be necessary. The army was therefore concentrated at Crown Point. Stores were landed and a hospital established. Fraser's corps was pushed forward seven miles and took up a position on the banks of Putnam's Creek on the western shore. On the eastern shore of the lake, the German Reserve held a similar position aligned with Fraser's left. A detachment of Indians with the Corps of Marksmen made a sweep on the eastern shore to collect forage.

By 30th June all was ready and Burgoyne issued a General Order saying, "The army embarks tomorrow to approach the enemy. We are to contend for the King and the Constitution of Great Britain, to vindicate law, and to relieve the oppressed—a cause in which his Majesty's troops and those of the Princes his allies will feel equal excitement. The services required of this particular expedition are critical and conspicuous. During our progress, occasions may occur in which nor difficulty, nor labour, nor life are to be regarded. The army must not retreat."

As events turned out, this last phrase proved singularly unfortunate and was used by Burgoyne's detractors to show that he had neither the skill nor the intelligence to manoeuvre, that he set his mind on going bull-headed to Albany. His aim in using the phrase was to impress on his army the vital importance of joining Howe. If the two armies met on the Hudson the war could be won; if only one army reached Albany the rebellion might drag on for years. Burgoyne was determined that the Canadian army should not fail Howe.

Reveille was not beaten the next day. Instead, at dawn, the ten drummers of each battalion beat "the General", the warning that the army was to march. An hour later the Assembly was beaten and the troops fell in in front of their lines. Their tents and baggage were immediately loaded and, as soon as men and stores were embarked, the great fleet of *bateaux* set off in two columns, British on the right, Germans on the left. "Some of the armed vessels accompanied us; the music[4] and drums of the different regiments were continually playing and contributed to making the scene and passage extremely pleasant."

Fort Ticonderoga was important because it controlled the most convenient route between Canada and the American colonies.[5] There could be no safety for Canada as long as the rebels held it. It was also a symbol of great significance. Nineteen years earlier, on 8th July 1758, a French garrison of 3,600 men under Montcalm had held it against an army composed of British regulars and American militia. The British commander, James Abercromby, decided to storm it out of hand. There followed, in the words of Sir John Fortescue, "such a scene as had not been witnessed since Malplaquet nor was to be seen again till Badajoz." The assault failed with two thousand casualties and when at last the retreat was ordered the survivors fled in panic. Although the fort was taken with little trouble in the following year, it remained a potent symbol to both British and Americans.

In 1777 the American garrison was 3,600 strong, the same as that with which Montcalm had successfully defended the place, but it was under some initial disadvantage. The French fort and its outworks, which were never as strong as they were reputed to be, had been sited to guard against an attack from the south. Burgoyne was approaching from the weaker rear of the original fortifications. Nevertheless, in the twenty-six months they had held it, the rebels had greatly extended and improved the defences.

The French fort, Fort Carillon, stands on a peninsula where the southern end of Lake Champlain bifurcates. The lake itself is on the east and round the southern end flows the outlet from Lake George. Carillon stood on a rocky plateau toward the end of the peninsula and the whole plateau was surrounded with breastworks, redoubts, batteries and blockhouses. The rebels had strengthened and repaired the old French works on this side but most of their work had been done on the eastern shore of Lake Champlain. Here, there is a considerable hill which they christened Mount Independence. This they had crowned with a star fort and a barracks, surrounding both with palisades, earthworks and batteries. Mount Independence would have been a very difficult feature to attack since it is covered on the west and north-west by the Lake and its tributary, the South River, and on the south and east by a marshy stream. Nor could it be ignored, since its guns commanded the waterborne access to the George river and its own bulk blocked the land route to Skenesborough.

Fort Carillon was joined to the fort on Mount Independence by a timber bridge which was protected by a substantial boom covered by artillery fire. The rebels had also built some blockhouses on the north bank of the George river to defend the only bridge across that river.

There were two other features which the Americans considered fortifying. One was the height, Mount Hope, to the north west of Carillon, on which Jeffrey Amherst had placed his batteries when he took the place in 1759. The American commander, St Clair, rightly refused to consider holding it as he had insufficient men to be able to spare a garrison and the men to support it. The second feature was Mount Defiance, a sugar loaf hill between the George and South rivers. This St Clair declined to occupy since he believed that it was inaccessible and that, even if it were not, guns sited on it would be out of range of the two forts. It might be imagined that the first supposition might have been disproved by an afternoon's reconnaissance. The second had been disproved in 1776 when Colonel John Trumbull, then adjutant general of the northern rebel army, had fired a shot from the fortress to the crest of Mount Defiance.

When Burgoyne looked at the fortress from the deck of the *Royal George* on 1st July, it seemed very formidable. "The enemy appeared to be posted as follows:—a brigade occupied the old French lines on the height to the north of Ticonderoga. These lines were in good repair and had several entrenchments behind them, chiefly calculated to guard the north-west flank, and were further sustained by a block-house." They had farther to their left, a post at the saw mills, which are at the foot of the carrying place to Lake George, a block-house upon the eminence above the mills, and a block-house and hospital at the entrance to the lake [George]. Upon the right of the lines, and between them and the old fort, were two new block-houses and a considerable battery close to the water's edge. It seemed that the enemy had employed their chief industry, and were in the greatest force, upon Mount Independence, which is high and circular, and upon the summit, which is table land, was a star fort, made of piquets and well supplied with artillery, and a large square barracks within it. The foot of the hill, on the side which projects into the lake, was intrenched and had a strong abbatis close to the water. This intrenchment was lined with heavy artillery, pointed down the lake [Champlain] flanking the water battery above described, and sustained by another battery about half way up the hill. On the west side of the hill runs the main river, and its passage is joined by the water which comes down from Lake George. The enemy here had a bridge of communication which could not at this time be reconnoitred. [It was later found to be] supported by twenty two sunken piers of timber at nearly equal distances; the space between were made of separate floats, each fifty feet long, and twelve feet wide, strongly fastened together with chains and also fastened to the sunken piers. Before this bridge was a boom, made of very large pieces of timber, fastened together with rivetted bolts and double chains, made of iron an inch and a half square . . . On the east side of the hill [Mount Independence] the water forms a small bay, into which falls a rivulet after having encircled in its course part of the hill to the south east. The side to the south could not be seen, but was described as inaccessible."

While Burgoyne was making this reconnaissance, the army was moving forward. The British went to Three Mile Point (so named from its distance from Carillon) and the Germans moved to a position opposite them on the east side of the lake. Both wings encamped, having to clear the ground of brushwood before the tents could be pitched. It seemed that they might have to stay there for several weeks. Feeling in the army was that "fortified as the enemy are, nothing but a regular siege can dispossess them."

The prospects for a regular siege were not good. Burgoyne's army was little more than twice the strength of the garrison, far from the superiority usually considered necessary for siege operations. It would be very difficult to cut the rebels' communications with the south so that they could easily be reinforced until they had parity or even superiority in numbers. They had, with their bridge, easy lateral communication while Burgoyne's army had to be divided in two by a mile wide river. The rebels would also have artillery superiority. Large as Burgoyne's siege train was, it was certain to be outgunned by the 128 heavy pieces behind the fortifications.

The only practicable plan was to start by taking Fort Carillon. Only when that was held could Mount Independence be attacked. A month seemed a short time to take the two forts and it did not help starting the operation that the *radeau*, which carried most of the siege guns, was sailing as badly as she had done in the previous year. She had to be warped forward from Crown Point several days behind the rest of the fleet.

While the plans were being made, the garrison started to behave unaccountably. Burgoyne reported that "about nine in the morning [of 2nd July] a smoke was observed towards Lake George, and the savages brought in a report that the enemy had set fire to the further block-house and had abandoned the saw-mills" on the George river. At the same time "a considerable body" of rebels was seen moving towards the British right. Phillips took forward a brigade and some light troops to meet them while some Indians and the Corps of Marksmen were sent round the enemy's left flank to intercept their retreat. Unfortunately the Indians had succeeded in getting hold of rather too much rum. They attacked the rebel flank, warning them of their danger. When the Americans retreated, the Indians followed, despite the efforts of Lieutenant Haughton, Fifty Third, who ran forward to recall them. He was wounded and blinded. The Indians suffered two casualties and ran to the rear. The rebels, who lost two officers, retreated across the George river in good order, burning the only bridge after they had crossed.

The next two days passed with no more than some desultory cannonading while preparations were made for the siege, and on 4th July, when the *radeau* finally caught up with the army, all was prepared to put the guns in their emplacements and open the bombardment of Carillon. Meanwhile, officers with spy glasses had been examining the rebel dispositions. What they saw astonished them. After burning the block-houses on the north bank of the George river, the Americans had withdrawn all their troops from the peninsula bounded by the South and George rivers and Lake George. There was no guard on the approaches to Mount Defiance.

Burgoyne reacted immediately. On the night of 4th July, a detachment of light infantry slipped across the George river and reached the crest of Mount Defiance without opposition. Lieutenant William Twiss RE, who went with them, rode back soon after dawn to Burgoyne and "reported this hill to have the entire command of the works and buildings both of Ticonderoga and Mount Independence, at a distance of about 1,400 from the former and 1,500 from the latter; that the ground might be levelled so as to receive cannon, and that the road to convey them, though difficult, might be made practicable in twenty four hours. This hill also commanded in reverse the bridge of communication; saw the exact situation of their vessels; nor could the enemy during the day make any material movement or preparation without being discovered, even having their numbers counted."

Already artificers were at work repairing the bridge over the George. Now Burgoyne told Phillips to take every man who could be spared from the lines to clear the two mile track to the summit. Phillips remarked that, "Where a goat can go a man can go and where a man can go he can drag a gun." By dawn on 6th July, two medium 12 pounders were on the crest. They did not have to open fire. The rebels had discovered what was afoot and St Clair called a council of war. It was decided unanimously that the fortress was untenable. Some light artillery was loaded on to boats and ferried up the

South river under the escort of a single regiment. The rest of the garrison took the road to Skenesborough, a roundabout track through the forest going by way of Hubbardton and Castleton. A hundred and twenty eight heavy guns and a mass of stores were abandoned. When daylight came the only rebels in Ticonderoga were four artillerymen who had been detailed to fire off the guns on Mount Independence when the British attempted to cross the bridge. In the event they found the attraction of a case of Madeira more compelling and were captured peacefully asleep.

Each night Burgoyne had taken up his quarters in the *Royal George* moored in mid-stream to be in touch with both wings of his army. Soon after dawn on 6th July an ADC from Simon Fraser came on board with the news that the enemy had decamped. Looking south down the lake the general could see the Advanced Corps moving across the slopes of Mount Independence and "the British colours which the brigadier had fixed upon the fort of Ticonderoga". To the left the German Reserve were struggling across the boggy stream to the foot of Mount Independence.

Burgoyne knew that Fraser could be trusted to conduct the pursuit and did not attempt to interfere with him, only ordering Riedesel to follow him with the German Reserve and to take overall command on that flank. He devoted his own energies to getting a force up to Skenesborough by the South river to cut off St Clair's retreat. The boats of the fleet rowed up to the boom and within half-an-hour a gap had been cleared through both the boom and the bridge beyond it. The *Royal George* and *Inflexible* sailed through immediately, followed by a swarm of gunboats. By mid-afternoon they had reached South Bay, three miles beyond Skenesborough. It had been an exciting voyage as "the communication was so narrow in some places that the ships' yards almost touched the precipices which hung over them. The enemy might have done great execution by leaving a detachment on shore to harass them."

As it happened they met no opposition until South Bay, "at which place the enemy were posted in a stockaded fort, and their armed vessels in the falls below. The foremost regiments, viz. the 9th, 20th and 21st, were immediately disembarked and ascended the mountains with the intention of getting behind the fort; but [the American] precipitate flight rendered this manoeuvre ineffectual. The gunboats and frigates continued their path to Skenesborough Falls where the [American] armed vessels were posted. Captain Carter, Royal Artillery, with part of his brigade of gunboats immediately attacked with so much spirit that two of the vessels very soon struck; the other three were blown up and the enemy, having previously prepared combustible materials, set fire to the fort, mills, storehouses, *bateaux*, &c. and retired with the detachments left for that purpose, the main body having gone off when the troops were ascending the mountain. A great quantity of provisions and some arms were here consumed and most of their officers' baggage was burned, sunk or taken. Their loss is not known; about 30 prisoners were made, among which were two wounded officers."

On the east bank of the South river Fraser had set off in pursuit at 4 am. At first he had only eighty men with him as, to save time, he had moved off with the piquets[6] of the brigade, leaving orders for the rest to follow as soon as they could be got under arms. Even when the whole corps was together Fraser had only about 850 men, as they had had to leave a garrison in Ticonderoga to save the dump of stores from the thieving fingers of the Indians. On the rough track towards Hubbardton they met no opposition but picked up many stragglers, some of whom were not averse to being captured. From these prisoners they heard that the rebel rearguard consisted of two good regiments, about 1,200 men, under Colonel Seth Warner.

After a nine hour march "in a very hot sultry day over a long succession of steep and woody hills", Fraser called a halt at one o'clock. While the troops were resting, Riedesel rode up, having pressed on ahead of the Germans. He agreed that Fraser should make another march that evening and attempt a dawn attack on the rebel rearguard. Then he rode back to spur on the Brunswickers. The Advance, in the cool of the evening, covered a further three miles before halting in "an advantageous situation where we lay that night on our arms".

At 3 am they moved on again. The piquets led the way, commanded by Major Robert Grant, Twenty Fourth, who was field officer of the day. When they had marched about two miles they came to a small stream, flowing in a wooded valley. As the leading files crossed the bridge they saw rebel sentries, who fired at them and immediately fell back on their main body, which was stationed on a spur to the east of the road to Castleton and Skenesborough. The American sentries had been alert but Warner's two regiments were surprised. They were cooking their breakfasts.

Assuming that Riedesel and the leading Brunswickers were not far behind, Fraser decided to attack at once. He sent the light infantry battalion to seize a rise on the left of the road. The rebels hastily attacked them but were driven back. Meanwhile the Twenty Fourth crossed the bridge behind a screen formed by Grant's piquets. Grant, trying to get a clearer view through the wooded country, climbed on to a tree stump. Seeing a body of rebels coming towards him he turned to his men but "hardly had he given his orders to fire when he was struck by a rifle ball, fell off the tree and never uttered another syllable. [He] fell a victim to the great disadvantage we experience peculiar to this unfortunate contest, opposing expert riflemen."

Fraser's third unit, the battalion of grenadiers under Acland, was sent forward on the right with orders to cut the road to Castleton behind the rebel left. To the Americans this road was vital. If it was held against them their only retreat would be to the east. They launched an attack at Acland's men but were driven back. They were fighting bravely and skilfully, but they could not stand against the disciplined volleys of the finest infantry in the world. Warner then sent them further to the left towards a very steep hill which would enable them to regain touch with the Castleton road. Acland saw what they were doing and moved quickly to frustrate them. He set the grenadiers to climb "an ascent which seemed almost inaccessible. The men were obliged to sling their firelocks and climb up the side, sometimes resting their feet upon the branches of a tree, sometimes on a piece of rock; had any been so unfortunate as to have missed his hold, he must inevitably have been dashed to pieces." The rebels reached the crest first but the appearance of the grenadiers threw them into confusion and they were driven down again.

Fraser had succeeded in cutting off the American retreat but in doing so he had dangerously overextended his small force. He had to detach men from his centre and left to plug the gap between the grenadiers and the Twenty Fourth. He was counting on the arrival of the Brunswickers and still they did not come. The Americans had a three to two superiority and the light infantry on the left was hard put to it to hold their ground against repeated attacks. Riedesel arrived alone, having done what he could to urge on his fellow-countrymen. One British officer who saw him "could not help feeling for his situation, for the honour of a brave officer who was pouring forth every imprecation against his troops for not arriving at the place of action in time to earn the glories of the day".

At last, as the position of Fraser's left was becoming desperate, the German advance guard arrived. There was only a company of jägers and a mixed detachment of eighty grenadiers and light infantry, about 200 men in all,[7] but Riedesel sent them at once to the left wing and they were enough to restore the situation. Disheartened by the strengthening of the opposition, the rebels drew back. Fraser's left, British and German together, swung forward and the Americans abandoned the fight. They made their way eastward in no very regular order to cross the mountains into the Connecticut valley. A few isolated parties remained and continued sniping until they were captured or driven away.

One very unfortunate incident took place. Two companies of grenadiers had been left at the foot of the steep hill to cover the rear of the battalion. As the fighting died down they "observed a number of Americans, to the amount of about sixty, coming across the field with their arms clubbed, which is always considered as a surrender as prisoners of war. The grenadiers were restrained from firing, commanded to stand to their arms, and showed no intention of hostility: when the Americans had got within ten yards, they in an instant turned round their muskets, fired upon the grenadiers and ran as fast as they could into the woods; their fire killed and wounded a great number of men, and those who escaped immediately pursued them, and gave no quarter."

The British casualties at Hubbardton were sixteen officers (including one Volunteer[8]) and a hundred and twenty rank and file killed and wounded. Burgoyne claimed that the rebels lost two hundred killed and six hundred wounded but this, like all estimates of enemy casualties, is certainly too high. It seems probable that they suffered about three hundred killed and wounded, including the brave Colonel Francis, whose death was regretted on both sides. There is no reason to doubt Burgoyne's claim to have taken 210 prisoners, including another colonel. This figure, however, includes stragglers and deserters picked up on the road from Ticonderoga.

One unfortunate side-effect of Hubbardton was a deterioration in the relations between the British and German troops. The Germans had been culpably late in reaching the fighting and no doubt the British, from Fraser downwards, had expressed themselves forcibly, if unofficially, on the subject.[9] General Riedesel, who was acutely aware of the delay, can not have been unaware of this ill-feeling and began to press Burgoyne for a chance to demonstrate that the Germans were the equals of their allies.

On 7th July, while Fraser was engaged at Hubbardton, Burgoyne heard from the people of Skenesborough that the rebels were flying south as fast as they could go. He therefore ordered Lieutenant Colonel John Hill of the Ninth Foot to take his battalion after them to seize Fort Anne, midway between Skenesborough and the Hudson river. The other regiments of Hamilton's brigade[10] were ordered to support him. The distance to Fort Anne is fourteen miles and Hill got his men forward at a very smart pace considering that "the roads were almost impracticable and the bridges broken."

"They had not proceeded many miles through the woods before they overtook some boats laden with baggage, women and invalids belonging to the Americans, rowing up Wood Creek; these were immediately secured." By nightfall Hill was within a quarter of a mile of Fort Anne and could see that it was strongly held. He took up the strongest position he could find and ordered the troops to lie on their arms all night. He had failed to realise how far he had outrun his support. The Ninth had been travelling light, while the other two battalions, encumbered with baggage and rations for themselves and the Ninth, were still manhandling the unwieldy *bateaux* over Skenesborough Falls.

Early next morning a deserter came out from the fort and told Hill that the place was held by a thousand men and that "they were in the greatest consternation, under the apprehension of the British attacking and storming them". Hill could see large numbers of men near the fort. He sent back to Burgoyne "that the enemy had been reinforced in the night by a considerable body of fresh men; that he could not retire with his regiment before them, but he would maintain his ground." Burgoyne accordingly sent instructions to the two supporting battalions to hasten their march and ordered General Phillips to take another battalion and two light guns to Fort Anne as fast as he could.

In the meanwhile, the self-styled deserter had vanished from the Ninth's position, the first of a long series of bogus deserters who plagued the British army.[11] This one was able to tell the rebels at Fort Anne that the Ninth were very weak in numbers[12] and appeared to be unsupported. The American commander, who had about a thousand men, decided to attack at once.

According to Hill's second in command, "At half past ten in the morning they attacked us with a heavy and well-directed fire; a large body of them passed the creek on the left and fired from a thick wood across the creek on the left flank of the regiment; they then began to re-cross the creek, and attack us in the rear; we then found it necessary to change our ground to prevent the regiment being surrounded; we took post on the top of a very high hill to our right." Hill, with great skill, pivoted his battalion on his right flank and took up a very strong position. According to Sergeant Lamb, "When the troops arrived at the summit of the hill they formed in Indian file [i.e. in single rank] and kept up a well directed fire till all the ammunition was expended; the enemy observing that the fire was ceasing was encouraged to press forward with redoubled vigour and endeavoured to surround us in order to cut off all retreat. Just at this critical moment a war whoop was heard which resounded through the wood; this sound, which was so obnoxious at that time to the Americans, threw them into the utmost confusion."

The American version of this incident is that they withdrew because they too had run out of ammunition but, whatever the cause, they retreated with great rapidity, leaving a block-house and saw mill intact. This was most fortunate for the Ninth who were not only without ammunition but without Indians or any other reinforcements. The war whoops were the production of Captain John Money,[13] Burgoyne's Deputy Quartermaster General, who had been sent forward with a party of Indians. When he heard the firing ahead he urged his followers to hurry but they hung back. He went on alone, imitating their war cry.

When Phillips and the reinforcements arrived they found the Ninth exhausted but triumphant on their hill. They had lost three officers and nineteen other ranks killed and wounded. They had thirty prisoners in their hands and had taken the colours of the 2nd Regiment of New Hampshire, "a very handsome flag of the United States, 13 stripes, alternate red and white, with thirteen stars on a blue field, representing a new constellation".

Burgoyne had every reason to be satisfied with the performance of his army in the first week of active campaigning. At a time when he could have been involved in a lengthy and expensive siege, which could well have lasted into August, his spearhead was fifty miles further on and separated from the Hudson by only fourteen miles of a low but woody watershed. It is true that the taking of Ticonderoga was largely attributable to the incompetence of the rebel command, but both Burgoyne and Phillips deserve great credit for the bold way they had exploited the advantage offered to them. The thrust to Mount Defiance was a particularly bold move. The best brigade in the army with two siege guns was hazarded across a substantial river. It would have been hard to support them if St Clair had had the courage to attack them. The risk paid off handsomely but it was not one that, for example, Sir William Howe would have taken.

Hubbardton was a most creditable action. Fraser and his men showed great determination and skill. Although outnumbered, they had succeeded in driving their opponents away in an eccentric direction which would remove them from the campaign for some time, while inflicting on them much heavier casualties than the British themselves had suffered. This was the more gratifying since it was just the type of action in which the Americans could have been expected to do well. There was nothing of the parade ground in the way that the Advanced Corps had fought. As a subaltern wrote, "The advantage of the ground was wholly on the side of the Americans, added to which the woods were so thick that little or no order could be observed in advancing upon the enemy, it being impossible to form a regular line; personal courage and intrepidity was therefore to supply the place of military skill and discipline."

Similarly the action at Fort Anne, with none of the specially trained flank companies present, gave good ground for optimism. Colonel Hill had been rash in advancing so far ahead of his supports, but his handling of the battle had been masterly and the Ninth had shown that their battalion companies were very highly trained.

As far as fighting was concerned, Burgoyne and his men had every reason for confidence. The general was, nevertheless, beset with many worries, not the least of which was a total absence of news from Howe.

The most immediate problem was presented by the Indians. They had contributed nothing to the pursuit from Ticonderoga since it was not possible "to draw them from the plunder of that place". They were constantly getting drunk. Increasingly stringent orders had to be issued to stop them obtaining alcohol. "The first person guilty of disobedience shall instantly have all their liquors and suttling stores destroyed and be turned out of camp, besides whatever corporal punishment a court martial shall inflict." The Indians who had joined at Bouquet river were from lower Canada and were reputedly of lower quality than "the Ottawas and other remote nations" who were due to join at Skenesborough. These, Burgoyne had been told, would "profess war not pillage". They proved no better than their predecessors.

Indians had a very positive value. They were unrivalled at scouting ahead of the army and their presence at the outposts of the army's camp was sufficient to stop rebel patrols from attempting to surprise the troops at night. On the other hand they showed no courage of a very obvious kind and they became increasingly grasping in their demands for rewards. As Burgoyne noted, "If, under the management of their conductors, they are indulged, in all the caprices and humours of spoiled children, like them they grow more unreasonable and importunate upon every new favour; were they left to themselves, enormities too horrid to think of would ensue, guilty and innocent, women and infants, would be common prey."

The truth was that, if Indians were to be used at all, they should have been given their heads. Burgoyne laid down strict rules for their conduct and succeeded only in earning the intense dislike of the Indians[14] without denying to the rebel propagandists opportunities for horror stories which they were not slow to exploit. The most notorious incident occurred while the army was at Skenesborough. An American girl, Jenny McCrea, was coming into the British camp to join her fiancé, a Loyalist officer. One of the Indians arrived in the camp carrying her bleeding scalp. Throughout the army it was assumed that he had killed her. Burgoyne demanded that the Indian be hanged but he was dissuaded by Fraser who told him that the execution would cause all the rest of the Indians to desert, thereby endangering the safety of the army. The Chevalier St Luc prophesied that the result would be an Indian revolt in Canada. The Indian was thus permitted to go free— a triumph for justice since subsequent evidence makes it certain that Miss McCrea was killed accidentally by a stray rebel shot.

It had always been foreseen that land transport would be a major problem. It was exacerbated by the quantity of baggage brought by the officers. As far as Skenesborough, water carriage had been available. From there forward the army would be dependent on an inadequate number of draught animals. Officers were told that, despite the orders given in Canada, "the regiments in general are encumbered with much more baggage than they can possibly be supplied with means of conveying when they quit the lakes and rivers;

warning is therefore given to the officers to convey by the *bateaux* which are soon to return to Ticonderoga, the baggage which is not indispensably necessary to them; or, upon the first sudden movement, it must inevitably be left on the ground.''

The German officers, brought up in the tradition of European warfare with good roads, were the worst offenders.[15] Burgoyne had to write to Riedesel urging him "to take measures that the spirit of the order respecting the sending back of the officers' baggage to Ticonderoga may have due force. The baggage of the British officers is already gone and many of them have only retained a small tent and one cloak bag.''

There were minor troubles between the British and German soldiers. On 16th July, there was a riot in which a German sentry was insulted by drunken British soldiers. The British felt that the Brunswickers had not done their share of fighting and were further incensed because their allies were requisitioning cattle for their own consumption while the British (who at that moment did not have the same opportunities for cattle stealing) were getting only salt meat.

It was some consolation that Loyalists were enlisting in substantial numbers, considering that the country around was thinly populated. In the first four days at Skenesborough, "some hundreds of men, a third part of them with arms, have joined me, professing themselves loyalists and wishing to serve, some to the end of the war, some for the campaign." Those with arms were incorporated into the two embryo Loyalist regiments which had marched with the army from Canada. The rest were used for clearing the road ahead, which the rebels had blocked with fallen trees and broken bridges.

At Skenesborough a crucial tactical decision had to be taken. In the *Thoughts for Conducting the War from the Side of Canada*, Burgoyne had favoured making the advance from Ticonderoga to the Hudson by way of Lake George, if it could be done without making elaborate naval preparations on that lake. This had been on the presumption that he would just have completed a lengthy siege of Ticonderoga. Events had turned out differently. A rapid pursuit had brought the army to within twenty-eight miles of the Hudson, the forward post at Fort Anne being half that distance from the river. The whole business of defeating the rebel row-galleys on Lake George would be avoided if the troops could seize Fort George at the southern end of the lake, thereby depriving the galleys of their base.

Burgoyne decided that he would take the army overland to the Hudson, leaving Phillips to bring the artillery and stores across Lake George as soon as the head of the lake was cleared of rebels.

The re-establishment of the road from Skenesborough was a formidable task. It took "six or seven days" to make the track to Fort Anne passable for waggons. "The toil of the march was great, but supported by the utmost alacrity. The country was a wilderness, in almost every part of the passage the enemy took the means of cutting large timber trees on both sides of the road so as to lay across and lengthwise with the branches interwoven. The troops had not only layers of them to remove in places where it was impossible to take any other direction, but also they had above forty bridges to construct and others to repair, one of which was of logwood over a morass, two miles in extent." Beyond Fort Anne the going was easier as "there was a very good road made by the rebels the year before, between Fort Anne and Fort Edward, in which road the rebels had cut down some few trees which took the provincials in our army some few hours to clear." Difficult as was the business of opening the road, it was estimated by one of the staff to have saved the army two weeks compared with taking the whole force back to Ticonderoga and starting again from there over the lake.

In any case there had to be a pause at Skenesborough while sufficient supplies were ferried up South Creek to enable the army to be fed while it moved to the Hudson and to live there until stores could be brought across the lake and over the difficult road from Fort George to Fort Edward. In this pause Riedesel and his Germans were posted on the east bank of the creek and ordered to raid towards the Connecticut, part of Burgoyne's policy of "giving a jealousy" in that direction. Riedesel found the inhabitants cooperative and pressed to be allowed to make a deeper penetration in search of supplies. He was also anxious to requisition horses to mount his dragoon regiment. Burgoyne could not agree to this proposal. If the Germans ran into trouble, the operation necessary to extricate them would consume the painfully accumulated reserve of stores and delay the main advance to the Hudson. He did, however, promise Riedesel that he should be permitted to make such a raid as soon as the army was once more on a regular supply line.

On 23rd July, Fraser's Advance marched forward to Fort Anne where they paused again for five days to allow a further build up of stores. Their presence there was enough to alarm the defenders of Fort George, who saw their retreat threatened. They abandoned the place and burned their rowgalleys. Phillips immediately set his first convoy of guns and stores sailing up the lake. It reached Fort George on 28th July, and on the same day Fraser's men occupied Fort Edward on the Hudson without opposition. Reports from deserters told them that the rebel army had retreated twenty-five miles to Stillwater.

It was very satisfactory to have reached the upper Hudson before the end of July, but on the following day, Burgoyne received the first of the many disappointments which crowded in on him in the days to come. He had written from Skenesborough to ask Sir Guy Carleton to find troops for the garrison of Ticonderoga. This was a very reasonable request. Nothing could make Canada more secure than Burgoyne's successful advance into New York. Burgoyne certainly expected Carleton to agree to do so and it seems probable that he believed he had received a half-promise to this effect before he left Montreal. When sending a progress report to Howe when the army was in front of Ticonderoga, he had written that that fortress "will be garrisoned from Canada". There is no plausible reason why he should have made such an assertion if he had not believed it to be true. Carleton, however, was not in a cooperative mood. He alleged that Lord George had specified Île de Noix as the most southerly post for the Canadian garrison and refused to spare any troops for the other end of Lake Champlain. He took the opportunity of adding some highly improper comments. "As to the grand division of troops, his Lordship [Germain] leaves no room for our reasoning . . . Whatever I may think of his Lordship as an officer or a statesman, I must respect his office, and as Secretary of State, signifying to me the King's pleasure, he must be obeyed . . . I am very ready to acknowledge that I think the whole of our minister's measures, civil and military, very strange; indeed to me they appear incomprehensible."

Sir Guy was within his rights to refuse this assistance to Burgoyne if he judged the situation in Canada justified keeping all his troops within the province. He was wrong to put on Germain's order a construction they would not bear. The tone of his letter suggests that he was swayed more by his hatred of Germain than by military considerations or by concern for the success of Burgoyne who was, and continued to be, his friend. One thing is quite clear from his letter. Carleton no longer regarded Burgoyne as being under his command and, consequently, his responsibility. Since Carleton had been told unambiguously that the King had appointed only two Commanders in Chief in North America, it followed that he considered Burgoyne to be under Howe's command. A further indication that Carleton felt little responsibility for Burgoyne's army once Canada was safe was that he withdrew the army's chief staff officer, his brother, Lieutenant Colonel Thomas Carleton, as soon as the news of the capture of Ticonderoga reached Quebec.

The result of Carleton's intransigence was that Burgoyne had to part with two battalions,[16] 910 rank and file, to garrison Ticonderoga. The army's strength in regular infantry was consequently down to 4,627 rank and file by the beginning of August. He wrote sadly to Carleton, "I must do as well as I can but I am sure your Excellency as a soldier will think my situation a little difficult. A breach in my communication must either ruin my army entirely or oblige me to return in force to restore [the communications] which might mean the loss of the campaign. To prevent a breach Ticonderoga and Fort

George must be in very respectable strength and I must beside have posts at Fort Edward and other carrying places. These drains, added to the common accidents and losses, will necessarily render me very inferior in point of numbers to the enemy, whom I must expect always to find strongly posted."

Lacking encouragement from Canada, Burgoyne was all the more anxious to hear from New York, but no message came. To Germain he wrote, "I have spared no pains to open a correspondence with Sir William Howe. I have employed the most enterprizing characters and offered very promising rewards, but of ten messengers sent by different routes not one is returned to me and I am in total ignorance of the situation or intentions of that general."

CHAPTER 10

"Depending on Adventure"

On 20th December 1776, Sir William Howe wrote to Lord George Germain proposing that, instead of employing "an offensive army" from Rhode Island to operate towards Boston as he had earlier suggested, he should take a force of ten thousand men to capture Philadelphia. This letter reached London on 23rd February. Since it included the phrase, "We must not look for the northern army [Burgoyne's] to reach Albany before the middle of September", it did not occur to the British government that Howe had no intention of implementing the long agreed plan for a joint operation from New York and Montreal to obtain control of the line of the Hudson river.

The defeat of the Hessians at Trenton on Christmas Day meant that Howe's forward positions were no longer within easy striking distance of Philadelphia but it should not take more than ten days to move ten thousand men from New York by sea to the lower reaches of the Delaware river. If Howe started his campaign as soon as the weather was suitable, which would be in April or early May, there was no reason why he should not be in possession of Philadelphia before the end of June. There would be plenty of time for him to switch troops back to the province of New York either by sea or through New Jersey, in time to cooperate with Burgoyne around Albany by the middle of September. On this reading of Howe's letter, Lord George, having consulted Burgoyne, replied on 3rd March, "I am now commanded to acquaint you that the King entirely approves of your proposed deviation from the plan which you formerly suggested."

Howe was not an industrious writer of letters. The next significant reference to his plans came in his letter of 2nd April which reached London on 8th May[1], accompanying a copy of his letter to Carleton written three days later. He did not mention the operation on the Hudson but repeated his intention of abandoning the move against Boston from Rhode Island. He said that, owing to the severe winter in New Jersey, "the campaign will not commence as soon as your Lordship may expect", and added that, 'My hopes of terminating the war this campaign are vanished." It is possible that Germain might have understood from this that Howe had abandoned hope of moving up the Hudson to meet Burgoyne in 1777 but Howe gave the contrary impression by writing that, "I think it probable that by the latter end of the campaign we shall be in possession of the provinces of New York, the Jersies and Pensylvania, tho' this may in some measure depend on the success of the northern army."

The province of New York stretches to the Canadian border north of Ticonderoga and it seemed inconceivable to Lord George that Howe could contemplate being in possession of the province unless he intended to use a strong body of troops to cooperate with Burgoyne. There was confirmation of his intention to do so in the letter to Carleton. "In the meanwhile I shall endeavour to have a corps upon the lower part of the Hudson's river sufficient to open the communication for shipping thro' the Highlands at present obstructed by several forts erected by the rebels, which corps may afterwards act in favour of the northern army." Germain could not believe that Howe expected Burgoyne's army to survive at Albany unsupported and Burgoyne's proposed movements would be clear to Howe as soon as he received a copy of Germain's orders to him which had been despatched to New York on 26th March.

Lord George had to believe either that Howe still meant to go up the Hudson after taking Philadelphia or that the Commander in Chief was totally irresponsible. In his reply he wrote, "As you must from your situation and military skill be a competent judge of the propriety of every plan, his Majesty does not hesitate to approve the alterations which you propose, trusting, however, that whatever you may meditate, it will be executed in time for you to cooperate with the army ordered to proceed from Canada and put itself under your command."

Letters between London and New York could take any time between five weeks and seven months. This one took three months and reached Howe on 16th August. By that time he, with his army, was at sea off Chesapeake Bay. Even if Howe had, by that time, felt any responsibility for Burgoyne's corps, he could have done nothing about it.

The army at New York was ready to move, and anxious to do so, from the end of March. The main body was still holding the small strip of New Jersey into which it had retreated after the reverses at Trenton and Princeton. Although Howe ordered a new bridge to be built over the Rariton river, he had given up the idea of advancing to Philadelphia over land. He had also decided that he must abandon New Jersey if he was to make a seaborne attack on Philadelphia, but he made no move to evacuate that province. Throughout April and May he claimed that he was unable to move because new camp equipment had not arrived from England. This deficiency would not have precluded him from withdrawing the troops into billets in and around New York.

The missing equipment arrived on 26th May. His first use of it was to make a series of ineffective passes in the hope of bringing Washington's army to decisive action in New Jersey. It was not until 30th June that the army embarked at Amboy and left New Jersey to the rebels. It was exactly at the time at which the Pennsylvania campaign should have been complete.

Howe had received his copy of Germain's orders to Carleton and Burgoyne early in June.[2] Although it was made clear that Burgoyne was to march to Albany and put himself under his orders, Howe gave no appearance of acknowledging that he had any responsibility for anything that might happen in northern New York. It was a month before he mentioned that he had received the copy. His only comment to London referred to a minor administrative point—whether Burgoyne's brigadiers should continue to hold temporary rank after the junction of the armies. On this he casually remarked that this could only "take place when the armies absolutely join, which I do not suppose can happen this campaign, as I apprehend General Burgoyne will find full employment for his army against that of the rebels opposed to him." He took no steps to stop Burgoyne, now his subordinate, from trying to force his way to Albany although he mentioned that he had received Burgoyne's letter of 14th May, which continued the phrase, "I shall have no view but that of joining you."

Howe's lack of concern for Burgoyne was the more surprising since, two days before he wrote to Germain, Henry Clinton had returned to New York from London. Clinton was fully informed about the government's intentions for the campaign and, having dined several times with Burgoyne before he sailed for Canada, knew what the northern army was proposing. He "lost no time, when asked, in delivering my opinion upon the intended move south [to Philadelphia] and with all deference suggested the many and superior advantages to be derived at the present moment from a co-operation of his whole force with General Burgoyne on the river Hudson. And I took the liberty at the same time to say it was highly probable the fleet was instantly gone to sea, Mr Washington would move with everything he could collect either against General Burgoyne or me [in New York] and crush the one or the other, as neither would be very capable of withstanding such superior force unless timely intelligence should bring the fleet back to our relief."

Howe was not to be shifted from his plans and preparations for going to Philadelphia. It was unfortunate that he and Clinton were not on closer terms. At this stage they did not dislike each other, but Howe was so taciturn and Clinton so touchy that although, in Clinton's words, "we had a favourable opinion of each other, by some cursed fatality we could never draw together."

It is hard to understand Howe's reasoning at this time. It is true that Germain had been negligent in not sending him explicit orders, but this is an inadequate excuse. Germain's orders to Carleton, Clinton's on the government's plans and Burgoyne's declared intention of joining Howe at Albany can have left him in no doubt as to what he was meant to do. If he was unable or unwilling to do it, the least he should have done was to send orders to Burgoyne instructing him to confine himself to the recapture of Ticonderoga and to such diversionary operations against northern New York and the Connecticut valley as would not commit him to a situation in which he would be dependent on supplies from New York.

Instead he wrote to Burgoyne on 17th July as follows:

"Dear Sir,

"I have received yours of the second instant [from Crown Point] on the 15th, have since heard from the rebel army of your being in possession of Ticonderoga, *which is a great event, carried without loss.* I have received your two letters, viz. from Plymouth and Quebec, your last of 14th May, and shall observe the contents. There is a report of a messenger of yours to me having been taken and the letter discovered in a double wooden canteen [water bottle], you will know if it was of any consequence; nothing of it has transpired to us. I observe the same rules in writing to you, as you propose in your letters to me. Washington is waiting our motions here, and has detached Sullivan with about 2,500 men, as I learn to Albany. My intention is for Pensylvania where I expect to meet Washington, but if he goes to the northward contrary to my expectations and you can keep him at bay, be assured I shall soon be after him to relieve you.

"After you arrive at Albany, the movements of the enemy will guide yours; but my wishes are that the enemy be drove out of this province [New York] before any operations take place in Connecticut. Sir Henry Clinton remains in the command here and will act as circumstances may direct. Putnam is in the Highlands with about 4,000 men. Success be ever with you."

Howe's expeditionary force was already embarked when this letter was written. Contrary winds held the fleet in New York roads until 23rd July, when they set out for the south. Howe was sailing for Philadelphia twelve weeks later than London had expected him to do and he had embarked 25%

more men than he had been authorised to take.[3] He can scarcely not have realised that he was sailing in a direction diametrically opposed to that in which the government wished and common sense dictated.

It is not only in retrospect that Howe's conduct seems incomprehensible. His own second in command found it so at the time. Clinton was being left in New York with an effective force which "did not exceed 7,200 (including 325 artillerymen, nearly 3,000 newly raised provincials and about the same number of foreign auxiliaries [Hessians])". He found Howe's plan incredible. "Notwithstanding my instructions and many other unequivocal demonstrations tended to show that Sir William Howe's army was destined for the expedition to the southward, I own I could not to the very last bring myself to believe it. For I was satisfied in my own mind that it was all a feint, particularly after the receipt of General Burgoyne's letter from before Ticonderoga, which other credible accounts at the time asserted he was in possession of. I could not help, therefore, telling the Commander in Chief on his taking leave of me that I was persuaded *he intended to deceieve us all, and though he was pleased to say he was going to sea with the present northerly, I should expect to see him return with the first southerly blast and run up the North* [Hudson] *river.*"

Howe had no intention to deceive. He was at sea for more than a month. He reached the mouth of the Delaware on 30th July. The navy assured him that he could land in safety at Reedy Island, near New Castle but, despite the opposition of his brother the admiral, he insisted on continuing south to the Chesapeake. The navy had no charts of Chesapeake Bay and the channel had laboriously to be sounded and buoyed. It was not until 25th August that the army started ashore near Head of Elk. They were slightly further from Philadelphia than they would have been had they landed at Reedy Island twenty-six days earlier.

Washington had, not unnaturally, been perplexed by Howe's irrational movements. When he heard of the landing at Head of Elk he wrote, "Now let all New England turn out and crush Burgoyne."

Howe's letter to Burgoyne was cut into thin strips and rolled into a quill. It was delivered at Fort Edward on 3rd August. Burgoyne found it a baffling document and it was some days before he made its contents known to his senior subordinates. It seemed that in his first direct order Howe was telling him to put his army in a situation where it must be destroyed. The Commander in Chief reiterated Germain's order to go to Albany while announcing his own intention of moving in the opposite direction. For good measure he added that the opposition to Burgoyne had been reinforced.

It seems likely that Burgoyne came to the same conclusion as Clinton had done—that the move to Philadelphia was a feint. The letter had been carried secretly through nearly two hundred miles of rebel-held territory and, in the letter, Howe had drawn attention to the danger of their correspondence falling into enemy hands. There was nothing inherently improbable in Howe sending him the main message—go on to Albany—in clear. The rebels were likely to know his destination since it had been the common talk of Montreal before he had reached that city in May. The rest of the message could be strictly for American consumption.[4]

It was obvious that Howe expected Burgoyne to go to Albany and Burgoyne was in no doubt that his orders from London left him no alternative but to do his best to get there. Howe, as Commander in Chief, could override the orders from London and send him back to Ticonderoga but he had clearly not done so. For Burgoyne to retreat on his own initiative might well wreck the whole plan for the campaign. If Howe (or Clinton) came up the Hudson and found that Burgoyne was not there to cooperate, the best that could happen was that the whole campaigning season would have been wasted. The worst was that the southern army could be overwhelmed by a concentration of all the rebel armies. It must be remembered that Burgoyne was under the impression that Howe had received definitive orders from London and that Clinton, who had discussed the plans with Germain and Burgoyne, would make sure that there were no misunderstandings in New York.

To Burgoyne the choice was clear. Either he went on to Albany and helped to win the war or he retreated. In that case the best he could expect was a court martial presided over by the twenty-year-old ghost of Admiral Byng. He would have no defence against a charge of disobedience to orders from both London and New York. He might get sympathy but he would get no support from Lord George Germain né Sackville. He decided that he must march on to Albany.

Immediate movement was impossible. Some reinforcements were on their way to join him[5] and he must again build up supplies. "From the hour I pass the Hudson river and proceed towards Albany, all safety of communication [with Canada] ceases." He dare not move before he had accumulated at least twenty five days' rations and the means to transport them forward.

As far as Fort George a steady flow of supplies was now coming forward over the lake. The next sixteen miles to the Hudson at Fort Edward were very difficult going, "the roads in some parts steep and in others wanting great repair. Of the horses furnished by contract not more than a third part was yet arrived . . . Fifty team of oxen which had been collected in the country through which I had marched were added to the transport." To make matters worse there was a shortage of wagons since many of those available, and their horses, "were necessarily detained at Ticonderoga for the purpose of dragging the boats and provisions over the carrying place between Lake Champlain and Lake George".

The most laborious part of the business was getting the *bateaux*, forty feet long and heavily built, over the pass to the Hudson. It was "often necessary to employ ten or twelve oxen upon a single *bateau* . . . exceedingly heavy rains augmented the impediments." The journey between the two forts took only "about six hours", but the difficulties of loading the boats on and off the wagons at the ends of the journey meant that each team could scarcely manage one loaded journey each day. "After the utmost exertion for fifteen days, there were not more than ten days of provisions before hand, nor above ten *bateaux* on the river."

The only chance of building up supplies more rapidly was to obtain them from the more fertile country which the army now approached. As Burgoyne wrote, "It was well known that the enemy's source of supplies in live cattle from a large tract of country, passed by the route of Manchester, Arlington and other parts of the Hampshire Grants, to Bennington, in order to be occasionally conveyed from thence to the main army [at Stillwater]. A large depot of corn and of wheeled carriages was also formed at the same place, and the usual guard was militia, though it varied in numbers from day to day. A scheme was formed to surprise Bennington. The possession of the cattle and carriages would certainly have enabled the army to leave their distant magazines and to have acted with energy and dispatch."

When Riedesel had raided into the Hampshire Grants while the army was halted at Skenesborough he had reported "the people frightened and submissive". He had several times recommended a raid in that direction. In particular, as Burgoyne wrote, "Major General Riedesel has pressed upon me repeatedly the mounting of his dragoons, the men were animated with the same desire, and I conceived it a most favourable occasion to give into their ideas and solicitations, because in exerting their zeal to fulfill their favourite purpose,[6] they necessarily would effect the greater purpose of my own."

The expedition was entrusted to Lieutenant Colonel Friedrich Baum of the dragoons, whom Burgoyne considered "an officer well qualified for the undertaking".[7] His force consisted of two hundred of his own dragoons, fifty men of the Corps of Marksmen, the fifty six Canadians still with the army, a skeletal Loyalist regiment, 150 strong, eighty Indians and two 3 pounders from the Hanau artillery, a total of 556 all ranks.

Baum was told that, "the object of your expedition is to try the affectation of the country, to disconcert the council of the enemy, to mount the Riedesel dragoons, to complete Peters' corps[8] and to obtain large supplies of cattles fit for slaughter, milch cows excepted,[9] which are to be left for the use of the inhabitants."

It was a small detachment to make a raid twenty-five miles into enemy territory but, according to the information available, the only opposition would be a small body of militia. In case some more powerful force of the enemy intervened, Burgoyne issued detailed tactical instructions for Baum to keep the regulars closed up behind temporary earthworks until the Indians and provincials had reconnoitred each successive move. "The instructions were positive to keep the regular corps posted while the light troops felt their way, and not to incur the danger of being surrounded, or having the retreat cut off."

The dragoon officers had no doubt that the task was within their capabilities. Lord Petersham, one of Burgoyne's ADCs "talked to Colonel Baum and with several officers under his command and they appeared perfectly satisfied, at least I heard no complaint from them; the only anxiety they expressed was lest their destination should become known to the enemy."

This was a very understandable cause for concern. Loyalists and pretended loyalists were daily coming into the camp and some of them slipped out again with news for the rebels. Burgoyne knew how difficult it was to keep any kind of secret from the enemy and had made his arrangements accordingly. The written orders called for a wide swing into Connecticut. "The route marked for this expedition is to Arlington and Manchester, and in case it should be found the enemy is not in too great force upon the Connecticut river, from thence to Brattlebury." Just as the expedition was about to set out Burgoyne rode into Baum's camp and gave him verbally a new route— "from the mouth of Batten Kill, east for two miles; then strike off south east for about fifteen miles to Cambridge; and so on about twelve miles to Bennington."

This was a shorter and safer route than that originally proposed but when he heard of the change General Riedesel, according to his journal, "expressed his fear and astonishment in regard to the danger attending it." If Riedesel did make so illogical a protest, Burgoyne overruled it, but added fifty German light infantry to Baum's force.

One British general had reservations about the expedition. Talking to Burgoyne's Acting Adjutant General, Simon Fraser expressed doubts about the abilities of the Germans to carry out their task. The staff officer urged him "if he saw any objections to his plan, to express himself fully and freely to General Burgoyne." Fraser, Burgoyne's closest friend in the army, declined to interfere but remarked that, "the Germans are not very active people; but it may do."

The expedition was an unrelieved disaster. The main reason for this was straightforward bad luck. There happened to be at Bennington one of the most active of rebel officers, Brigadier General John Stark. His presence was not only fortuitous, it was in direct defiance of his orders. He had been instructed to join the main army at Stillwater. He refused, claiming that only the legislature of New Hampshire could compel him to serve there. The Congress condemned this attitude as being "destructive to military subordination" and they requested New Hampshire to instruct him "to conform to the same rules which other generals of the militia are subject to whenever they are called out at the expense of the United States". Nevertheless in mid-August, Stark was at Bennington and had gathered there almost two thousand militia.

Baum had reported on 13th August that there were said to be 1,800 rebel troops at Bennington and had undertaken to be "particularly careful on my approach at that place". In fact, having gained some easy successes on his approach march, Baum threw caution to the wind and forgot all Burgoyne's careful tactical injunctions. On 15th August, he got his small body of regulars far too close to Bennington without any serious attempt to discover the rebel strength in the town.

His situation was made no easier by the gullible enthusiasm of Philip Skene, the proprietor of Skenesborough, who was accompanying him to arrange for the enlistment of Loyalists. Skene had been in the hands of Congress early in the rebellion but had made his way to England where he had spread tales of Loyalist enthusiasm all over the colonies. The government had appointed him lieutenant governor of Crown Point and Ticonderoga (a district which, at the time, was wholly under rebel control) and had placed him on Burgoyne's staff. Although the army had already had bitter experience of bogus Loyalists, Skene seems to have been wholly unselective in his enlistments. He administered the oath of allegiance to all-comers and told them to wear white papers in their hats to show the troops that they were friendly.

On the morning of 16th August, Baum had his force entrenched in a good position about three miles from Bennington. Skene was much gratified to see two bodies of men, each about two hundred strong and all wearing white papers in their hats, take post in the left and right rear of Baum's position. He was less pleased when Stark launched a frontal attack and the paper-hatted gentry poured a heavy fire into the rear of the dragoons. The Indians took to their heels at the first shot and most of the Canadians followed them.[10] The remainder fought grimly on hoping for relief, but none came.

During the night of 14th/15th August, Burgoyne realised that Baum might be getting himself into difficulties and at dawn he set Colonel Breymann with the German Reserve to march from Batten Kill to the help of the dragoons. Breymann had twenty-four miles to cover and most of his troops were light infantry or jägers. After marching for thirty-two hours he was still two miles short of Baum's position. By that time Baum had been mortally wounded and his men had come to the end of their ammunition. The survivors either surrendered or made the best of their way back to Batten Kill. Trying to force his way forward, Breymann's advance guard was attacked by Stark's victorious men and very severely handled, losing two guns.[11] The Reserve retreated in some disorder to Batten Kill.

Why Breymann, who was a competent and brave officer, took so long to reach his objective is a matter for speculation. His own explanation was "bad weather, bad roads, tired horses and other impediments". Fraser had said that, "the Germans are not very active people", and certainly Breymann had been slow in coming up with Fraser's men at Hubbardton. The army had a less charitable explanation. "A report is current that an old pique between Breymann and Baum might occasion his tardiness, as he was heard to say, 'We will let them get warm before we reach them', when he heard the firing. This, of course, was only rumour, but there is some evidence that Breymann allowed his men two hours to cook their breakfast on the morning of 16th August. This time, as it happened, was long enough to have made the difference between the success and failure of his rescue attempt.

Burgoyne wrote confidentially to Lord George, "Had my instructions been followed, or could Mr Breymann have marched at the rate of two miles an hour any given twelve hours out of two and thirty, success would probably have ensued, misfortune would certainly have been avoided." It is impossible to dissent from this verdict. Burgoyne's responsibility for the reverse was only that he chose for the operation two brave and competent officers who both underestimated their enemy. As a result Baum moved too fast[12] and Breymann too slowly.

Whoever was the fault it was undeniable that the operation had miscarried very seriously, greatly to the encouragement of the rebels. The army had lost four field guns, though these were quickly replaced from Canada, and 26 officers and about four hundred other ranks from the troops which had marched from Canada.[13]

The reverse also brought to a head the resentment which had been smouldering among the Indians since they realised that Burgoyne's rules for their conduct were to be enforced. Led by the Chevalier St Luc, they held a "congress" and informed Burgoyne that they intended to go home. Through an interpreter, they said, "(speaking figuratively in the Indian fashion) that on their first joining his army, the sun arose bright and in its full glory; that the sky was clear and serene, forboding conquest and victory; but then that great luminary was surrounded and almost obscured from the sight by dark clouds, which threatened in their bursting to involve all nature in a general wreck and confusion." A party of ninety of the most enterprising warriors was induced to stay; the remainder went home, accompanied by St Luc, who might well have been charged with desertion, but who returned unmolested to spend his time abusing Burgoyne for his strict treatment of the Indians.

The defeat at Bennington was not offset by any good news from the Mohawk river. It will be remembered that Colonel St Leger had been sent, as a diversionary move, to the Mohawk by way of Lake Ontario in order to meet Burgoyne near Albany. He had about six hundred regulars[14] and a force of Loyalists and Indians which gave him a total strength of 1,700.

To reach the Mohawk, St Leger had first to capture Fort Stanwix. By the last intelligence available in Canada, the place was a stockaded post designed only to resist Indian attacks. When St Leger came before it he found the fortifications had been greatly improved and that it had a garrison of six hundred men. His artillery, two 6 pounders, two 3 pounders and four $4\frac{1}{2}$ inch howitzers, was unsuitable for siege work but, if St Leger was to get through to join Burgoyne, he had to capture the fort. He invested it on 3rd September and three days later his Loyalists and Indians ambushed a relieving force, eight hundred strong, near Oriskany. There were heavy casualties on both sides but the rebels were forced to withdraw. A simultaneous sortie by the garrison caused damage in St Leger's camps but did not make him raise the siege.

On 22nd August he had to withdraw. A stronger rebel force under Benedict Arnold was coming up the Mohawk and Arnold, more subtle than his predecessor, had prepared the way by sending messengers to St Leger's Indians greatly exaggerating his strength. Having broken into the rum store, the Indians decamped in a body. Hopelessly outnumbered, St Leger withdrew his regulars and guns, intending to join Burgoyne by way of Ticonderoga.

Although St Leger's retreat was unknown to Burgoyne in the immediate aftermath of Bennington, the general had little to cheer him. He found "daily reason to doubt the sincerity of the professing Loyalists. I have about 400 (not half of them armed) who may be depended upon; the rest are trimmers merely actuated by self-interest. The great bulk of the country is undoubtedly with the Congress, in principle and zeal." He knew that St Leger was stuck in front of Fort Stanwix and, worst of all, "no operations have yet been undertaken in my favour [from New York]; the Highlands have not yet been threatened. The consequence is that Putnam has detached two brigades [from the Highlands] to Mr Gates, who is now strongly posted near the mouth of the Mohawk with an army superior to mine in troops of the Congress [regulars] and as many militia as he pleases. He is likewise far from being deficient in artillery."

As for his own army, he was back in the dilemma he had tried to solve by the raid to Bennington, but in a more acute form. The campaigning season was more advanced and his army was weaker. "The prospect of the campaign is far less favourable . . . When I wrote more confidently, I little foresaw that I was to be left to pursue my way through such a tract of country and hosts of foes without any cooperation from New York; nor did I think the garrison of Ticonderoga would fall to my share alone."

His military judgment told him that he should retreat. His duty, as expressed in his orders from Germain and Howe, told him that if he did not go on he would ruin the grand strategy for suppressing the rebellion. "Had I a latitude in my orders, I should think it my duty to wait in this position [Batten Kill] or perhaps as far back as Fort Edward, where my communication with Lake George would be perfectly secure, till something happened to assist my movement forward; but my orders are positive to "force a junction with Sir William Howe.' I apprehend I am not at liberty to remain inactive longer than shall be necessary to collect twenty five days' provisions, and to receive the reinforcements now (and unfortunately only now) on Lake Champlain. The waiting the arrival of this reinforcement is on indispensible necessity because, from the hour I pass the Hudson's river and proceed towards Albany, all safety of communication ceases. I must expect a large body of the enemy from my left will take post behind me. I have put out of the question the waiting longer than the time necessary for the foregoing purposes, because the attempt, then critical, depending on adventure and the fortune that often accompanies it, and hardly justifiable but by orders from the State, would afterwards be consumatedly desperate. I mean that by moving soon, though I should meet with insurmountable difficulties to my progress, I shall at least have the chance of fighting my way back to Ticonderoga, but, the season a little farther advanced, the distance increased, and the march unavoidably tardy because surrounded by enemies, a retreat might be shut by impenetrable bars or the elements, and at the same time no possible means of existence remain in the country.

"I do not yet despond. Should I succeed in forcing my way to Albany and find the country in a state to subsist my army, I shall think no more of retreat, but at the worst fortify there and await Sir W. Howe's operation.

"Whatever may be my fate, I submit my actions to the breast of the King and to the candid judgment of my profession, when all the motives become public; and I rest in confidence that, whatever decision may be passed on my conduct, my good intent will not be questioned."

The Advanced Corps had crossed the Hudson to establish a bridgehead while the Bennington expedition was in progress. They had used an ingenious bridge of logs chained together, built under the supervision of Captain George Laws of the Royal Highland Emigrants, who had accompanied the army in charge of the artificers. There was torrential rain from the 15th August and the river started to run strongly. On the 17th, the bridge broke in the middle and Fraser's men had to be ferried back to the east bank in *bateaux*. Their artillery was brought across in "a large scow".

Even when the rain stopped the weather continued to be trying. "The heat in this region," wrote a German officer, "is uncommonly great and exceeds very noticeably the hottest summer day in our fatherland. Almost every day there are thunder showers which, though violent, are soon over. On the other hand, it does not cool off after them and at night, expecially towards morning, such a heavy dew or mist falls that it penetrates the tents and soaks the blankets."

Four weeks were needed after Bennington to bring forward the essential stock of provisions and *bateaux*. The main magazine was established at Duer's House, opposite the ruins of Fort Miller and seven miles downstream from Fort Edward. This was just below the last obstacle to navigation on the river. "The falls of Fort Miller, though of no considerable length, make it necessary to unload the boats, to place the contents in carts and replace them in fresh boats at the place where the river again admits of navigation. The boats unloaded, return to Fort Edward against a rapid stream." Between Forts Edward and Miller, eighty to a hundred boats were needed and each of them had to be brought over the hills from Lake George. Further boats were needed beyond the Miller Falls round which they were "carried 2 or 300 yards on rollers by fatigue parties", before being re-launched. The attempt to bring a gunboat over the hills to act as an escort to the *bateaux* failed owing to the steepness of the road.

Towards the end of August the transport situation was eased by the arrival of a further five hundred horses from Canada, but every possible economy was practised. Since "the preservation of the live cattle requires the most particular attention, they are to be slaughtered for the sick, and in such cases only as absolutely requires it." To ensure that the ranks were filled as far as possible, officers' servants were to be "considered as effective in the ranks". The promised reinforcements, three hundred British and 222 Germans, at last arrived on 3rd September. They were allocated to battalions and put through a quick training course. "The additional men are to be exercised from seven to nine each morning and from three to five every afternoon. In their exercising they will fire ball occasionally."

With very few Indians still with the army, the Corps of Marksmen was strengthened "with one non-commissioned officer and sixteen men from each British regiment of the line (the 53rd excepted[15]); they are to take two from each [battalion] company [and should be] men of good character, sober, active, robust and healthy: they are to be provided with a very good firelock."

Despite the long pause in the campaign, the army was confident and in good spirits. A German officer wrote, "Probably never did an army have less deserters than ours has had and in this connection you must remember that the rebels try to seduce our men to desertion by their emissaries, some of whom are English and some Germans . . . We shall be in a position to move on towards Albany. The soldiers desire it. The unhappy occurence at [Bennington] has not dispirited us. We regret nothing but the loss of brave friends and men . . . Fighting in wild woods and bushes is a serious business, and one detachment may easily have better or worse luck that another."

Part of this optimism was based on the rumours that took the place of the real news which failed to arrive. On 18th August, the same German had reported a story, current in the camp, that Lord Cornwallis was leading a corps of Howe's army up the Hudson and another that St Leger had taken Fort Stanwix. News of St Leger's retreat came to the army in the first week of September. Burgoyne immediately took steps to help him get forward from Ticonderoga. "I desire to have two *bateaux* with their oars buried as quietly as possible at Fort Edward. It would be as well to shovel earth upon them; and to give them still more the appearance of graves, a cross might be placed upon each hillock. All this must be done at night and only by trustworthy soldiers. The use for which these *bateaux* are intended is to help Lt. Col. St Leger in crossing the river. This officer has been forced by the bad conduct of the Indians to retreat on the road to Oswego . . . and he is now on the road to join us."

Burgoyne was less confident than his army. He knew that his next move was crucial. He had no reason to believe that forces from New York were not going to cooperate with him. "The want of communication with Sir William Howe is . . . a most embarrassing circumstance; of the messengers I have sent, I know of two being hanged, and am ignorant of whether any of the rest arrived." The last order he had had from Howe, which arrived early in August, told him to go on to Albany. If he obeyed it, he ran the risk of losing his army; if he fell back unnecessarily his only defence could be that he believed the Commander in Chief was behaving with criminal irresponsibility and had abandoned him to his fate. It was a poor excuse to put before a court martial.

Had Burgoyne only known it, the letter which would have solved his dilemma and saved the army had been sent from New York on 10th August. Clinton had written to say that Howe had sailed away to the south and that the garrison of New York was too weak to undertake an operation up the Hudson. This letter never reached Burgoyne. Clinton must bear a heavy share of blame for what followed, because he despatched only a single messenger with this letter. If three or four copies had been sent by different routes, one at least might have got through. A single messenger had little chance. Such negligence would have been characteristic of Howe, who seems to have persuaded himself that Burgoyne's fate was no concern of his. Clinton, however, knew the whole plan and had discussed it with Burgoyne. He must know that Burgoyne would follow his orders unless he received instructions to the contrary.

Meanwhile the enemy were concentrating to the north of Albany. Their army was nine thousand strong and their successes at Bennington and Fort Stanwix were ensuring that a steady stream of militia units joined them. They were well on the way to recovering from the shocks they had suffered in early July. Their main trouble was their commander. Political intrigue had removed the competent, if physically frail, Phillip Schuyler and replaced him with General Horatio Gates.

"Gates," wrote Horace Walpole, "was the son of a housekeeper of the second Duke of Leeds who, marrying a young husband when very old, had had this son by him. That Duke of Leeds had been saved, when guilty of Jacobite plot, by my father, Sir Robert Walpole, and the Duke was very grateful and took great notice of me when I was quite a boy. My mother's woman was intimate with that housekeeper and thence I was godfather to her son, though I believe I was not then ten years old."

After service as a Volunteer, Gates had been given a commission in the Sixtieth (Royal Americans). As a captain he was present at Braddock's defeat by the Monongahela river and seven years later distinguished himself for personal bravery at the taking of Martinique. General Monckton sent him to London with despatches and, as was usual with officers who brought home news of a victory, he was given a brevet majority. Although he was under the patronage of General Cornwallis, the uncle of Howe's corps commander, Gates' promotion languished after the peace of 1763 and he became more and more dissatisfied. He joined the rebel army and was made Adjutant General. He was an excellent administrator but, when raised to field command, he showed a mediocre talent, his moral courage falling far short of the bravery he had demonstrated in the field.

The position he had chosen to resist Burgoyne was based on the islands at the mouth of the Mohawk. When Benedict Arnold, his subordinate, returned from relieving Fort Stanwix, he chose a position six miles forward on high ground near Stillwater. The key to the position was a plateau, roughly square and about two hundred feet above the Hudson, known as Bemis' Heights. The right of the heights was protected by the river and the front was covered by a substantial re-entrant, the Mill Creek, beyond which there was a ridge on which stood Freeman's Farm. It was true that the heights could, in theory, be turned on the west, but Arnold realised that Burgoyne would be dependent on the river for his supplies and that, in consequence, the danger from the west would be minimal. He entrusted the fortification of the heights to a Polish exile, Thadeus Kosciuszko, who was later to make an imperishable name as a resistance fighter in his own country, but who was then an engineer officer in the Continental army, and started to put the troops into position. All Arnold's arrangements were admirable but, since he had omitted to consult Gates, it is not surprising that the two men were never again on good terms.

As soon as Burgoyne's supply position was in hand, he made preparations for his next move forward. The rear formations of the army and the heavy artillery were brought up to Fort Miller. Thirty days' supplies were loaded on to *bateaux*. A naval officer, Lieutenant John Schanck, had designed a new bridge of great ingenuity and on 12th September it was sailed into place and joined together by a party of sailors commanded by Midshipman Edward Pellew.

"On the 13th we passed the Hudson's river and encamped on the plains of Saratoga, at which place there is a handsome and commodious dwelling house, with outhouses, and exceedingly fine saw- and grist mills, and at a small distance a very neat church, with several houses round it, all of which were the property of General Schuyler. This beautiful spot was quite deserted, not a living creature on it. On the grounds were great quantities of fine wheat, as also Indian corn; the former was instantly cut down, threshed, carried to the mill to be ground, and delivered to the men to save our provisions; the latter was cut for forage for the horses."

Next day, "General Phillips called the officers of the artillery together and exhorted them to be cautious in expending their ammunition, reminding them of the impossibility of a fresh supply and requesting them to recollect that one action would probably not decide the campaign. He therefore begged that they would avoid firing on a retreating enemy unless almost certain of great success."

Burgoyne had decided that he was bound to advance. He had no illusions about the risks he was running but believed he had no option. It was inconceivable that Howe would urge him to Albany and then leave him to his own devices. The choice was agonising but he had to take it alone. After he had met disaster he wrote to London, "I think it a duty of justice to take upon myself the measure of passing Hudson's river. I did not think myself authorised to call any men into council."

He had the thirty days for which the army had rations to discover whether his trust in Howe was misplaced.

CHAPTER 11

"The Course of Unsuccessful Events"

It was nine miles from the camp near Saratoga to the rebel position on Bemis' Heights. The advance had to be a deliberate business. The ground was seamed with watercourses and, covered by the Advanced Corps, the artificers had to precede the army repairing the bridges so that the artillery could get forward. On the first day, 15th September, the camp was not struck until noon and the day's progress was only two and a half miles. The guns used the only road available, with the British battalions on their right and the Germans, in the meadows between the road and the river, on their left. On the river were the *bateaux*, loaded with the provisions and reserve of ammunition under the guard of six companies of the Forty Seventh.[1] The German Reserve brought up the rear, while abreast of them the sailors sailed Schanck's floating bridge down the river in sections.

The night of 15th/16th September was spend round a large farmstead called Dovecote,[2] and, "it being found that there were several bridges to repair, that work was begun under strong detachments, and the opportunity was taken to reconnoitre the country". Burgoyne, with Generals Phillips and Fraser, spent the day on horseback far ahead of the army under the escort of the Brunswick dragoons, about forty strong, "shabbily mounted and attired". It was no easy task to plan operations as the country was broken and thickly wooded.

On 17th September, the army moved forward a further three and a half miles and reached Sword's Farm. Again there was a day's halt while the artificers did their work on the road ahead. "The enemy appeared in considerable force to obstruct the further repair of bridges and with a view, as it was conceived, to draw on an action where artillery could not be employed. A small loss was sustained in skirmishing but the work of the bridges was effected."

As next day, 19th September, seemed likely to be one of battle, the morning's orders included instructions for coordinating the two wings of the army.

"In case of an action, the Lieut. General will be found near the centre of the British line, or he will leave word *there* where he may be followed. One orderly subaltern is to be sent from each of the following corps, viz-: one from the British line, one from Brigadier Fraser's corps, and one who speaks French from the left [German] wing. These officers are to be on horse back." Burgoyne had seen, while reconnoitring, that the earthworks on the left of the rebel position on the heights were far from complete. Since this end of the plateau was higher than the side near the river, possession of the left would make the rest of the heights untenable. He therefore planned to envelope the rebel flank with his best and most mobile troops before making a combined attack from front and flank. As Arnold had foreseen, he could not manoeuvre as widely as he would wish. He was tied by his left foot to his irreplaceable stores and *bateaux*. At all costs he must prevent a rebel attack breaking through between his columns and reaching the river. He had inevitably to keep a very substantial force on his own left.

He formed the army into three columns. On the right was Fraser with the Advanced Corps, including the Marksmen, supported by Breymann and the German Reserve. With Fraser went the remaining Indians, about eighty, a hundred Canadians and two hundred Loyalists, all that could be supplied with arms. Their field battery, four 6 pounders, four 3 pounders and two $5\frac{1}{2}$ inch howitzers, moved with them.

In the centre was the British line brigade, four weak battalions, Twentieth, Twenty First and Sixty Second Foot, with the Ninth in reserve. They had with them Captain Jones' four light 6 pounders. This was the column destined to make the frontal attack when Fraser's men had worked their way on to the rebel flank. Burgoyne rode with this centre column so that he could, as far as was possible in the broken country, coordinate the whole operation.

On the left, commanded by Riedesel, were four German regiments, those of Rhetz, Specht and Riedesel[3] from Brunswick, and the regiment of Hesse Hanau. Captain Pausch with six 6 pounders and two 3 pounders provided the artillery support.

Stationed in rear of the left wing was the artillery park with the heavy guns and four howitzers. General Phillips was in charge of the park and of the boats on the river and their escort of the Forty Seventh.

Fraser's column marched out of camp at nine o'clock in the morning. The head of the column started almost due west, moving up a track leading through the low wooded hills towards Saratoga lake. After they had covered two and a half miles they wheeled southward and their Indians, Canadians and Marksmen fanned out to cover their front. An hour later, at ten o'clock, the centre column left Sword's Farm and started up the same track. They, however, turned south a mile earlier than Fraser had done. Their route was shorter than Fraser's but across it lay "a deep ravine with a run of water sufficient to run a saw mill in the middle. Here, the enemy having neglected to destroy a small bridge, we passed without opposition." The head of the column reached the ridge on the far side of the ravine about noon and halted, throwing out piquets towards the enemy. There was some bickering between the piquets and rebel scouts. Near the river bank the Germans, followed by the heavy artillery, moved forward keeping level with the centre column.

The first serious fighting took place on the front of the centre column. At about 12.45 pm, Burgoyne ordered the combined piquets, twenty-five men from each of the four battalions under Major Gordon Forbes of the Ninth, to probe forward across the next valley and occupy Freeman's Farm on the high ground beyond. They found the buildings strongly held by riflemen, who counter attacked and drove the piquets back in disorder, wounding Forbes. Unfortunately fire was opened on the retreating piquets by their own comrades who took them for enemy. A tentative attempt by the rebels to follow up their success was checked by the main body of the column deployed into line and by some light infantry sent down by Fraser from the right. Soon afterwards, at about three o'clock, signal guns were fired from all the three columns indicating that they were in the positions allotted to them. The right and centre columns then began their advance.

Meanwhile there was dissension in the American camp. Gates believed that his best course was to keep his whole force within the entrenched camp and to wait until the British mounted a full-scale attack on it. Bunker Hill had shown what such an assault would cost them and Gates could argue that Burgoyne's outnumbered army could not afford this cost without reducing itself to impotence. Benedict Arnold commanded the American left and knew, better than Burgoyne, how little progress had been made with the fortifications on that side. After bitter argument, Arnold obtained a grudging permission to take three thousand men, including Daniel Morgan's Riflemen, to swing round the flank of the British advance. It so happened that he believed that it was Burgoyne's right which was menacing Freeman's Farm. He drove through the screen of Indians and skirmishers and marched headlong into Fraser's position. Taken by surprise, his advance guard was severely handled, especially by the artillery, and fell back. Realising his mistake, Arnold left a small force to keep Fraser in check and turned east towards the farm.

The Americans had evacuated the farm when Burgoyne's guns fired two roundshot through the main building. The infantry were already crossing the valley. They "passed a bridge (over a hollow way or large gutter apparently made by heavy falls of rain) and took post at the skirt of a wood a little beyond it. The enemy, being in possession of the wood, almost immediately attacked the [brigade] which took post beyond two log huts on the farm." Four guns were brought forward and stationed in pairs on the brigade's flanks.

During the next three hours the three battalions forming the front line withstood a series of attacks. In the intervals they were subjected to rifle fire and musketry from hidden marksmen in the surrounding woods. The rebel attacks were greeted by devastating volleys and grape shot from the guns. No assailants could stand against this fire but the redcoats could only drive them away as far as the edges of the wood. To pursue further would be to lose cohesion among the trees. Their task was to hold the farm that they had taken and, in doing so, they were confined by the technological limits of their weapons. They had to stand shoulder to shoulder to produce enough fire power to beat off the attacks. This made them prime targets for the rebel marksmen, but if they dispersed to lessen the target they presented, they could not hope to resist the onslaught of Arnold's formed bodies of men. Naturally they suffered heavy casualties.

From the right Fraser did what he could to relieve them but his freedom of action was limited. His first task must be to hold his position on a hill which prevented rebel forces sweeping round the British right and taking the whole army in the rear. He deployed Breymann's Germans in the gap between his left and the right of the Ninth Foot and made a series of limited counter attacks to clear the right of the troops at the farm. He could do nothing to assist their hard-pressed left.

Help for the Sixty Second and the Twentieth, who were on the left, had to come from the riverside column who were more than a mile away and out of visual touch because of the trees. Phillips was the first to react. He sent four 12 pounders to march towards the farm and rode up to join Burgoyne. Riedesel, while anxious to help, was in a quandary. He knew that the rebel army outnumbered the British by two to one. He did not know of Gates' extreme reluctance to release any troops from the entrenched camp. The Germans had in their care all the stores and heavy artillery. If those were lost the army would have to surrender. If Riedesel sent too many troops to help the centre column, a frontal attack by the rebels (who knew where the vital *bateaux* were) could break through, capture the stores and bring the campaign to an early and calamitous end. He sent an ADC to Burgoyne for orders and, meanwhile, sent two companies of the Rhetz regiment to take stations on a knoll on his right so as to form a link between his inner flank and Freeman's Farm. He could hear a continuous storm of musketry and cannon fire from the right but he received reports of formed bodies of rebels in front of his line.[4]

It was not until five o'clock, two hours after the battle at the farm had become serious, that his ADC returned from Burgoyne with orders to make his position by the river as secure as possible and to march to the left of the centre column with all the troops he could spare. Riedesel marched off immediately with his own regiment, the two companies of Rhetz, already detached, and two of Pausch's field guns.

Relief for the left of the British line at the farm was needed desperately. The Twentieth and the Sixty Second were dwindling away rapidly. Even more serious were the casualties among the gunners. Of the twenty-two men who manned the two guns on the left, nineteen were killed or wounded. Their commander borrowed a gun crew from the right (being shot through his hat while doing so) but the new crew lasted no longer than their predecessors. The slackening of the cannon fire encouraged the rebels to renew their attacks. The Twentieth were driven back, leaving the full strength of assault to be borne by the Sixty Second, already much reduced. They charged with the bayonet, lost another twenty-five men and "had begun to get into confusion".

At this moment relief arrived. The four 12 pounders which Phillips had sent forward arrived, unlimbered and opened a devastating fire with case shot. Phillips rallied the Twentieth and led them forward again. A staff officer who was with him recalled that, "the ranks appeared to be very thin, the regiment were much fatigued by the length of the action, but moved to the charge with spirit."

The Twentieth made a most gallant attack and enabled the Sixty Second to re-form and move back to a new, less exposed position. Two 6 pounders had to be left where they stood since there were neither horses nor gunners to move them.

This was the turning point of the action. Fraser had sent the Twenty Fourth across to extend the flank of the German Reserve towards Freeman's Farm. This enabled the Ninth to be moved behind their comrades to reinforce the left. They reached their new station just as Riedesel arrived with fresh infantry. Together they counter-attacked, recovering the ground which had been lost and with it the two 6 pounders. Fraser sent the grenadier battalion against the rebel left. Arnold's attack was broken and his men streamed away to the cover of their entrenchments on the heights. "By this time it was nearly dark and no further pursuit was attempted."

The British believed that they had won a victory and, in an immediate tactical sense, they had. They had beaten off Arnold's spoiling attack and captured Freeman's Farm. But, as Burgoyne wrote, "It was soon found that no fruits, honour excepted, were attained." They had not succeeded in capturing the hill on the left of the American camp, which alone could enable them to break through to Albany. "The enemy worked with redoubled ardour to strengthen their left: their right was already unattackable."

The British infantry was terribly reduced. The four battalions had gone into action 1,100 strong. Their casualties were, "seventy six killed, rank and file, between two hundred and forty and two hundred and fifty wounded and twenty eight or thirty prisoners". The Sixty Second had only seventy men left in the ranks.

There were, nevertheless, the Germans and the Advanced Corps substantially intact. If another attack could be mounted immediately the hill could still be seized before it became impregnable. Burgoyne gave orders for the army to be ready to move the next day as early as was possible after having brought in the wounded at first light. All night the troops lay on their arms and "lit fires as we were almost froze with cold".

There was a thick mist at dawn and, before the advance could be started, Fraser rode across to Burgoyne and told him that, "the grenadiers and light infantry, who were to lead the attack, appeared fatigued by the duty of the previous day and that if he would suspend the operation until the next day he was persuaded they would carry the attack with more vivacity."[5] Burgoyne had absolute confidence in Fraser's judgment and agreed to the postponement. As a result the second attack was never mounted. During the following night the long awaited messenger from Clinton arrived with the first news from New York that had reached the army for seven weeks.

Clinton had written, "You know my good will and are not ignorant of my poverty. If you think two thousand men can assist you effectually, I will make a push at Montgomery [the principal fort in the Highlands] in about ten days, but ever jealous for my flanks. If they make a move in force on either of them I must return to save this important post. I expect reinforcements every day. Let me know what you would wish."[6]

This message was embodied in an apparently trivial letter and could only be read correctly if a pre-arranged mask was laid over it which left only the essential words visible. Disastrously, Burgoyne's copy of the mask had been lost on the advance. He and his staff were left to guess which of the words in the covering letter were significant. They disentangled the part which dealt with the proposed attack on Fort Montgomery in the Highlands which was due to start at about the time they received the message. They did not realise the small scale of the attack intended. Since the earlier letter had failed to arrive they were indeed "ignorant of Clinton's poverty". Howe, they believed, had left Clinton with orders to attack up the Hudson. It was unimaginable that he would not have left him with enough troops to do so.

The news that Clinton was, at last, on his way, changed the whole prospect for Burgoyne's army. Before its arrival Burgoyne had been intent on making a further attempt to break through to Albany as directed by his orders. If that failed he would have no alternative to retreating at least as far as Fort Edward until he heard definite news of a move to assist him from the south. With Clinton advancing on the Highlands, his only course was to stay where he was. It would waste lives to renew the attack until part of the enemy's strength was drawn away to face Clinton. To retreat would allow Gates to use the bulk of his army to oppose Clinton. Burgoyne gave orders to entrench the position won at Freeman's Farm.

That night, Sergeant Taylor, who had brought Clinton's message from New York, set out on the return journey with a letter which read, "I have lost the old cypher; but from the tenor of your letter, as I thought you would have it to read—an attack, or even the menace of an attack upon Fort Montgomery, will be of use; it will stir them from in front of me, and I will follow them close."

Two officers, Captains Campbell and Scott, followed Sergeant Taylor on successive nights with further information for Clinton. Most of this information was to be given verbally and, as Clinton understood it, was that Burgoyne, "had lost his communication with Canada, that he had provisions until the 20th [October], described the situation of his own army, that though the rebels were strongly posted likewise, he made no doubt of being able to force them, and of getting to Albany; but doubted whether he could subsist there, as the country was drained, and that therefore he could not think of going there without I could open a communication with it; could name the day on which I would be there, and being there would answer for keeping the communication open with New York: he further desired [Captain Campbell] to tell me he awaited my orders whether he should attack the rebels or retire across the lakes while they were clear from ice: that, if he did not hear from me by the 12th he should retire."

These letters and messages show that Burgoyne's faith in cooperation from the south was now strained to breaking point. As long as he was confident that Howe was sending an army to share the task of establishing the King's troops in Albany, Burgoyne's letters were full of cheerful confidence. He had a clearcut task to perform and, provided that the rebels were being squeezed between two British forces, he rightly foresaw no insurmountable difficulties in fulfilling it. Howe's airy letter which reached him on 4th August had worried him, but had not deflected him from his aim since Howe had confirmed that aim. Six weeks later his credulity was being overtaxed. It was the middle of September, the time when Howe had expected him to reach Albany, and the army in New York was only contemplating an attack on the Highlands, in itself only the first step in the planned cooperation. He delivered an ultimatum. Either he had some new orders or he would retreat to preserve his army.

It is important to understand how little Burgoyne knew, or could know, of what was going on in New York. He knew that Howe had gone to Pennsylvania but he did not know how large Howe's army was nor how many men had been taken from New York for the southern expedition. Before leaving London he would have seen Howe's letter in which he proposed to take ten thousand rank and file. From Clinton's letter he had not been able to elucidate how many troops were available in New York. "I did *not* know Sir Henry Clinton's force. I *did* know that a considerable reinforcement might then be expected at New York from England." Had he known the "damn'd starved defensive" in which Howe had left Clinton he would have retreated. As it was he would assume that Clinton had at least enough men to undertake the task that Howe had said he had prescribed for him, "to open the communication for shipping thro' the Highlands". On the assumption that that communication was to be opened, there was no valid reason why Burgoyne should disobey his original instructions, confirmed by Howe, "to force his way to Albany".

Pending orders or further news from Clinton, his best course was to stand his ground as long as his supplies allowed. Opinion among his staff was that "on the approach of Sir Henry Clinton's army, the enemy could not stand against us, but would cross the river and go towards New England." This belief was reinforced when spies reported that Gates had built a bridge across the Hudson behind his right flank. According to Robert Kingston, who was acting as Adjutant General, no senior officer "considered retreat necessary".

Burgoyne said that from the moment Clinton's letter arrived, "I was in hourly expectation, I thought a justly founded one, of [Clinton's attack on the Highlands] operating to dislodge Mr Gates entirely or to oblige him to detach a large portion of his force. Either of these cases would probably have opened my way to Albany. In these circumstances could the preference upon these alternatives[7] admit of a moment's reflection? To wait so fair a prospect of effecting at last the great purpose of the campaign, or to put a victorious army under all the disadvantages of a beaten one by a difficult and disgraceful retreat; relinquishing the long-expected cooperation: and leaving Sir Henry Clinton's army, and probably Sir William Howe's, exposed with so much of the season to run, to the whole force of Mr Gates, after he should have seen me on the other side of the Hudson."

Clinton's position in New York was unenviable. Having failed to persuade Howe to abandon his southern expedition, he was left in command at New York with a force which in "rank and file fit for duty did not exceed 7,200 (including 325 artillerymen), nearly 3,000 newly raised Provincials, and much about the same number of foreign auxiliaries".

He was also oppressed by foreboding. While he was concerned about Burgoyne's position, he was even more so about the safety of New York. "I had the strongest reasons for thinking my situation most critical, especially while Mr Washington continued in such force [in New Jersey]. Because, should he have possessed himself of the heights of Morrisania (near which, or any of those between City Island and Hell Gate, no ship of war can possibly lie), how easily might he have landed—under cover of batteries raised there—on the plains of Haarlem? And when there and in possession of Brooklyn and Staten Island, it will readily be admitted, I believe, he could without difficulty have rendered my hold on New York very precarious, or at least destroyed my magazines and burnt the town."

His last information from Burgoyne was a letter written on 6th August from Fort Edward. "This letter," wrote Clinton, "showed [Burgoyne] to be in the highest spirits, and did not contain an expression that indicated the expectation or desire of cooperation from the southern army." This reading of Burgoyne's letter was, at best, ingenuous. Clinton knew that Burgoyne was expecting cooperation from the south. The two men had discussed the operation in London. He knew that Burgoyne's plans "were based on the supposition that it is the sole purpose of the Canada army to effect a junction with General Howe." Why else had Clinton spent so much time trying to convince Howe to move up the Hudson?

In the second week of September, Clinton mounted "a desultory move" (his own phrase) into New Jersey. This resulted in the capture of "some horses, about four hundred head of cattle and the same quantity of sheep, together with twenty milch cows, which afforded a seasonable refreshment to the squadron and army". Before this raid started he heard, through rebel sources, of the action at Bennington. At the same time he heard a rumour that Burgoyne's men had won a compensating success on the other bank of the Hudson. On this scanty evidence, he convinced himself that Baum's defeat had been "the cause of the most material success. For the rebels have detached to follow their blow on the supposed *avant garde* of Burgoyne's army, and he with his gross has penetrated by the Hudson's river."

It was not until the "desultory operation" was under way that it occurred to him that the northern army might "be in want of some little diversion". He then started the three day task of drafting the message to Burgoyne offering to attack Fort Montgomery. Four days after despatching it he reported to London and expressed the hope that Burgoyne "will not advance to Albany till we can cooperate with him. By 'we' I do not mean myself. I cannot in the whole muster up above 7,700, one half of which are Provincials . . . I cannot leave an extended coast, of near two hundred miles altogether, to less than five thousand, and with the other three thousand attempt to break through such a country as the Highlands, opposed by double that number already there [and by] every difficulty that nature and art united can bring against me, with no probability of holding it if I succeed, and every risk of consequence fatal to this important post [New York] if I fail. Nothing can tempt me but Burgoyne's great success—or his distress—to risk anything while the rebels are in force."

On 24th September Clinton's expected reinforcement—1,700 British and German recruits—landed at New York. Four days later Sergeant Taylor returned from Burgoyne with the message that "an attack or even the menace of an attack upon Fort Montgomery will be of service." By 3rd October Clinton had embarked three thousand men and began sailing up the Hudson. He had taken care to put around the information that he was again raiding into New Jersey.

At dawn on 5th October, he landed a force at Verplanck's Point, some miles south of Fort Montgomery and on the opposite bank of the river. The garrison was so surprised that it fled without firing a shot. It was at that juncture that Captain Campbell, Burgoyne's second messenger, came out to Clinton on board ship and gave him an account of the real situation of the northern army and passed on Burgoyne's request for orders.

Clinton's reaction to Campbell's message showed both the strong and the weak parts of his character. As far as physical action was concerned he was magnificent. He immediately put in hand a serious attack on the forts in the Highlands which, despite the total absence of artillery support, succeeded beyond any possible expectation. By 8th October, the whole of the Highlands were in British hands. He made immediate arrangements to exploit this success.

When it came to moral courage Clinton failed utterly. His letter to Burgoyne would have been a disgrace if it had been written to a stranger. To a friend it was unforgivable. Fortunately it was never delivered.

"Not having received any instructions from the Commander in Chief relative to the northern army, and ignorant of even his intentions concerning its operations (excepting his wishes that it may get to Albany), Sir Henry Clinton cannot presume to send orders to General Burgoyne. But he thinks it impossible that General Burgoyne could really suppose Sir Henry Clinton had any idea of penetrating to Albany with the small force he mentioned in his letter of the 11th September. What Sir Henry Clinton offered in that letter he has now undertaken. He cannot by any means promise himself success, but he hopes the move may be serviceable to General Burgoyne, as his letter of the 21st intimates that even the menace of an attack will be of use."

While Clinton must be given credit for the movements he made to help Burgoyne and the skill with which they were carried out, nothing can excuse the tone of this impersonal letter in which he washed his hands of Burgoyne's fate. Granted that Howe had left him in an extremely difficult position, Clinton was still responsible for Burgoyne's army. He was Howe's second in command and by that commission, as well as by the date of his rank in the army, he was Burgoyne's senior officer. From 23rd July, when Howe had disappeared over the horizon to the south, Clinton had been in charge of Burgoyne's army and, consequently, was responsible for it. It could be no excuse that Howe had affected to feel no responsibility for the northern army. Howe could plead, however unconvincingly, that he had been given no explicit order to co-operate with Burgoyne. Clinton could raise no such plea. He was fully informed, at first hand, of the intentions of both Lord George Germain and of Burgoyne. When he had been left in charge at New York, having failed to convince Howe of the necessity of moving up the Hudson, Clinton had an inescapable duty—to order Burgoyne to retreat. He could not shuffle that responsibility on to Howe or Germain or Burgoyne.

Clinton was not equal to his task. Howe had been out of touch for eighteen days before Clinton made his first attempt to communicate with Burgoyne. It failed, largely through Clinton's fault in sending only a single messenger. Even if it had succeeded, it contained information rather than instructions. It would not have relieved Burgoyne of the responsibility for failing to comply with his orders from London and New York. It gave some of the facts and left Burgoyne to draw his own conclusions.

Clinton had been responsible for seven weeks before he wrote again to Burgoyne. This time the letter got through. Clinton could not be held responsible that Burgoyne had lost the vital mask so that, when he read the letter he was delighted rather than appalled. He could have sent a verbal message but, perhaps because the bearer was not an officer, he did not. Even if Burgoyne could have read the message as it was written, it would not have given him the message Clinton should have sent him—retreat, we have changed the plan.

It may well have been the ghost of Admiral Byng that stopped Clinton asserting his power, just as it drove Burgoyne onwards.

By the end of September Burgoyne's position at Freeman's Farm was strongly fortified. A German officer wrote, "We entrenched the camp including all the outposts and piquets, made a line round the camp and fitted it with redoubts and batteries. Even behind the camp we laid out two great redoubts for the defence of the magazine, train and hospital. We felled thousands of trees to clear fields of fire for the guns . . . To do this we moved out every morning an hour before dawn and this caused trouble with the enemy. At that time one could enjoy the fresh morning air, with a very heavy hoar frost; that was followed by a mist which you could actually grasp with your hands and which rarely dispersed before nine o'clock. In the middle of the day there was enough heat to melt you . . . Things began to get very scarce. Nothing came through from Ticonderoga; there is nothing in this desert and the Americans would not let anything come to us from Albany. A bottle of poor red wine cost two reichsthaler, eight silver gröschen in our money, and a pound of coffee came to one reichsthaler, twenty two gröschen, sugar about the same. There was no hope of getting any clothes, although we were tearing ours to pieces every day in this wilderness. Never can the Jews have longed more for the coming of the Messiah than we longed for the arrival of General Clinton. From time to time news of his arrival passed round the camp. It was only rumours though they helped to keep up our spirits."

A British subaltern wrote, "Our present situation is far from being an inactive one, the armies being so near that not a night passes but there is firing and continual attacks upon the advanced piquets, especially those of the Germans. It seems to be the plan of the enemy to harass us with constant attacks, which they are able to do without fatiguing their army, from the great superiority of their numbers . . . Beyond the ground where we defeated the enemy on 19th September, all is hostile and dangerous in an alarming degree. The nature of the ground is peculiarly unfavourable in respect to military operations, it being difficult to reconnoitre the enemy and to obtain any intelligence to be relied upon: the roads, the situation of the enemy, the grounds for procuring forage, of which the army is in great want and all parties are in quest of, are often attended with the utmost danger, and require great bodies to cover them."

Bad news from the north reached the army on the last day of September. Burgoyne had always been concerned about the possibility of an attack on his communications from the east. Now it came. A rebel force marched on Ticonderoga by way of Hubbardton. The garrison, far from the fighting, had relaxed their vigilance. Four companies of the Fifty Third were captured at the portage from Lake George. Mount Defiance was lost. The boats of the lake fell into American hands. Fortunately the Brunswickers on Mount Independence were more alert and stood their ground, as did the rest the Fifty Third in Fort Carillon. Using the boats they had captured, the rebels next attacked Diamond Island. Here they met their match. The two companies of the Forty Seventh in garrison there under Captain Thomas Aubrey repelled the attack and recaptured most of the boats and all the guns which had been seized at Ticonderoga.

Although messengers could still get through from Canada, it was now clear that laden *bateaux* and wagons could not. There were still rations with the army until 12th October but, despite a flood of rumours and reports from deserters, no news of Clinton's progress. To prolong the time for which they could hold their ground, Burgoyne ordered the issue of rations to be halved. "There is reason to be assured that other powerful armies of the King are actually in cooperation with these troops, and although the present supply of rations is ample, it is highly desirable to be prepared for any continuance in the field that the King's service may require, without the delay of bringing forward further stores. For these purposes, the ration of bread or flour is for the present fixed at one pound."

It was typical of Burgoyne's constant care for his troops that simultaneously ordered the ration money deducted from the men's pay to be correspondingly reduced. He risked serious trouble with the Treasury by doing this since, not being a Commander in Chief, he had no authority to make the additional cash payment.

Four days later another action was fought. It was one of the most confusing battles in military history. Only one thing emerges clearly from the accounts. It was a disaster for Burgoyne's army.

On the morning of 7th October Burgoyne assembled a force of 1,500 muskets for a reconnaissance of the American left. His two objects were to discover whether there was a way of moving round the American flank and to reap a large field of grain to eke out the supplies for men and horses. His force was composed of detachments, as each battalion had to leave a proportion of its strength to guard its sector of the fortifications. The Advanced Corps provided seven hundred men, the German Reserve, much reduced since Bennington, and both the British and German line brigades provided about five hundred each. Six guns and two howitzers moved with them.

Soon after noon, the force marched off in column with the Germans in the centre and the British in front and rear. At about a mile south-west of Freeman's Farm, they halted and deployed into line "within three quarters of a mile of the enemy's left" and somewhat short of the valley of the Mill Creek. The Indians and the Marksmen were sent forward "by secret paths in the woods to gain the enemy's rear, and by showing themselves to keep them in check".

The main position lay across a tract of open ground. The left was held by the grenadier battalion under Major Acland. On their right were, in succession, the detachments of the Hanau infantry and the regiments of Rhetz and Riedesel. Next came the detachments of the British line, and Fraser held the extreme left with the Twenty Fourth and the Light Infantry. The German Reserve moved out beyond the left flank to act as a support for the Indians and Marksmen. Two Hanau 6 pounders were stationed fifty yards in front[8] of their compatriots "on a piece of ground somewhat elevated and commanding an advantageous and clear position". Two British 12 pounders were a short distance from the right of the German guns, separated from them by a small wood. Two 6 pounders were with Fraser on the left. A ring of piquets was in front of the guns to give warning of any rebel approaches and, in rear of the position, the batmen[9] started to cut the standing grain and load it on to the baggage horses.

Half an hour after the army had deployed reports came in of American patrols probing all along the front. On the hills to the south large bodies of rebels could be seen leaving the fortifications "at a 'double quick' and in squares, two strong columns, one towards our right and the other towards our left wing".

The first blow fell on the left. The Americans "advanced madly and blindly in face of a furious fire" from the grenadiers. In front of the line, they could make no progress but, being in great strength, they started to work round the left flank. Acland ordered his grenadiers to wheel back to form a flank *en potence*, facing east. This was a difficult manoeuvre to perform under sustained attack and there was some confusion. Some men broke their ranks "but some *aid du camps* calling to them 'For Shame', they marched away to their station in good order." Seeing this disorder among the grenadiers, the Hanauers on their right broke and fled.[10] Their artillery commander wrote, "They retreated—or to speak more plainly—they left their position without informing me, although I was fifty paces in advance of them. I looked backward toward the position still held, as I supposed, by our German infantry but not a man was to be seen. They had all run across the road into the fields and thence into the bushes, and had taken refuge behind the trees."

Riedesel and his staff rallied the broken troops and brought them up again, "an *aid du camp* and a brigade major with their drawn swords keeping them up". Their defection had left the grenadiers with both flanks in the air and they were suffering crippling casualties. To extricate them Burgoyne ordered Fraser to bring the Twenty Fourth and the Light Infantry across from the right. At the same time he sent orders for the artillery to retire. Unfortunately the ADC with this last message was mortally wounded and fell into rebel hands before he reached the guns. The gunners defended themselves most gallantly, the two German 6 pounders fired off three wagon loads of ammunition, but, there being no horses left alive, all the guns were overrun and captured.

Hardly had Fraser left his position on the right when an American brigade, the fourth to be committed, swept round the flank of the British line detachments and seemed certain to break into the lightly held camp. Checking his march, Fraser counter attacked but was mortally wounded as the rebel onslaught was held. His men succeeded in bringing him into camp but they were forced to leave Major Acland, who was also seriously wounded.

The British position was now desperate. Both flanks were threatened and, on the left, the grenadiers were disintegrating under continuous attack from overwhelming numbers. Burgoyne ordered Phillips and Riedesel "to cover the retreat while such troops as were most ready for the purpose returned for the defence of the lines." Burgoyne himself galloped back to camp and set about improvising a defence, posting the troops as they came in. The rearguard, the detachments of the British line, "retreated hard pressed but in good order", but ahead of them came a disorderly mob headed by the batmen who "came galloping into camp, having thrown off their forage to save their horses and themselves by flight." Riding on his last ammunition wagon, Captain Pausch of the German artillery, "met all the different nationalities of our division running pell-mell—among them Captain Schöll with whom there was not a single man left of the Hanau regiment. In this confused retreat, all made for the camp and our lines."

The Americans were hard on their heels. Needless to say, Benedict Arnold was their moving spirit. Deprived of his command by Gates he had accompanied the attack as a volunteer and now he took over the direction of the pursuit. He flung a brigade at the redoubt of the Advanced Corps. Fortunately that post was sufficiently manned as much of the rearguard had fallen back to it. Thwarted, Arnold swung his attack to the left and assaulted the most easterly redoubt, the position of the German Reserve. There were only about two hundred men in it. The detachment which had gone out in the morning had, for the most part, not succeeded in returning to it. Those who remained in garrison were not the best of the soldiers. The Canadians who were stationed to guard the flanks were quickly overwhelmed. Arnold launched a full brigade at the earthwork. Some of the defenders fired a single volley and fled. The rest fought desperately, inspired by Colonel Breymann who, it is said, cut down several of his own men when they attempted to escape. Arnold was seriously wounded; Breymann was killed. The redoubt was stormed.

With the loss of Breymann's redoubt the whole security of the camp was endangered. Burgoyne and Riedesel tried to organise an immediate counter-attack with the Rhetz regiment, but darkness had fallen and too few formed men could be collected to make the attempt possible. Burgoyne could not risk a dawn attack round the rear of his position. He ordered the army to swing its right back so that it held a close perimeter around the stores and hospitals. Both flanks were secured on the river.

The battle of Bemis' Heights cost Burgoyne about four hundred casualties among his regular infantry[11] and about a hundred and fifty of the auxiliaries were also lost, the remaining Indians deserting in a body. In particular there was a heavy loss among the officers, notably Fraser, Acland and Breymann.

The position on the river bank could only be temporary. Rebel troops could be seen moving northward on both sides of the Hudson to get between the army and Canada. The army's situation would be much strengthened if they could rest their southern flank on the Fishkill stream. Burgoyne ordered a retreat to Saratoga to be carried out on the night of 8th October.

"The army began to move at nine o'clock at night, Major General Riedesel commanding the vanguard and Major General Phillips the rear. This retreat although within musket shot of the enemy and encumbered by all the baggage of the army was made without loss but a very heavy raid and the difficulties of guarding the *bateaux* which contained all the provisions, occasioned delays which prevented the army reaching Saratoga till the night of the 9th and the artillery could not pass the fords of the Fishkill till the morning of the 10th." As a regimental officer wrote, the troops, by the time they reached the new position were "in such a state of fatigue that they had not the strength or inclination to cut wood or make fires, but rather sought sleep in their wet clothes and on the wet ground under a heavy rain that still continued."

By the time the men reached their new position, few of them had had any sleep for forty-eight hours. They had been on half rations for several days, they had suffered a sharp defeat with heavy loss and they had made a tedious night march under constant rain and the menace of a superior and victorious enemy. The high level of discipline which was maintained must reflect the highest credit on their general, their officers and the soldiers. Their only regret was that it had been impossible to move the wounded, as there were not enough wagons. General Gates treated them with the greatest consideration.

As soon as the army was in position a new ring of earthworks was begun.[12] There was a strong rebel force to be seen on the east bank of the Hudson so that there was no possibility of crossing to that side to continue the retreat. The main body of Gates' army had moved up to the Fishkill and other rebel forces were moving round the west face of the new camp.

The only way back to Canada was on the west bank of the great river and on 11th October a party of artificers, with a covering force consisting of the Forty Seventh and the Marksmen, were sent out to repair bridges along that road. Hardly had they left camp when the rebels formed columns as if to attempt the crossing of the Fishkill. The Forty Seventh and the Marksmen were immediately recalled to the entrenchments and the artificers, left to the protection of a party of Loyalists, refused to work and returned to camp.

No attack across the Fishkill developed but the Americans made a series of small attacks on the loaded *bateaux*. Some they captured but prompt action recovered most of them. A counter-attack led by Edward Pellew recaptured a *bateau* loaded with five hundred barrels of food. Nevertheless the army could not afford to have its small store of food under constant attack. The remaining provisions were unloaded and carried up to the scant security of the slopes. By this time there was no part of the position that could not be reached by rebel fire.

On 12th October, Burgoyne called Phillips and Riedesel with Brigadier Hamilton into a Council of War. He outlined the rebel position and estimated their strength at about fourteen thousand men. His own army consisted of 1,900 British and 1,600 German infantry. "The provisions of the army may hold out to the 20th; there is neither rum nor spruce beer." The latest intelligence from the south was encouraging but unconfirmed. "The intelligence from the lower parts of Hudson's river is founded upon the concurrent reports of prisoners and deserters, who say it was the news in the enemy camp that Fort Montgomery was taken [by Clinton] and one man, a friend to government, who arrived yesterday, mentions particulars of the manner in which it was taken."

Burgoyne pointed out that the only escape route was "by the ford at Fort Edward, or taking to the mountains in order to pass the head of Hudson's river and continue to the westward of Fort George all the way to Ticonderoga; it is true this last passage was never made but by Indians or very small bodies." Unless the bridges could be repaired, artillery could not be taken up the west bank.

The Council decided that "to retreat by night, leaving the artillery and baggage and, should it be found impracticable to force the passage [at Fort Edward] with musketry, to attempt the upper ford or the passage round Fort George, is the only recourse, and to effect it the utmost secrecy and silence is to be observed and the troops are to be put in motion in the still part of the night, without any change in the disposition." Whether this would be possible depended upon "the delivery of six days' provisions in due time and upon the return of scouts, which had been sent forward to examine what route the army could move the first four miles undiscovered, whether the plan could take place that day or on the morrow."

The plan was never implemented. "The scouts returned with intelligence that the enemy was intrenched opposite those fords and had a camp in force between Fort Edward and Fort George with cannon, and had posts so near to us upon our side of the water as must prevented the army moving a single mile without being discovered. In this situation the army took the best position possible and fortified, waiting until the 13th at night in the anxious hope of succours from our friends, or the next desirable expectation, an attack from our enemy. During this time the men lay continually on their arms and were cannonaded in every part, even with rifle shot and grape shot came into all parts of the line, though without any considerable effect. At this period an exact account of the provisions was taken. Only three days upon short allowance were in store. The regular troops had been reduced by losses from the best part to 3,500, not 2,000 of which were British . . . I called into Council all the generals, field officers and captains commanding corps. By their unanimous concurrence and advice, I was induced to open a treaty with Major General Gates."

Burgoyne's conduct of the negotiations was a diplomatic triumph. His position was hopeless. Fortunately the Americans did not realise how hopeless it was. He was also helped because the Americans believed, as Burgoyne no longer did, that powerful British forces were coming up the Hudson. Clinton was keeping up the pressure. He had dashed back to New York, assured himself of its safety, scraped together some reinforcements, commandeered some transports and loaded them with six months provisions for five thousand men. On 13th October, he was back in the Highlands and ordered his second in command, General Vaughan, to embark two thousand men and sail up the river. Next day Vaughan, who met no opposition, passed Kingston. Gates, who did not realise Vaughan's weakness, was intent on forcing Burgoyne to surrender as soon as possible and was prepared to make concessions to encourage him to do so.

When Burgoyne asked permission to send a staff officer to the American outposts, Gates sent his ADC forward. The ADC left an account of the meeting. "At the hour appointed, I repaired to the advanced posts. The bridge across the Fishkill had been destroyed, but the sleepers remained. We did not wait many minutes before the *chamade*[13] was beat at the advanced guard of the enemy and an officer, descending the hill, stepped across the creek on one of the sleepers; he called out it was 'Major Kingston[14] with a message from Lieutenant General Burgoyne to Major General Gates'.

"I named myself to him 'Colonel Wilkinson,[15] on the part of General Gates, to receive the message.'

"He paused for a moment, pulled out a paper, looked at it and said, 'My orders direct me to Major General Gates.'

"'It is to save you time and trouble that I am authorised to receive the message you bear.' He then took General Gates' note to General Burgoyne from his pocket, read it and said,

"'General Gates has agreed to receive this message and I am not authorised to deliver it to any other person.'

"'Well then, sir, you must submit to being hoodwinked.' He affected to start at the proposition and objected on the grounds of it being an indignity.

I could but smile and observed that I had understood that there was nothing more common than to blindfold military messengers when they were admitted within the walls of a place or the guards of a camp. He replied, 'Well, sir, I will submit to it but under the express stipulation that no indignity is intended to the British arms.'

"I then carefully bound up his eyes with his own hankerchief; he took my arm and in this way we walked upwards of a mile to headquarters. Major Kingston appeared to be about forty; he was a well formed, ruddy and handsome man, and expatiated with taste and eloquence on the beautiful scenery of the Hudson's river, and the charms of the season.

"When I introduced him into General Gates' tent and named him, the gentlemen saluted each other with 'General Gates, your servant,' and 'Ah, Kingston, how do you do,' and a shake of the hand. Being seated a few minutes, Kingston arose and observed he had certain communications to make to Major General Gates from Lieutenant General Burgoyne, and to guard against inaccuracies of memory, he had committed them to paper and, with permission, would read them. The general consented, and the major took from his pocket and read.

"'After having fought you twice, Lieut. General Burgoyne has waited for some days in his present position determined to try a third conflict against any force you could bring to attack him.

"'He is apprized of the superiority of your numbers, and the disposition of your troops to impede his supplies and render his retreat a scene of carnage on both sides. In this situation he is impelled by humanity and thinks himself justified by established principles and precedents of state and war to spare the lives of brave men upon honourable terms. Should Major Genl. Gates be inclined to treat upon that idea, General Burgoyne would propose a cessation of arms during the time necessary to communicate the preliminary terms by which, in any extremity, he and his army mean to abide.'

"So soon as he had finished, General Gates, to my utter astonishment, put his hand in his side pocket, pulled out a paper and presented it to Kingston, observing, 'There, sir, are the terms on which General Burgoyne must surrender.'

"The major appeared thunderstruck but read the paper whilst the old chief surveyed him attentively through his spectacles. Having finished the perusal of the propositions, Major Kingston appeared exceedingly mortified and said to the general, 'I must beg leave to decline delivering this paper to General Burgoyne because, although I cannot speak for him. I think the propositions it contains cannot be submitted to.'

"The general observed that he might be mistaken, and there could be no impropriety in his delivering them. Kingston requested that they might be sent by one of his own officers, which the general declined and remarked 'that as he had brought the message, he ought to take back the answer,' to which the major reluctantly consented, took leave and I again filletted him, and at his request conducted him to our advanced guard. Very different was his conversation in returning, he complained of General Gates' propositions, to which I was still a perfect stranger; talked of the pride and spirit of his army, and called my recollection to the feats performed by the six British regiments at Minden. I felt for his chagrin, and said nothing to increase it; and having passed him beyond our guards, I hastened back to headquarters, filled with uneasiness by the course General Gates had adopted."

The propositions sent by General Gates were brutally simple. Burgoyne's army was to march out of its camp, ground arms and surrender as prisoners of war. Officers would be granted parole but, if they broke it, they would be closely confined.

This was rejected out of hand. "Lieut. General Burgoyne's army, however reduced, will never admit that their retreat is cut off while they have arms in their hands." Rather than surrender, "they will rush on the enemy determined to take no quarter."

This was bold talk. Astonishingly, it succeeded. Burgoyne sent Gates a set of counter proposals which were accepted. By a Treaty of Convention, a phrase carefully chosen to avoid the word "capitulation", the troops were not to be prisoners of war. They were to leave their camp, lay down their arms and then set out, under their own officers, to march to Boston. There they were to be embarked in British transports and taken back to Europe "on condition of not serving again in North America during the present contest". All Canadians "and persons belonging to the Canadian establishment" were to be sent back to Canada. The enlisted Loyalists were to be treated as members of the British army, thus avoiding the chance of being treated as rebels to the United States.[16]

On the morning of 17th October, Burgoyne's army marched out of the entrenched camp and laid down its arms on the banks of the Hudson river. Then they set off for Boston with their bands playing. There were 2,442 British of all ranks (exclusive of twelve staff officers) and 2,198 Germans. Thirty-seven guns and howitzers were left in the fortifications.

When that sad ceremony was over Burgoyne turned his horse and rode to the American camp followed by his generals. The American army, 17,091 effective of all ranks, were drawn up to receive him. General Gates was waiting to greet him and "they had approached nearly within swords length, when they reined up and halted. General Burgoyne, raising his hat, said 'The fortune of war, General Gates, has made me your prisoner.' To which the conquerer replied, 'I shall always be ready to bear testimony that it has not been any fault of your Excellency.'"

On the same day General Vaughan, with his two thousand men, reached Livingstone's Manor, the highest point on the Hudson which big ships could reach. He was forty-six miles from Albany.

PART VI

Aftermath

CHAPTER 12

"Ministerial Ingratitude will be Displayed"

The signing of the Convention left Burgoyne "sunk in mind and body". "I have been obliged to deliberate upon the most nice negotiations and political arrangements that required the most undisturbed reflection, under perpetual fire, and exhausted with laborious days and sixteen almost sleepless nights, without a change of clothes, or other covering than the sky. I have been with my army in the jaws of famine; shot through my hat and waistcoat; my nearest friends killed round me; and after all these combined misfortunes and escapes, I imagine I am reserved to stand a war with ministers who will always lay the blame upon the employed who miscarries."

He realised that he would be cast as the scapegoat for what he then believed to be the errors of ministers. "I expect ministerial ingratitude will be displayed, as in all countries and at all times is usual, to remove the blame from the orders to the execution." At this early stage it did not occur to him that Howe was the author of his misfortune and he wrote to that general that "I think it not impossible that the persons who are most bound to vindicate me will be the first to attack my reputation, those for whom I cheerfully under-took a forlorn hope,[1] and who would have crushed me if I remained inactive, I expect to find my accusers for rashness."

He was in no doubt that he could justify his conduct. It had never occurred to him that his orders were other than mandatory. He was "to proceed with all expedition to Albany and put himself under the orders of Sir William Howe". He had discussed the orders with Germain before leaving London. Carleton had agreed with his reading of them. Howe had confirmed that he should go to Albany in the only two letters Burgoyne had received from him. With his public despatch he sent a confidential letter to Lord George out-lining his defence. "I rest my confidence in the justice of the King and his councils, to support the general they thought proper to appoint to as arduous an undertaking, and under a direction as positive as perhaps cabinet ever framed. It will, I am sure, be remembered that a preference of exertions was the only latitude given to me, and that to force a junction with Sir William Howe, or at least a passage to Albany,[2] was the principle, the letter and the spirit of my orders. Indeed the appearance at the time I passed the Hudson's river, though subject to doubt in some instances as I wrote to your Lordship were such as upon a general view such as I am persuaded would have rendered inaction censurable had my orders, instead of being peremptory, been discretionary . . . The expediency of advancing being admitted, the consequences have been honourable misfortunes . . . Will it be said that in the exhausted situation described, and in the jaws of famine and invested by quadruple numbers, a treaty which saves the army for the state for the next campaign, was not more than could have been expected?"

Remembering the editing of Clinton's Charleston despatch in 1775, Burgoyne took precautions "in case the Ministry should mangle or curtail any part of it in the Gazette." He sent additional copies of the public despatch to his nephew Lord Derby and his friend Charles James Fox. All these and the confidential letter to Lord George were entrusted to his ADC, Lord Petersham, who had the advantage that he was a Member of Parliament, beside being the son of a distinguished general.

There were small gleams of light in the gloom that surrounded Burgoyne. He could feel that the terms he had secured for his army minimised the loss to the country. As long as the army remained in the care of Gates' men, every attention was being paid to them. "The treatment of the officers and troops in general is of so extraordinary a nature, in point of generosity, that I must suppose it proceeds from some other motive than mere kindness of nature." The army, despite its hardships and discouragements, remained loyal and devoted to its general. After a month in captivity, a German wrote home from Cambridge, Massachusetts that, "You can be sure that neither the army nor its conduct is to blame, and it can still look other more fortunate armies frankly and boldly in the face. Nor can the army complain of its general, but believes that he will justify his conduct before the King, his country and the world."

There was consolation too in a letter from Carleton commiserating with his misfortune and confirming his view that Burgoyne's orders had left him no discretion. "This unfortunate event, it is to be hoped, will in future prevent ministers from pretending to direct operations of war in a country at 3,000 miles distance, of which they have so little knowledge as not to be able to distinguish between good, bad, or interested advices, or to give positive orders in matters which from their nature are ever upon the change: so that the expedience or propriety of a measure at one moment may be totally inexpedient or improper in the next."

Soon after the Convention he began to learn, from rebel sources in the first place, how impossible it would have been for Clinton to have fulfilled the southern part of the joint plan. In astonishment, Burgoyne wrote to Howe that "it is now demonstrable that even a relief from famine would not have effected my junction with Sir H. Clinton. His strength and his situation were not such as to oblige Gates to desist, and my force was much inadequate, and the country much too strong to cut my way thro' the whole."

He did not realise the full extent of Howe's responsibility until he received a letter from Clinton telling how he had tried to persuade Howe to abandon the Philadelphia expedition. "I feared indeed, and was not silent upon the subject, that when our force was removed out of the power of cooperating with you, such numbers would press upon you from the four contiguous provinces as might overwhelm you. I had still, however, a hope that the Commander in Chief might get possession of Philadelphia and send me reinforcements from thence early enough to enable me to try something in your favour . . . As for your having applied to me for orders, I never could be expected to give you any, ignorant as I was of your plans and those of the Commander in Chief, except his wishes that you should approach Albany." It would not have escaped Burgoyne that Clinton was being somewhat disingenuous about his own failings but it was now very clear that it was Howe who had left the northern army in the lurch.

Meanwhile the situation of the "Convention Army" was deteriorating. It was only to be expected that the troops would meet a measure of hostilities from the civilian population as they were marched through New England. What was more disturbing was that, as they moved further away from the influence of General Gates, the attitude of the American soldiery changed for the worse. In particular General Stark, the victor of Bennington, showed himself in a most regrettable light, declaring publicly that he would give any officer "two hundred lashes, without the benefit of a court-marital" who moved more than ten rods (55 yards) from his quarters. Sergeant Lamb recalled that during the nights on their march, "it was not infrequent for thirty or forty persons, men, women and children, to be indiscriminately crowded together in one small open hut, their provisions and firewood on short allowance; a scanty provision of straw their bed; their blankets their only covering. In the nightime those that could not lie down, and the many who sat up from the cold, were obliged frequently to rise and shake from them the snow which the wind drifted in at the openings. General Burgoyne, ever attentive to the welfare of his army, remonstrated in a letter to General Gates." The behaviour of one American officer, Colonel Healy, was so brutal that Burgoyne succeeded in having him brought to a court martial. He was acquitted, despite overwhelming evidence of his guilt.

Most depressing of all was the steadily accumulating evidence that the

Congress did not intend to be bound by the terms of the Convention. It is easy to see that the treaty would be displeasing to the Americans once the immediate pressures which led to it had passed away. Congress, however, had commissioned General Gates as their commander in the north and it might be supposed that they would feel bound to honour his pledged word. Instead they announced that, since 648 soldiers had retained their cartouche boxes, the British had broken the treaty and it was no longer binding on the Congress.[3]

By February Burgoyne was a sick man and it was obvious that the army was not going to be repatriated. He applied to General Washington and the Congress for leave to return to England to recover his health and to defend his reputation against "all the aspersions and erroneous interpretations that the malevolent, the prejudiced, or the misinformed may choose to cast upon it". Congress gave him leave to return on parole and he agreed "that should the embarkation of the troops of the Convention of Saratoga be by any means prolonged beyond the time apprehended, I will return to America, upon demand and due notice given by Congress, and will re-deliver myself into the power of the Congress of the United States unless regularly exchanged."

He embarked in mid-April at Rhode Island in the frigate *Juno*, Captain Hew Dalrymple. Thirty-one years later another Hew Dalrymple was to sign the Convention of Cintra, a treaty even more generous to the French than that of Saratoga was to the British. Much as the British government and people, headed by George III, disliked the Convention of Cintra they did not hesitate to honour it.

As he embarked, Burgoyne received a letter from General Riedesel which must have been especially pleasing to him and which must cast great doubt on the subsequent criticisms made of Burgoyne by the general and his wife. As with the rest of the correspondence between Riedesel and Burgoyne, it was in French.

"My heart overflows at the departure of your Excellency. Words cannot express my gratitude for the letter your Excellency has written to my master, H.S.H. the Duke of Brunswick about myself and my soldiers. Your kindness goes far beyond my deserts except on the subject of my zeal on behalf his Majesty the King and the sincere devotion I have to yourself, a devotion I shall retain to the end of my life. My natural diffidence [*ma défiance sur mon propre devoir*], the difficulties in the languages of the troops of two nations, have often made me afraid of displeasing you and of failing in my duty and in that of the service; these doubts have been heightened by the strength of the attachment, esteem and deep respect which I bear towards your Excellency.

"Your Excellency's generous letter fully reassures me on this matter; it also puts me under the greatest obligation and wholly justifies my conduct in the eyes of my Most Serene Master . . .

"I take the liberty of begging your Excellency to accept this letter as a mark of thanks from myself and all the Brunswick officers for all the courtesy and kindness you have shown us throughout the period in which we have had the privilege to serve under your orders. Although success has not crowned your efforts, we well know that the fault has not been yours and that the army has fallen a victim to the misfortunes of war."

It had been an unhappy summer for ministers in London. They had started the year with the reasonable confidence that the plan to cut the colonies in half by taking the line of the Hudson would cripple the rebellion. It was 8th May before they began to be uneasy. Howe's letter of 2nd April said that his "hopes of terminating the campaign this year are vanished". However, his addition that "I still think it probable that by the latter end of the campaign we shall be in possession of the provinces of New York, the Jersies and Pensylvania, tho' this in some measure must depend on the success of the northern army", gave hope that 1778 should see the end. It still seemed that Howe intended to cooperate with Burgoyne. Certainly he had said nothing to suggest that he intended to abandon Burgoyne.

There followed a long silence. At the end of June, Germain was complaining that, "I cannot guess by Sir William Howe's letters when he will begin his operations, or where he proposes carrying them on." The silence lasted well into August. Meantime, on 2nd August, a merchantman from the St Lawrence brought news that Ticonderoga was surrounded by British troops, which suggested to Lord George that "we may expect a glorious campaign". Two weeks later a ship arrived from New York. She carried no letters from Howe but an officer, returning on private business, told Germain that the army was still at New York but that the hope there was "that Sir Wm. Howe is going to Boston and not to the southward, but everything is kept a profound secret."

A batch of letters from Howe, written before the army left New York, reached London on 22nd August. In one of them, written on 7th July, Howe remarked casually that he did not suppose the northern and southern British armies could join hands in that year, "as I apprehend General Burgoyne will find full employment for his army against that of the rebels opposed to him." He added that he was leaving Clinton at New York with 7,367 rank and file, including Loyalists, with orders to act on the defensive but with discretion to take the offensive provided the safety of New York was assured. He reported having received Burgoyne's letter from Quebec but considered that it did not contain "anything more material than that the artillery stores designed for the northern service, together with a reinforcement for that corps and the victuallers from Cork had not then arrived". He had overlooked the extremely "material" phrase in which Burgoyne had said that "I shall have no view but that of joining you." The fact that Burgoyne was intent on joining Howe on the Hudson did not seem to Howe to be any reason why his own army should not set off in the opposite direction.

At the same time there arrived another letter from Howe, written nine days later, which set out to allay any fears the earlier letter might have aroused in London. "I apprehend General Burgoyne will meet with little interuption otherwise than the difficulties he must encounter in transporting stores and provisions for the supply of his army . . . If General Washington should march with a determination to force General Burgoyne, the strength of General Burgoyne's army is such as to leave me no room to dread the event." Having said, in the earlier letter, that he expected Burgoyne to "find full employment for his army against that of the rebels opposed to him", he now viewed with equanimity Burgoyne's chances against the northern and southern rebel armies combined. This could scarcely be reassuring, but he added two undertakings. He would reinforce Clinton's force at New York and he would go to Philadelphia "up the Delaware, in order to be nearer [New York] than I should be by taking the course of Chesapeak Bay, which I had once intended". He failed to abide by either of these undertakings.

Germain was now helpless. If he immediately sent orders to Burgoyne, warning him of Howe's insouciance, the earliest they could be expected to reach him near Ticonderoga would be the end of October and by that time it could easily be (and would have been) too late. That he did not do so was probably explained by the arrival, on the day following his receipt of Howe's letters, of Captain Gardner with Burgoyne's despatches announcing the victories at Ticonderoga, Hubbardton and Fort Anne. Since the myth of Ticonderoga's strength was still potent, this information induced a mood of euphoria in the Secretary of State. He wrote, "Burgoyne is fortunate and deserves it. His account of his success is not exaggerated and we have reason to hope that his progress will be rapid."

In writing this, Germain was overlooking the fact that the rebels still had a powerful army in the north. He was also believing Howe's assurances that Clinton was at New York with "a strong force" and that the southern expeditionary army was going to the Delaware rather than on the long seaborne trip to the Chesapeake. He was also assuming that Howe "will take those measures which are most for the public benefit". On all these points he had been misled.

Some lurking suspicion on these points may have been on his mind. When he congratulated the King "upon the great and glorious success of Lieutenant

General Burgoyne in taking Ticonderoga", he witheld from the King Burgoyne's private letter which accompanied the despatches. This letter drew attention to the disappointing performance of the Indians and lamented "that my orders do not give me the latitude I ventured to propose in my original project for the campaign." Germain was already shying away from any suggestion that Burgoyne's orders were positive about marching to Albany. When the King proposed that Burgoyne should be given the Red Ribband, Germain supported the idea. Fortunately for all concerned, Lord Derby, acting on previous instructions, declined the honour on Burgoyne's behalf.

About a month later Burgoyne's report of his arrival at Ford Edward on the Hudson reached the American department. Germain reported to the King, "The progress of General Burgoyne is as rapid as could be expected and the difficulties he has surmounted do him great honour. In a private letter the general says that nothing has happened since he last wrote to change his sentiments of the campaign; he complains of not hearing from Sir Wm. Howe, or knowing anything of his operations; he has despatched ten messengers to New Yorke and not one has returned."

There was no more news from Howe until 28th October. In the nine week interregnum government and public had to make do with rumours of doubtful foundation brought by the crews of merchant ships. At the end of September the captain of a transport reported that Howe had divided his army between Baltimore and Chesapeake Bay; "that Washington had marched his army to Philadelphia; that Burgoyne was below Albany; that Clinton was preparing an expedition supposed to meet him." On 6th October, an Edinburgh newspaper reported that "a vessel at Clyde from Quebec, sailed the 24th Sug., and letters say that Arnold with 12,000 men had surrendered." This, commented Governor Hutchinson, "is only corroborating former reports. But the state of Howe's army, and the time spent this summer without effecting anything material gives the most concern."

On 28th October, despatches from Howe, Burgoyne and Clinton reached London. Howe reported that his army was ashore at Head of Elk and had defeated Washington at Brandywine. Burgoyne's letter was dated 20th August. It reported the reverse at Bennington and set out his doubts about continuing his advance without news or orders from New York. It also recorded his intention to persevere. Clinton's letter, addressed to the Adjutant General, said that Burgoyne "has hitherto acted so judiciously that we have everything to expect from his good conduct. I hope, however, that he will not advance beyond Albany till we can cooperate with him."

These three letters opened Germain's eyes to the seriousness of the situation in America. At the same time he received a letter from Brigadier

Maclean, commanding at Montreal. This gave an incomplete account of the battle of Freeman's Farm. He wrote to his Under Secretary, "I am sorry to find that Burgoyne's campaign is so totally ruined; the best wish I can form is that he may have returned to Ticonderoga without much loss . . . What alarms me most is that he thinks his orders to go to Albany and form a junction with Sir William Howe are so positive that he must attempt at all events the obeying of them."

Lord George was starting to erect his defences against the outcry which the failure of the year's campaign must call down on his own head. He knew that the blame for Burgoyne's plight lay with Howe but Howe was the King's favourite and he, Germain, had strongly supported his appointment. Moreover Howe, always a popular favourite, had just won a victory and news that he had seized the rebel capital was expected at any moment. It was impracticable to blame Howe on both political and military grounds, the more so since Howe's disgrace would inevitably lead to the resignation of his brother, the naval commander in chief.

Nor was Lord George prepared to accept responsibility for the failure of the campaign. In the first place, he did not believe that he was responsible. He believed that the plan for subduing the colonies had been both right and practicable but that it had been wrecked by Howe. Germain was not prepared to be dismissed a second time with scarcely less ignominy than he had, unjustly in his view, suffered after Minden. He also saw it as his duty to stay in office. If he resigned, the government would collapse. There was no one else who had the abilities to hold the American Secretaryship. Even his bitterest enemies could not plausibly deny that he had done marvels in making the creaking machinery of war administration work. If he left office, Britain must inevitably lose the war.

Even if he was wholly blameless, Burgoyne was expendable. A scapegoat had to be found and he was the obvious choice, since he was the general who was likely to be defeated. If he was, he would probably, since he was known to be a brave man, be killed. If he was not he would spend several years as a prisoner. Either way he would be in no position to tell his side of the story. It was an unjust decision but one which was demanded by public necessity. Better governments than that of Lord North have discarded unsuccessful commanders in all centuries.[4] Privately Germain made his view clear. He "owned to Lord Hertford that General Howe had defeated all his views by going to Maryland instead of waiting to join Burgoyne." Publicly, Burgoyne was going to bear the blame.

Throughout November there was little definite news from America, but a vague apprehension of disaster spread through Britain. Early in the month the opposition in Parliament pressed for information about Burgoyne's progress.

Although the government's majorities remained firm, ministers were glad
to have a week's break in the House before the State Opening of Parliament.
The King's speech on 18th November made no mention of the sombre
rumours that were circulating. In the debate that followed, ministers, whatever their fears, took an optimistic line. Lord George claimed that, "There
is every reason to hope for success in America." He began, nevertheless, to
deploy his defensive gambit in case the worst should happen. "With regard
to the Canada expedition, the honourable gentleman was under a mistake
when he imagined that General Burgoyne had orders to fight his way to New
York, and there join Sir William Howe: his orders were to clear the country
of rebels as far as Albany, which town was prescribed to him as the boundary
of his expedition, unless circumstances might make it necessary to cooperate
with General Howe, in which case he was to assist him to the utmost of his
powers." There was a subtle shift of emphasis in this description of Burgoyne's
orders. Instead of Albany being his objective, it became "the boundary of his
expedition".

The country's sense of foreboding was not decreased. Edward Gibbon, a
steady government supporter in the Commons, wrote on 2nd December,
"Opposition is very lively, and though in the House, we keep up our numbers, there seems to be a universal desire for peace even on the most humble
conditions." Two days later he wrote, "Dreadful news indeed. You will see
them partly in the papers and we have not yet any particulars. An English
army of near 10,000 men laid down their arms and surrendered prisoners of
war on condition of being sent to England and of never again serving against
America. They had fought bravely and were three days without food.
General Fraser with 2,000 men killed. A general cry for peace."

That news had come from a rebel ship which had docked in France and
from a letter from Carleton, who wrote that he had heard from rebel
deserters that Burgoyne had surrendered and that he believed the report to be
true. According to Horace Walpole, on 3rd December, "Charles Fox and
Burke pressed Lord George to know if the capture of Burgoyne's army was
true. He was forced to own he believed it, though he did not know it
officially. The Opposition, instead of receiving such a national indignity with
serious lamentations, insulted the Ministers so much that the majority
appeared less dejected than on former days of the session."

Two days later Burgoyne's old patron Lord Chatham called for the orders
sent to both Burgoyne and Howe in the House of Lords. "He lamented the
fate of Mr Burgoyne in the most pathetic terms; and said that that gentleman's character, the glory of British arms and the dearest interests of this
undone disgraced country, had all been sacrificed to the ignorance, temerity
and incapacity of ministers . . . He spoke with great candour of General

Burgoyne; he might, or he might not be an able officer; but by everything he could learn, his fate was not proportionate to his merit; he might have received orders it was not in his power to execute . . . Lord Chatham returned to the situation of General Burgoyne and paid him, indeed, very high complements. He said his zeal in the service was unquestioned." The government's majority in the Lords was as firm as it was in the Commons.

Throughout the country there was a discernible rally in support for North's government. Partly this was due to the instinct for national unity which has marked most periods of English history. Partly it was due to the feeling among the independent members that no acceptable alternative government was in sight. The decisive factor was an issue of principle. Few members believed that Lord George was being wholly frank about Burgoyne. Fewer still believed in the disinterestedness of the opposition. Very few would wish to see men like Shelburne, Barré, Fox, Burke or Wilkes in power. Their open joy at the military reverses alienated many who might otherwise have wished to see changes in the cabinet.[5] Moreover, it was no secret that Howe's conduct had greatly contributed to the *debâcle*. Clinton criticised him strongly in his letters home to friends and relations who were members of both Houses. Many junior officers in Howe's own army were scathing in their comments on their commander's conduct. On 1st December, Hutchinson had noted that "Howe's going round to Chesapeake instead of going to join Burgoyne is censured much; and it now begins to be said that he has not the capacity for the place he is in." Three days later he added, "Where the blame will lay seems undetermined. Howe's leaving Burgoyne after he knew he was on his way to Albany, and going upon the southern expedition is not at present accounted for."

The opposition were significantly silent about Howe. They spoke warmly in defence of Burgoyne but they evaded the question of Howe's responsibility. Both the Howe brothers had acted with the Opposition before they sailed for America. If Germain was concealing his own errors, the opposition were turning a blind eye to the far more serious errors of their allies, the Howe brothers. Faced with a choice of hypocricies, the independent gentlemen unhesitatingly chose the lesser. A classically educated Parliament had no difficulty in accepting that *Salus populi suprema lex esto*. They could not bring themselves to believe that the preservation of the state lay in defending the tarnished reputation of Sir William Howe or in installing the spendthrift Fox at the Treasury.

All doubts about Burgoyne's fate were resolved on 15th December when Captain James Craig arrived with a copy of the final despatch from Saratoga.[6] Germain forwarded the papers with a note which left no doubt about the line he intended to take. "Lord George is sorry he cannot send you

Majesty better accounts, the positive orders which Lt. General Burgoyne refers to, your Majesty will remember, but it was never understood that at such a distance any order could be positive. In the present case the words of the order will not bear the strict construction the general puts upon them." The King was not convinced. He promoted Captain Craig, a reward normally given only to officers bringing despatches announcing a victory. The King could scarcely have shown more clearly his approval of Burgoyne's conduct.

There were demands for an enquiry into the failure of the expedition. The government, while willing to have an enquiry, were concerned that it should not put the blame on them. They favoured one with strictly limited terms of reference. The King disagreed. Writing to Lord North on Christmas Day, he said, "I confess I am still of the opinion that I threw out to you yesterday; that if on consideration it should be thought right to enquire through the medium of a Board of General Officers into the defence laid by Lt. G. Burgoyne that his orders were positive (which I much incline to) the reference ought to extend to the failure of the expedition and what is now proposed make only a part of it; Lord G. Germain may be contented with an enquiry into what bears upon himself, but when my name is mentioned it should be a candid and not a partial enquiry."

In his public despatch Burgoyne had played scrupulously fair with ministers. His complaints about being left to his own devices had been reserved for his private letters to Lord George. It was only in an occasional isolated phrase that his discontent could be glimpsed by a critic hostile to government—phrases like "the peremptory tenor of my orders", "disappointed in the last hope of any timely cooperation from other armies", and "the expedition I commanded was evidently meant at first to be *hazarded*". A general enquiry, such as the King was suggesting, would certainly have to dig deeper than this and, if as the King himself was inclined to believe that Burgoyne's orders were positive, there was little chance that ministers should escape censure. Faced with the prospects of losing his ministers or sacrificing Howe, the King was quickly brought to agree that there should be no enquiry in the immediate future. Nevertheless he agreed reluctantly. "I cannot help expressing some surprise that so many of the Cabinet have doubted the propriety of bringing the unhappy fate of Lt. G. Burgoyne's expedition to an enquiry, though I thought there might be a diversity of opinion as to the mode and extent of such an enquiry; in the state of it yesterday I think Lord G. Germain judged right in not for the present moment pressing the affair further."

Lord George summed up the situation when he wrote, Burgoyne's "conduct requires and ought to undergo an inquiry but it should be an inquiry by officers, and it should await his arrival. After what he has sought fit to lay to the charge of others [i.e. his orders], he had no right to complain if ministers do not expose themselves in his behalf to even a temporary censure . . . The defence of the expedition, as far as it relates to the administration depends upon showing that the object to be obtained was important, that it was attainable with the force employed, that the necessary preparations were made, that the orders left sufficient discretion to the commander."

To establish these points, all of which were more than dubious, Lord George hit on the expedient of releasing to Parliament Burgoyne's *Thoughts for conducting the War from the side of Canada*. He said that the advantage of doing this would be that "it accounts for the conciseness of the instructions which did not require to be very ample when they only related to a plan formed by the person to whom they were addressed. It also appears from this paper that a cooperation of Howe's army was not expected, but the expedition undertaken as an independent enterprize to be executed by the force allotted to it."

Germain's intention was to give the impression that Burgoyne had written his own orders. This was to be made easier because the government had no intention of releasing the actual orders sent to Carleton in Canada, the more so since they could not release the complementary orders to Howe which, of course, did not exist. Thus it would be impossible for members of Parliament to compare what Burgoyne had written with what he had been told to do. Naturally there would be no mention of the fact that the *Thoughts* had been written at a time when Clinton was designated as commander of the northern army. To make the revelation more convincing, the *Thoughts* were released to the Commons in apparent error. As Horace Walpole wrote, "The Court had very maliciously delivered among the papers [related to Fox's motion that no more of the pre-war regiments be sent out of the kingdom], one sent over by General Burgoyne and called his 'Thoughts on the Canadian war'— a clear symptom of their intending to inculpate him." Since no explanation was offered as to how the *Thoughts* came to be written, the idea was allowed to get abroad, and sedulously cultivated, that Burgoyne had offered the paper spontaneously in the hope of supplanting Carleton.

The ice over which Germain was skating at this point was not as thin as it appears. The opposition could not press him too far on this point without incriminating Howe and this he knew they would never do. It was impossible to build up a case which would exculpate both Burgoyne and Howe. The opposition could not have it both ways. The government supporters and the independent members might feel that Burgoyne was being shabbily treated, but they were still determined to win the war and this could not be done by defeating the government. Moreover, the danger of war with France was growing steadily. On 13th March, the French Ambassador informed Lord Weymouth that his country had concluded a Treaty of Commerce with the United States. He did not add that a Treaty of Alliance had been signed at the same time, but the British government realised that was intended and, that night, sent orders to Paris recalling their ambassador. Many men, inside and outside Parliament, who disapproved of the government's American policy, rallied to their support as soon as war with France seemed certain.

On 4th February, Sir William Howe's resignation had been accepted. He had offered it on 22nd October, as soon as he had heard of Burgoyne's surrender. He must have suspected that if he did not resign he would soon be dismissed. He accompanied his resignation with a tendentious letter attempting to prove that Burgoyne's isolation had been the fault of Lord George rather than himself. He declared that he had "positively mentioned" in his letter to Carleton before Burgoyne left Canada, "that no direct assistance could be given by the southern army." It was useful political ammunition for the Opposition and some of it was at least half true.

The King did his best to retain Howe in command. Ministers were determined not to lose the chance of disposing of him. The King's refusal to accept his resignation would have given Lord North the chance he had been looking for to retire in private life. George III knew, as well as the independent members did, that he could not afford to change the government. Reluctantly he agreed to Howe's replacement by Clinton. He was now in the same dilemma as the opposition. Since it was impossible to exonerate both Howe and Burgoyne one of them had to be sacrificed. Howe was an old friend, some said he was the King's close relation. He had, moreover, won a series of victories even if none of them approached being decisive. By the spring of March 1778, King and government had decided that Burgoyne must be the scapegoat. The independent members of Parliament had decided that they must support the government as the lesser of two evils. The opposition would use Burgoyne as a stick to beat ministers but only as far as was constant with protecting Howe from blame. It was not a cheerful prospect for Burgoyne.

Burgoyne reached Portsmouth in the storeship *Grampus* on 13th May 1778. As soon as he landed he sent a letter to Lord George requesting a court martial. He did not realise how the cards had been stacked against him. It never occurred to him that Germain of all men would refuse him a court martial. Nor did he doubt that a court martial would find that Howe had abandoned him to his fate. He had not reached London before he realised that he was being over-optimistic.

According to Nicholas Wraxall, who claimed to have the story from "a high living authority", "the Opposition, apprehensive of his taking part with Administration, and fearful that he might accuse the adherents of Congress in this country with having contributed by their language in Parliament, if not by other means of encouragement, to the resistance that produced the disaster at Saratoga, determined if possible to gain him. For that purpose Fox went down privately to Hounslow in a hired post-chaise, where he met Burgoyne soon after he had landed, on his way from Portsmouth to London. In the course of a long confidential interview, Fox convinced him so thoroughly that the ministers would not support him, that Lord George must accuse him in order to exculpate himself, that the King had imbibed very strong prejudices against him, and that the Administration could not last a twelvemonth, as to induce the general to transfer his charges of misconduct from the Opposition to the Treasury Bench." Governor Hutchinson heard the story of this conversation rather differently and probably more correctly. "Charles F. asked [Burgoyne] his plan? 'To charge Howe with leaving him to be sacrificed.' 'If that's your plan, we must forsake you; we are determined to support H[owe].'"

It is clear from both these versions that the opposition feared that Burgoyne would become a supporter of the government. The indications are that they were right in that fear. In Burgoyne's private letter to Germain after Saratoga he had seemed to blame government for making his orders too positive. Germain had taken his counter-measures accordingly. Since writing that letter, Burgoyne had heard how Howe had left Clinton with too few men to act when he went off on a wild goose chase to the south. As soon as he realised this, Burgoyne's resentment turned against Howe. He knew of Howe's resignation and it seemed to him that there was no reason why, with Howe as no more than one of the least articulate members of a factious opposition, Burgoyne's reputation should not be restored, a consummation that would have the additional effect of removing the odium of Saratoga from Lord George and his colleagues.

Charles Fox had been Burgoyne's friend for many years but they had never been political allies. It is unlikely that the arguments he used at Hounslow carried much weight. The qualified support he offered was unlikely to be of much assistance. If Burgoyne joined the opposition he would have their help in clearing his reputation, but only to the point where Howe's interests conflicted with his own. This meant that he must admit to undertaking an operation which he knew to be impracticable—supporting his army at Albany through the winter of 1777–78 without supplies from New York. His honour might be cleared but his military reputation must be destroyed.

The following morning Burgoyne called on Lord George at his office in Pall Mall. "It will naturally be supposed that the state in which I stood was the first subject of conversation; on the contrary, I was received with much apparent kindness; explanations passed, but they were friendly; I was heard attentively, through a report of all the transactions subsequent to the Convention of Saratoga, and I was led by degrees, and without suspicion of insidiousness, to the most confidential communication, on my part, of facts, observations and opinions, respecting very important objects."

It seemed that Fox had been wrong in his description of the government's attitude towards Burgoyne. The general was confirmed in his belief that Germain would help to clear his reputation by bringing to light Howe's irresponsible conduct. At this moment Burgoyne was ripe to become a staunch and valuable ally to the government, the ideal counter to the charges that Howe was bound to bring when he returned to England. Unfortunately Germain had misread the situation. Perhaps he felt that his own responsibility for the situation was greater than the facts suggest. Perhaps, remembering the implicit reproaches in Burgoyne's confidential letter of 20th October, he was convinced that Burgoyne could only be an enemy. "After the matter of my communication was exhausted, the Secretary of State drew from his pocket an order, that I should prepare myself for an enquiry: at which I expressed my fullest satisfaction, till he followed with the information . . . that I was not to appear at Court. A Court *etiquette* had been invented, the foundation of which in reason or precedent I am not acquainted with, *viz.* that the persons whose conduct was so put in question should not appear at Court pending the enquiry."

The Board of Enquiry promptly convened but it did not probe the causes of the Saratoga failure. Instead Burgoyne was asked to explain the terms of his parole. Next day it reported that the terms were such that Burgoyne, being technically in the power of the Congress, could not be subject to military law in Britain. Thus no meaningful enquiry or court martial could be held as long as the parole was valid. By the "Court *etiquette*", Burgoyne must continue to be barred from Court.

Denied the chance to put his case to the King or to a court martial, Burgoyne took the only other course open to him. He resumed his seat in Parliament. Horace Walpole noted that on 21st May, "General Burgoyne appeared in the House of Commons, but said nothing, nor was anything said to him; but two days afterwards appearing there, Mr Vyner[7] declared he should desire leave to ask him some questions. Burgoyne replied that he should be very ready to answer any, and should even declare some things that would astonish everybody. He had intended to have Charles Fox question him in order to bring out what he wished—a step that showed that he thought himself, as it made him, desperate with the Ministers."

On 26th May Vyner, moved for a "Committee to take into consideration the state of the army under the Convention of Saratoga". The government immediately moved to clear the galleries of "strangers". Burgoyne protested that they should be permitted to stay and hear his defence, but the House was duly cleared. Burgoyne then seconded Vyner's motion for an enquiry, reviewing the whole course of the expedition and begging the House to remember that "these transactions should be considered as they appeared at the time".

He made a long speech, but the kernel of his defence was that Germain had rejected from the plan as suggested in the *Thoughts* the discretion that he, Burgoyne, had proposed should be left to the commander. "The orders became absolute by these variations. If anyone can suppose they imply a latitude, they must examine Lord George's letter of the 26th March 1777 [to Carleton], extracts of which were [Burgoyne's] only instructions, at the end of which there is a saving clause for the protection of the minister . . . The orders until his arrival [at Albany] are clear and distinct; the clause of discretion did not relate to the main object, but to such collateral and eventual operations as might be thought advisable to make an impression upon the rebels till he joined General Howe." Now, he claimed, the minister was trying to pretend that at all times during the expedition the general had the right to modify his orders as he saw fit. This was not the kind of support he was used to receiving from his superiors. He compared Germain's conduct unfavourably with that of Count La Lippe in Portugal in 1762. When sending him on a desperate venture, La Lippe had told him that, "he had only to persevere and be confident of his protection".

As Walpole retailed the speech, Burgoyne "gave an account of his conduct, said nothing hard on General Howe, did great justice to the Americans and complained much of being forbidden the King's presence." Burgoyne was in a very weak position. He was having to explain orders which the House had not been allowed to see (although they had been shown his *Thoughts*), and he could not say anything "hard on General Howe". He was fighting with one hand tied behind his back. The committed ministerialists were already against him. The government would willingly expel him from the House. He must, at all costs, retain the support of the opposition if he was to keep his seat. As long as they were behind him they could threaten the kind of imbroglio which the expulsion of Wilkes had caused in the last decade. The price of opposition support was oblivion towards Howe.

Even the incomplete defence he was able to deploy was fortuitously overshadowed by an altercation which dominated the House for three hours in the middle of the debate. Ever since he had come to office in 1775, Lord George had been subject to a barrage of offensive illusions to Minden. By superhuman self control, he had kept his notoriously high temper in check. On this day, he boiled over. Temple Luttrell,[8] the nastiest of the opposition members, favourably "compared the conduct of Burgoyne with that of Lord George who, he said, had been promoted for disobedience and timidity. Lord George started up in the most violent rage and, clapping his hand to his sword, said that though he was an old man he would not hear such an insult from a young man who was an assassin and of the most wretched character. Luttrell went out of the House that they might not be prevented fighting; but they forced him back by the order of the House, when he would not retract a syllable, and said he would be sent to prison rather than retract. Lord North said a few faint words for Lord George, though he owned he had been disorderly. . . . Lord George made apologies and called Luttrell his *noble* friend, which the latter rejected with great indignation. The confusion lasted above two hours, when Luttrell was forced to disclaim any further resentment." By the time all this excitement was over, Burgoyne's defence was quite forgotten and the motion for an enquiry was rejected by 144 votes to 95.

Two days later David Hartley, MP for Kingston upon Hull, moved that the House should adjourn rather than be prorogued in view of the dangerous crisis facing the nation. Burgoyne seconded this motion and was violently attacked by the Paymaster to the Forces, Richard Rigby, a man not widely admired, who "spoke *with great animosity against Burgoyne* and promised that he himself would move that he should have a trial", a promise that he failed to keep.

In the same debate the Solicitor General, Alexander Wedderburn, queried Burgoyne's right to sit in the Commons, alleging that, as a prisoner of war, he was ineligible. If Wedderburn had succeeded in his purpose, Burgoyne would have been deprived of all chance of putting his case. As it happened the move had been insufficiently well planned. The Speaker was able to quote the precedent of Lord Frederick Campbell who had been captured in the Seven Years War and released by the French on parole. He had taken the precaution of asking his captors whether they would object to his taking part in debates while on parole. They replied that they might just as well "prohibit him from begetting a child lest it should live to fight against them." The question of ineligibility was allowed to drop.

Baulked of silencing Burgoyne in the Commons, ministers tried to get him out of the country. On 5th June, the Secretary at War wrote to him that, "his Majesty is pleased to order that you should repair to Boston as soon as you have tried the Bath waters." Burgoyne replied deferentially that, "the remedies prescribed for me are repose, regimen of diet and repeated visits to Bath: my intention, in consequence, was to remain some time in this country, to repair to Bath for a short time next month, and to return thither for a

much longer space in the most proper season. But whatever may be the benefit of all or any of this plan, I am persuaded that to expose my constitution to
the next American winter is, in all probability, to doom me to the grave."
This reply received no more than a formal acknowledgment.

Parliament having been prorogued from June to November, there was
little that Burgoyne could do except to publish at his own expense the two
long speeches he had made in the Commons. His anger at the government
was now at its zenith and was not in the least abated in July when Howe
returned from America and was immediately and favourably received by the
King.

In the following session of Parliament he was on his feet, in and out of
season, drawing attention to the plight of his army, still held by the Americans, and attacking ministers for their conduct towards himself. He made
very little impression, nor could he hope to do so if he was inhibited from
attacking Howe.

It was not until May 1779, that chance of putting the record straight
seemed to appear. Isaac Barré, Shelburne's henchman in the House of
Commons, proposed a Committee of the House to examine the ill-success of
the expedition which led to Saratoga. Since a similar committee had already
sat, inconclusively, on Howe's conduct, the independent members considered that it would be unjust to Burgoyne to deny him a parliamentary
enquiry. Ignoring the protests of North and Germain, a committee was
voted, sat and heard evidence.

Burgoyne presented his case with skill, supporting it with all the relevant
documents, many of which, including Germain's orders for the expedition,
had not been put before the House before. Such witnesses as could be spared
from active service made statements and answered questions. The question
of Howe's responsibility was never explicitly stated but it was clear, to those
who wished to see it, in the documents. It seemed, at last, as if the truth must
emerge.

Unable to stop the committee meeting, the government decided to ignore
and muffle it. No member of the government attended. Lord George produced no papers and questioned none of the witnesses. Before the committee
could report, Parliament was prorogued and the committee automatically
lapsed. Burgoyne was reduced to having the proceedings printed at his own
expense as "A State of the Expedition from Canada, as laid before the House
of Commons by Lieutenant General Burgoyne and verified by evidence with
a collection of authentic documents and an addition of many circumstances
which were prevented from appearing before the House by the prorogation
of Parliament." He dedicated it to Major General Phillips and the other
officers who served in the army under his command and added, "My errors

may have been numberless; your conduct has been uniform—faithful, gallant and indefatigable. Debarred of the power of doing you justice before the King, these testimonies are the only means to which my gratitude and esteem can resort."

Still the government was anxious to get Burgoyne out of the way. A new Secretary at War tried to use threats. "I am commanded by the King to acquaint you that your not returning to America and joining the troops, prisoners under the Convention of Saratoga, is considered as a neglect of duty and disobedience of orders, transmitted to you by the Secretary at War in his letter of 5th June 1778."

This was a clumsy manoeuvre. As Burgoyne pointed out the orders in the letter of June 1778 had been conditional on the recovery of his health. He had not completely recovered and could bring medical evidence to prove it. Besides, supposing they did establish disobedience, what could ministers do about it? Having claimed that, as a prisoner of war, he was not amenable to military law, they could scarcely bring him to a court martial. "It may be remembered that I am deprived of a court martial upon my conduct in America, because I am not supposed to be amenable to the justice of this kingdom: the King is told I have disobeyed his orders, in the same breath I am stated not to be accountable to him: by this doctrine it seems supposed that I am not capable of receiving orders for the public justice, but am perperfectly subject to all such as have a tendency to my own destruction."

Once more he asked for a court martial on his conduct in America and added, "if not allowed an early trial, or by the King's grace restored to a capacity of service, I find myself compelled to request his Majesty to accept of my resignation of my appointments upon the American staff; of the Queen's regiment of light dragoons; and of the government of Fort William, humbly desiring only to reserve my rank of lieutenant general in the army to render me the more clearly amenable to a court martial, and to enable me to fulfill my personal faith, should I be required by the enemy to do so."

He was not allowed a court martial and the attempt to order him back to Boston was dropped. His resignation from his commands was accepted and, since the rank of general without an appointment on the staff carried no pay, he had renounced all his emoluments.

Eighteen months later, in April 1781, the American Congress formally asked for his return. In the event, they did not enforce the demand but allowed him to be exchanged for 1,047 private soldiers. This bargain was completed in February 1782 and by that time Lord George Germain was on the point of resignation and Lord North's government was tottering to collapse. In the next month a new ministry, headed by Lord Rockingham, came to power, dedicated to making peace with the Americans. Sir William

Howe was appointed Lieutenant General of the Ordnance and Burgoyne became Commander in Chief in Ireland. Both became Privy Councillors. In the circumstances, Burgoyne could scarcely renew his call for a court martial which must inevitably blame the disaster on Howe.

Epilogue

When Burgoyne was appointed Commander in Chief in Ireland he was sixty years old. A younger contemporary wrote that, "In his person he rose above ordinary height, and when young must have possessed a distinguished figure; but years had enfeebled him though he was cast in an athletic mould. He seemed more fitted for the drawing room or for the closet than for the camp, for pleasing in society than for commanding armies. No man possessed more pleasing manners."

He was not totally enfeebled. He formed an association with a singer, Susan Caulfield. The first of their four children, a son, was born in August 1782, four months after Burgoyne was appointed to Dublin. He was christened at St Anne's, Soho, as John Fox Burgoyne. Charles James Fox being godfather. He lived to see the reputation of the British army re-established at Busaco, Badajoz, Salamanca and Vitoria and died in 1871 as a much respected Field Marshal.

In the same year John Burgoyne's second professional play was produced at Drury Lane. This was *The Lord of the Manor*, written in 1780 "to relax a mind which had been engaged in more intense application". *The Lord of the Manor* had a disastrous first night. It was hurriedly substituted for another play which had not been completed. "Miss Farren[1] was ill, and Mr John Palmer could not be found; Miss Collett read for the former and Mr R. Palmer for his brother. The play had never been published, and they were obliged to use a manuscript copy, each with a candle in hand, delivering the manuscript alternately to each other. Palmer came to a passage so interlined that he could not proceed. The audience hissed violently. Mr Palmer requested the book might be examined by any gentleman in the pit, to see if the fault could be attributed to him. The gentleman who examined it, declared it illegible. The audience loudly applauded, and the book being returned, permission was given to pass over the obscure passages." The play had greater success when more painstakingly produced and, being published

219

anonymously, was attributed by many to Richard Brinsley Sheridan. Even then its troubles were not at an end as it attracted the unwelcome attention of the Lord Chamberlain because of some of its cynical comments about the army's recruiting system.

Burgoyne's term as Commander in Chief in Ireland was not a particularly happy or useful period of his life. He attempted to reform some of the more flagrant abuses of the Irish military establishment without noticeable success. He came over to England as often as possible to attend to his duty as MP and, no doubt, to see Miss Caulfield. This caused dissension between him and the Secretary at War and he had, on several occasions, to be dissuaded by his friends from resigning. He wrote another musical play. This was an English adaptation of Grétry's *Richard Coeur de Lion*. His first biographer said that the "work possesses no more literary merit than any ordinary libretto of a modern Italian opera done into English." It achieved a modest success due, in part, to the performance of Dorothea Jordan in one of the principal roles.[2]

Another step in his military reinstatement was his reappointment as colonel of a regiment. His own regiment, the Sixteenth Light Dragoons, had been given to the former lieutenant colonel William Harcourt, who continued as its colonel until his death in 1830. In June 1782 Burgoyne was made colonel of the 4th Foot. This was not considered as great a distinction as to be colonel of the regiment he had resigned three years earlier and efforts were made to secure a cavalry regiment for him. In April of the following year, he received notification from Lord North, then Secretary of State from the Home Department, that the King intended to give him the Eighth Dragoons. Unfortunately General John Severne, the Colonel of the Eighth, was not only still alive but lived another four years. Burgoyne had to be content with the Fourth Foot until his death.

He resigned from the Irish command in January 1784, immediately after his friend Fox left office and the younger William Pitt formed his first ministry. His successor was Lieutenant General William Augustus Pitt, no close relation to the new Prime Minister but the brother-in-law of Sir William Howe, who succeeded in keeping his office of Lieutenant General of the Ordnance through all the changes of government until 1804.

For the last eight years of his life Burgoyne held no public offices but those of Colonel of the King's Own Regiment of Foot and member of Parliament for Preston. He was an assiduous rather than an effective member of the House. His oratorical style, garnished with classical tags, was not such as to make him a political giant. In private life it was different and he was much sought after by hostesses for his beautiful manners and the wit of his conversation.

He had, however, one more success. In 1785 he wrote *The Heiress* which was produced at Drury Lane in the following year with Miss Farren in the lead. It was a great popular success. It was produced on thirty nights in 1786 and quickly ran through ten editions in its published form, and was translated into German, Spanish, French and Italian. One measure of its success was that it even converted the most obstinate of Burgoyne's critics, Horace Walpole. "Burgoyne," he wrote, "has written the best modern comedy." He paid it the compliment of reading it twice in a single day and declared that, "I like it better than any comedy I have seen since *The Provoked Husband* . . . Burgoyne's battles and speeches will be forgotten, but his delightful comedy of *The Heiress* will still continue the delight of the stage."

On the evening of 3rd August 1792, Burgoyne went to the theatre. Next day he died. He had left careful directions for his funeral. "Whenever I may happen to die, it is my desire that my body may be interred in the cloisters of Westminster Abbey, as near as may be to the remains of my late estimable wife, Lady Charlotte Burgoyne. Should I die at a distance, the body to be conveyed to Westminster at the cheapest rate that decency will permit, namely if a convenient mode should not offer by sea for the whole way to the river Thames, I would have a hearse drawn by four horses only, and attended by one carriage only with the same number of horses, for the conveyance of my menservants out of livery and my housekeeper, and no attendants on horseback except my footman, George Gosling. I desire that my funeral may be equally private."

On 13th August, he was buried, as he wished, in the cloisters of Westminster Abbey. "One coach only attended with four gentlemen; a lady was likewise present, whose convulsive agitation showed her to have that within which passes show."

No tablet shows where Burgoyne of Saratoga is buried.

Appendix

Order of Battle of "The Canada Army" June 1777
(Regular Troops Only)

Commander of the Forces
  Major General (local Lt. Gen) John Burgoyne MP (promoted Lieutenant
    General 29th August)
Aides de Camp
  Lt. & Capt. Sir Francis Carr Clarke, Bart., 3rd Foot Guards (also acted
    as Military Secretary) (died of wounds, 17th October)
  Captain Henry Gardner, 16th Light Dragoons (sent to England with
    despatches, 12th July)
  Captain Lord Petersham MP, 29th Foot (from 12th July)
  Lt Richard Wilford, 2nd Dragoon Guards
Staff
Adjutant and Quartermaster General
  Lt. Col. Thomas Carleton, 20th Foot (recalled to Canada, August)
Deputy Adjutant General
  Capt. (B/Maj) Robert Kingston, Irish Invalids (B/Lt. Col. 29 August)
Deputy Quartermaster General
  Captain John Money, 9th Foot (P/W 7th October)
Asst. Quartermaster General.
  Capt. George Preston Vallancay, 62nd Foot
Deputy Quartermaster General for German Troops
  Capt. Heinrich Gerlach, Brunswick Artillery
Judge Advocate General
  Capt. James Henry Craig, 47th Foot
Commanding Royal Engineer
  Lt. William Twiss RE
Paymaster General
  David Geddes (acting)

Commissary General
  Jonathan Clarke
Waggonmaster General
  Robert Hoakesly (appt'd 12th July)
Advanced Corps   Lt. Col. (Brig. Gen.) Simon Fraser, 24th Foot (died of
  Wounds 8th October)
  Grenadier Battalion Major John Acland MP, 20th Foot (wounded &
  P/W 7th October)
  Grenadier coys of 9th, 20th, 21st, 29th, 31st 34th, 47th, 53rd, 62nd Foot
  Light Infantry Battalion Maj. the Earl of Balcarres, 53rd Foot
    Light Companies of same regts as grenadier
  24th Foot (10 coys) Maj. Robert Grant
    (Killed in Action 7th July)
    Maj. William Agnew (from 7th July)
  Corps of Marksmen (Fraser's Rangers)
    Capt. Alexander Fraser, 34th Foot
RIGHT WING. Col. (local Maj. Gen.) William Phillips MP, RA (promoted Maj. Gen. 29th August)
    ADC Capt. Charles Green, 31st Foot
1st Brigade.   Lt. Col. (Brig. Gen.) James Inglis Hamilton, 21st Foot
  (Comd'g at Ticonderoga 6th July–14th August)
  9th Foot (8 coys) Lt. Col. John Hill
  47th Foot (8 coys) Lt. Col. Nicholas Sutherland
    (2 coys detached to Diamond Island, Lake George from late August)
  53rd Foot (8 coys) Maj. Paul Æmilius Irving
    (Garrison of Ticonderoga from 10th August)
2nd Brigade. Lt. Col. Henry Watson Powell, 53rd Foot
  (Comd'g at Ticonderoga from 15th August)
  20th Foot (8 coys) Lt. Col. John Lind
  21st Foot (Royal North British Fuzileers) (8 coys) Maj. George Forster
  62nd Foot (8 coys) Lt. Col. John Anstruther
    (Garrison at Ticonderoga 6th July–10th August)
LEFT WING. Maj. Gen. Friedrich Adolph Riedesel, Freiheer von
  Eisenbach
    ADC Lt. Friedrich Christian Cleve
1st Brigade. Col. (Brig. Gen.) Johann Friedrich Specht
  Regiment of Rhetz (5 coys) Maj. Balthasar von Lucke
  Regiment of Specht (5 coys) Maj. Carl von Ehrenkrock
  Regiment of Riedesel (5 coys) Lt. Col. Ernst von Speth
    (P/W 7th October)
2nd Brigade. Col. (Brig. Gen.) Wilhelm von Gall

Regiment of Prinz Friedrich (5 coys)
Lt. Col. Christian Prätorius
(Garrison of Ticonderoga from 6th July)
Regiment of Hesse-Hanau. (?6 coys) Lt. Col. Lentz
German Reserve. Lt. Col. Heinrich Carl Breymann
(Killed in Action 7th October)
Grenadier Battalion. (Grenadier coys from the four Brunswick regts)
Maj. Otto von Mengen
Light Infantry Battalion (4 light infantry & 1 jäger coys) Maj. Ferdinand
von Barner
Unbrigaded. Prinz Ludwig's Regiment of Dragoons (dismounted)
Lt. Col. Friedrich Baum
(Died of Wounds as P/W, 18th August)
Capt. Adolph von Schlagenteuffel (from 16th August)
ARTILLERY. Col. (local Maj. Gen.) William Phillips MP, RA (pro-
moted Major General 29th August)
Brigade Major, RA Capt. Thomas Blomefield RA[1]
Field Brigades.
1st Brigade (attached to Advanced Corps)
4×6 pdrs, 4×3 pdrs, $2 \times 5\frac{1}{2}''$ howitzers
Capt. Ellis Walker RA
2nd Brigade (attached to Right Wing)
4×6 pdrs
Capt. Thomas Jones RA (Killed in Action 20th September)
3rd Brigade (attached to Left Wing)
6×6 pdrs, 2×3 pdrs
Capt. Pausch, Hanau Artillery
Park of Artillery. Maj. Edward Williams RA[1]
Left Brigade. 2×12 pdrs, 2×6 pdrs, $1 \times 8''$ howitzer, $1 \times 5\frac{1}{2}''$
howitzer
Capt. Thomas Hosmer RA
Centre Brigade. 2×24 pdrs
Capt. John C. Carter RA[1]
Right Brigade. 2×12 pdrs, 2×6 pdrs, $1 \times 8''$ howitzer, $1 \times 5\frac{1}{2}''$
howitzer
Capt. Walter Mitchelson RA
Infantry attached to Royal Artillery
Detachments of 33rd Foot and other regiments at New York
Lt. Anson Nott, 33rd Foot

Notes

PROLOGUE

[1] Various glosses have been put on Burgoyne's orders in the hope of showing that they were only discretionary. As editor of the correspondence of King George III, Fortescue would not have overlooked, as many others have done, the King's own opinion that the orders were positive. Writing after the disaster was known in England, the King referred to "the defence of Lt. G. Burgoyne that his orders were positive (which I much incline to)".

CHAPTER 1. Britain in the Seventies

[1] As, for example, Chippenham and High Wycombe, both of which had populations of not more than 2,500.

[2] One of the candidates who refused to subscribe in this way and consequently failed to be elected was Colonel Thomas Gage, later to command the British army in Massachusetts.

[3] It was said that the 45 Scots members were elected by 3,963 voters.

[4] So empty that, despite living modestly, he ran steadily into debt while he was Prime Minister. In 1777 the King insisted on paying his debts and North estimated them at £18,000.

[5] When assailed violently in the House by Colonel Barré for losing an empire and ruining the country, North seemed to be dozing on the Treasury Bench. Barré complained that the first minister was asleep whereupon, North opened one eye and remarked, "I wish to God I were."

[6] Among them the Young Pretender's friend and saviour Flora Macdonald who, however, remained obstinately loyal to the Hanoverian king during the American Revolution until forced to return to Scotland in 1779.

[7] During the boycott following the imposition of the Townshend duties of 1767, Boston had a very poor record. While New York reduced imports of British goods by 85%, Boston only achieved 50%.

CHAPTER 2. "They have a great resource in our incapacity"

[1] The Chancellor of the Exchequer would not normally be a member of the cabinet. Lord North combined that office with that of First Lord of the Treasury.

[2] When the cabinet wanted military advice they could call in the Master General of the Ordnance. Lord Townshend, who was Master General in North's time was seldom consulted since he was seldom sober.

[3] The principal enemies, however, were France and Austria, both Southern Department's responsibilities.

[4] There were two establishments, one for Britain and one for Ireland. The rates of pay were less in Ireland for all ranks.

[5] Each of the three Guards regiments had two battalions, and the Household Brigade totalled 64 companies. Line battalions had only ten companies. Two line regiments (1st, Royal, and 60th, Royal Americans) had two battalions, the remainder only one. There was an additional small unit, 214 strong, in west Africa.

[6] After Bunker Hill, regiments posted to America were augmented by 17 privates to each company, giving the battalion a musket strength of 580.

[7] Only two British (light) dragoon regiments served in America. The assumption was that their lighter horses could be replaced from the countryside.

[8] The only other ranks available for engineering works comprised a single company, 93 strong, of 'soldier-artificers'. They were stationed permanently in Gibraltar.

[9] First Lords of the Admiralty were frequently considerable professional figures in the Navy. Admiral Lord Anson, the circumnavigator, had held office 1751–56 and 1762 and Admiral Sir Edward Hawke 1766–1771.

[10] The peerage was insufficiently philoprogenitive to fulfil the expectation of historians. In the peacetime army of 1775 there were about three thousand officers on the active list. There were only 170 peers of the United Kingdom, say three hundred including the peerages Scotland and Ireland. Even if the peerage had not provided large numbers of sons to the navy, the church, diplomacy and government, they would have been hard put to it to provide even 10% of army officers.

[11] In 1761 the MP for Chichester wrote that, "one of the tacit obligations upon a member of parliament was to keep the place he represented as free as he could from being pesterd [sic] and burthend [sic] with soldiers."

[12] This was the "Old English Long" musket used by 90% of the infantry. The light infantry used the "Short Land Service" pattern, weighing only 10 lbs and having a 40-inch barrel.

[13] "Harmless" because they were armed only with swords and had neither pistols nor carbines.

[14] Legend has turned this into thick woodland, but this was not the case.

[15] Two light infantry units did survive, the two battalions of the Sixtieth (Royal American) Foot which had been raised in America in 1755. The ranks were largely filled with Germans and Swiss and they were usually stationed in the West Indies.

CHAPTER 3. Dragoon and Guardsman

[1] The Wroxall estate, then amounting to 1,850 acres, was sold by the widow of the 2nd baronet in 1713. The purchaser was Sir Christopher Wren.

[2] Roger Benson (1676–1731) was Chancellor of the Exchequer, 1711–14. He was created Baron Bingley in 1713 and subsequently became Treasurer to the Household of George II. He married Elizabeth Finch, daughter of 1st Earl of Aylesford. They had one daughter.

[3] Sir Roger, the 6th baronet, put John Burgoyne into the entail for his estate previous to the birth of his own son. The 7th baronet, eventually Lt. Gen. Sir John Burgoyne, Colonel 58th Foot, made him his executor.

[4] In the 1774 Parliament there were 94 OWs in a House of 558, although only two of the 45 Scots members were at the school.

[5] James Stanley was incorrectly known as Lord Strange, that title having been borne by the eldest sons of the 7th, 8th and 9th Earls of Derby. However, the barony of Strange, together with the overlordship of the Isle of Man, passed in the female line to the Duke of Atholl. James Stanley's courtesy title was Lord Stanley.

[6] When a regiment had its establishment of officers increased the vacancies were not subject to purchase.

[7] Fonblanque (op. cit.) says that Burgoyne obtained a captaincy in the 13th Dragoons in 1744. On the other hand, Huddlestone maintains that the captaincy was in the Royals on 1st July 1745. I have followed the very reliable C. T. Atkinson in his *History of the Royal*

Dragoons (p 479), who gives the date as 1747. A close study of the vacancies occurring in the Royals convinces me that this is correct.

[8] William Wentworth was given a cornetcy as a child after his uncle's death, as a cornet in the regiment in 1702. His subsequent promotions were Lieut. 1719; Capt/Lieut. 1730; Capt. 1738.

[9] Fonblanque (p8) says that they were married in about 1743, but he prints a letter of Burgoyne's (p134) dated 1775 in which he says he has been married 24 years. Another letter in HMC Sackville ii 23, dated March 1776 also says that he had been married for 24 years. If they were married in 1743 Lady Charlotte must have been very young. The exact date of her birth seems uncertain but her elder sister was born in 1726, so that in 1743 Lady Charlotte can have been no more than sixteen and was probably younger. Fonblanque also says that the couple met when Burgoyne was stationed with the 13th Dragoons at Preston. The 13th were never at Preston during the forties (though they were at Prestonpans), but the Royals were there in 1748.

[10] Ramsay went to Rome at the end of 1754. There would have been a bond of fellow-feeling between Burgoyne and Ramsay, who had also made a runaway marriage. He had eloped with the daughter of Sir Alexander Lindsay and the niece of Lord Chancellor Mansfield. Her cousin, Lord Balcarres served under Burgoyne in America.

[11] Until 1803, the colonel, lieutenant colonel and major of each regiment each had the command of a company. Since the colonel (who was usually a general officer) seldom served with the regiment, his company was commanded by a captain-lieutenant, who ranked as a captain but was paid as a lieutenant.

[12] In particular, great animosity arose between Sackville (later Germain) and one of the naval commanders, Commodore Richard Howe, who was to become Admiral Lord Howe and to command on the American station during the War of Independence. At the time of the Cotentin raid, Howe was already Viscount Howe since his brother had been killed near Ticonderoga, although the news had not yet reached England.

[13] Burgoyne says that the French first appeared "by the time the rear brigade had gained the beach". It is not clear whether he means the last brigade to arrive or the rear brigade of the army as formed which would, of course, be leading the retreat to the beaches.

[14] The term "division" was loosely used at this time. It usually meant some part of a battalion, frequently half a company. In this case it is probably used for two or three companies grouped together.

[15] He did not become colonel of the regiment until 18th March 1763, after he had greatly distinguished himself in the field. He became a brevet colonel (i.e. colonel in the army) six months earlier.

[16] In 1788 Burgoyne wrote to William Pitt the Younger saying that he owed his command of the Sixteenth Light Dragoons to Pitt the Elder (Fonblanque p452).

[17] The difference between the three guineas paid to the recruit and the five guineas which could be charged to the Treasury was supposed to allow officers to recoup themselves against the inevitable "bounty jumpers" who took the three guineas and deserted. It also covered the cost of recruiting, which consisted of buying beer for likely recruits.

[18] This paragraph is based on the instructions for another regiment but there is no reason to suppose that those for the Sixteenth differed from these.

[19] A temporary regiment, known as the Duke of Kingston's Light Dragoons was formed and did good service in Scotland during the Forty Five. It was disbanded but reformed as the Duke of Cumberland's Dragoons. It was again disbanded in 1748. Light troops were added to eleven dragoon regiments in 1755.

[20] To avoid invidious re-numbering of dragoon regiments, converted regiments were renamed Dragoon Guards. The remaining regiment of Horse, the 1st, became the Royal Horse Guards. Four regiments on the Irish establishment did not become Dragoon Guards until 1788.

[21] A "bucket" is a long leather sleeve hanging beside the saddle into which the muzzle of the carbine is inserted when not in use.

22 The British Minister in Lisbon, the Hon. Edward Hay, had been Burgoyne's contemporary at Westminster.

CHAPTER 4. Honourable and Gallant Member

1 Warrant men were those who appeared on the Royal warrant for pay but did not actually exist. Technically they were tolerated to compensate colonels for the cost of clothing lost by deserters. In reality it was a device to increase the pay of colonels, which had been stationary since the reign of Queen Anne, without drawing parliamentary attention to the increase. The pay of regiments was voted by Parliament in a lump and, since they were habitually under strength, the small number of warrant men attracted no attention since, in Treasury terms, it was not an expense but merely failure to declare a saving, a less serious matter in terms of annual accounting.

2 Burgoyne was not, in fact, a major general until six years later.

3 Burgoyne also attacked those in Britain who adopted the "many absurdities" of the Prussian uniform, who "adopt the fopperies as the essentials and make everything give way to them . . . All minutiae of the system are dispersed throughout the world, and a thousand practices are introduced under the sanction of [the Prussian] parade that are frivolous, whimsical and inconvenient."

4 Newton was at the disposal of the Legh family of Lyme. At least one seat at Clitheroe was nominated by the Curzons. The Duke of Portland was cultivating Wigan and secured both seats there in 1768.

5 Sir Henry was the father of Maj. Gen. Daniel Hoghton who was killed in action at Albuera in 1811.

6 The corporation of Preston continued to dispute the validity of the wider franchise at successive elections until a special Act of Parliament was passed in 1786 which established an electorate of about 600.

7 In another letter, dated the same day, Junius gives the sum at £4,000.

8 William Harcourt (1743–1830), Lieut. Col. 16th Light Dragoons 1770. Became Colonel of the regiment when Burgoyne resigned in 1779. MP for Oxford 1768–74. Groom of the Bedchamber. Later became first Governor of the Royal Military College (1800). Succeeded his brother as 3rd Earl Harcourt 1809.

9 The London office of the Company was in Leadenhall Street.

10 John Burgoyne's cousin Roger, the 6th baronet, married Lady Frances Montagu, daughter of the Earl of Halifax. Her half sister, Lady Lucy, was Lord North's mother.

11 "There is a new puppet-show at Drury Lane, as fine as scenes can make it, called *The Maid of the Oaks*; and as dull as the author could not help making it." The Oaks was a country house of the Stanley family, near Epsom. The classic horse race was named after it by the 12th Earl of Derby who also gave his name to the Derby Stakes.

CHAPTER 5. "A Professional Tragedy"

1 He resigned the two colonelcies he held, those of the 15th Foot and the 60th (Royal Americans), but was appointed as Colonel, 3rd Foot, in November of the same year.

2 General Clinton's two sons, Henry and William, served as generals under Wellington in the Peninsula and were also "querulous, fussy and ineffective".

3 Jenkinson at this time held only the sinecure position of Vice Treasurer of Ireland but was one of Lord North's principal "political fixers". He later became 1st Earl of Liverpool and the father of the steadfast Prime Minister who led the government to victory over Napoleon.

4 Philip Yorke, 2nd Earl, the son of the Lord Chancellor of the previous reign. He was a classical scholar and a noted man of letters. Although a Privy Councillor, he held no public office except High Steward of the University of Cambridge.

5 George Monck (1608–70), Cromwellian general who contrived the restoration of Charles II in 1660.

CHAPTER 6. "Unactivity and Want of Spirit"

[1] Her father was a lieutenant general and her uncle, Sir David Colyear was both a lieutenant general in the British service and a marshal in the Dutch. He was created Earl of Portmore (in the peerage of Scotland) by William III.

[2] It had frequently been suggested that the reading of the sentence at the head of every regiment is evidence of the King's personal malice against Sackville. In fact all General Orders were read to the troops on parade since, with most of the soldiers illiterate, there was no other way of communicating information to them. The sentence of such an important court martial would naturally be incorporated in a General Order.

[3] He represented Dover until 1761. From 1761 to 1768 he sat for Hythe, and from then until he was raised to the peerage in 1782, East Grinstead. Dover and Hythe are Cinque Ports and his father was Lord Warden until his death in 1765. The Sackvilles were the most influential landlords in and around East Grinstead and nominated both members.

[4] The letters which passed between the Howe brothers and Lord George when they were appointed to the American commands on sea and land respectively go far beyond even the strict demands of formal eighteenth century courtesy.

[5] Ladies Margaret and Mary Stanley were Charlotte Burgoyne's elder sisters. Lady Mary recovered and lived until 1795.

[6] In January 1776, Burgoyne had written to Germain enclosing a plan for augmenting all the light dragoon regiments with "one cornet, one sergeant, one corporal and twenty three men per troop, these augmented men to be dismounted (riding behind their comrades) and to serve as infantry in conjunction with the mounted dragoons." This plan was turned down as impracticable.

[7] These vacancies would be offered, in the first instance, to cornets on half-pay. If there were not enough available they would probably go to young gentlemen who could raise the necessary fifteen recruits in exchange for a free commission.

[8] "Sir Guy Carleton dislikes Ld. Amherst so much that it is not easy to employ him." (HM to North, 30 April '79)

[9] Their uniform was to be the same as that of the Black Watch except that their sporrans were to be of racoon skin.

[10] The Eighth Foot was stationed around Lake Ontario and could not be withdrawn.

[11] Simon Fraser was the younger son of a highland laird and made his way in the army entirely by his own merits. He had been first commissioned into the Scots brigade in the Dutch service and had received his first wound at Bergen-op-Zoom in 1747. He was given a lieutenancy in the Royal Americans when they were raised in 1755 and was with Wolfe at Quebec as a captain in the 78th (Fraser's Highlanders). It was a Captain Fraser of the 78th who answered the French challenge as the attacking force rowed down to the Anse de Foulon, but he was by no means the only Captain Fraser in the regiment.

[12] There were also some 3 pounder "battalion" guns on shore but Williams considered them useless. "I hope I shall never see any more . . . but in the hands of the enemy or at Woolwich."

[13] According to Major Williams the fleet sailed on 13th June and reached a point a mile east of Nicholet the same evening. The unknown officer whose diary is published under the title *For Want of a Horse* says that the fleet sailed at 1 am on 14th June.

[14] It is fair to Carleton to add that Christie had previously succeeded in quarrelling with General Murray, the governor before Carleton.

[15] The quarrel is explored thoroughly in two articles in the *Canadian Historical Review*: A. L. Burt's, "The Quarrel between Germain and Carleton: An Inverted story" (1930) and R. Arthur Bowler's "Sir Guy Carleton and the Campaign of 1776 in Canada" (1974). Following Donne's edition of George III's letters some historians (e.g. Alan Valentine in his *Lord George Germain*) have claimed that Germain sought Carleton's dismissal in February 1777. He may well have wished to be rid of him but Donne had misread the original letter, which shows that it was Cramahé, the lieutenant governor he wished to dismiss. The name is given correctly in Fortescue's 1927 edition.

[16] It was in April 1775 that Dr Johnson, a staunch supporter of Britain's rights over the American colonies, referred to patriotism as "the last refuge of a scoundrel". He was referring to members of the Opposition who posed as defenders of their country against the Royal Prerogative. He probably had Burke and Fox particularly in mind.

CHAPTER 7. "To Finish the Rebellion in One Campaign"

[1] Fonblanque puts Burgoyne's visit to Bath after 28th February, which is unlikely as the evidence is that he was in London during the following month. It is possible that he did not, in the event, go to Bath at all. A search of the "Arrivals in Bath" in the local papers does not show his name in the first quarter of 1777, although many people of lesser consequence are listed and Burgoyne's name appears several times on the news pages. He may have spent the time in London and at Knowseley settling Lady Charlotte's estate.

[2] In the event only 2,500 reinforcements could be sent.

[3] It would no longer be practicable when France and, later, Spain joined the Americans. Then the Royal Navy's predominant task became to secure the British Isles against invasion.

[4] Most historians have assumed that Burgoyne submitted this paper on his own initiative in the hope of securing the command of the northern army for himself. The timing strongly suggests that he wrote it at Germain's request. Howe's letter was received on 23rd February. The *Thoughts* were delivered to Germain five days later. After a further three days Germain replied to Howe. It would seem that Germain was following sound administrative practice and collecting all relevant opinions before taking his decision. Further, in many places, the *Thoughts* are more comprehensible if they are read as being for the guidance of another officer (i.e. Clinton) than if Burgoyne was going to command himself.

[5] A clear indication of the paper's function as an *aide-memoire* is the passage dealing with the accommodation of the troops in their concentration area round St John's. Burgoyne recommended that they shoud be put into cantonments rather than tents as, "at that season of the year (May), the ground is very damp, and consequently very pernicious to the men, and more especially as they will have been for many months before used to lodgings, heated with stoves or between the decks of ships". Such advice would be quite unnecessary if Burgoyne was to be in command himself as he would be able to make the necessary arrangements. Clinton, on the other hand, knew nothing of the Canadian winter and might not have considered the problem. The recommendation is, incidentally, typical of Burgoyne's concern for his soldiers' welfare—the kind of attention which gained him the name "Gentleman Johnny".

[6] Faden's map, engraved by Medcalfe, was published in 1780 but, since it appeared in London, can only have been compiled before 1775.

CHAPTER 8. "Directed to Make a Junction"

[1] This transfer of 770 regular rank and file from the "operating army" to the static garrison makes it plain that the stories circulating after Saratoga and subsequently repeated by historians that Burgoyne had drafted his own orders cannot be true. He was most unlikely to have deprived himself of this body of men.

[2] Stoneland Lodge (now called Buckland), near Tunbridge Wells, was Germain's weekend retreat. He rented it from his nephew, the Duke of Dorset, whose seat was near by at Knole. Germain's principal country house was at Drayton in Northamptonshire, too far from London for weekend visits.

[3] Christian D'Oyley was Deputy Secretary at War but worked in the American office. He was a close friend of General Howe.

[4] While the outline of this story is undoubtedly correct, the details are somewhat suspect, possibly because it was written not less than five years after the event. A garbled version of the story, less creditable to Germain, is recorded by Lord Shelburne. It seems unlikely that Lord George was going to his weekend house at the time as the day on which the orders were completed was a Wednesday.

[5] His resignation was accepted, but since a new governor could not reach Canada that year, he had to stay in office until relieved by Sir Frederick Haldimand in July 1778.

[6] He had recently written, "I shall be glad of an opportunity of applauding his conduct this campaign."

[7] Fonblanque (p 234) claims that it was not until 7th June that Burgoyne started concerning himself about the supply of horses. This is most improbable. In the unlikely event of his having forgotten the need for draught animals it is inconceivable that Phillips, his active and efficient artillery commander, would have done so. The exchange of letters printed in State xxviii has all the appearance of a preconcerted exchange designed to force the governor's hand. There is also evidence that Burgoyne had been pressing for horses at least two weeks earlier.

[8] British battalions consisted of eight "battalion" companies and two "flank" companies, grenadiers (on the right) and light infantry (on the left)—ten companies in all.

[9] The number of guns with the force is somewhat obscured by naval guns carried in the fleet, field guns lent to the fleet, and guns captured at, or installed in, Ticonderoga. The figures given seem to be the correct one for the guns which accompanied the army on the march. The guns captured from the force up to 1st October were replaced from Canada.

[10] The complete Order of Battle of the army is shown in the Appendix.

[11] Powder and paper were at this date issued to companies to be made up into cartridges.

[12] The Ninth Foot carried their colours throughout the campaign and Colonel Hill concealed them in his baggage at the surrender. It is possible (though unlikely) that the Twentieth also took their colours.

[13] It was impossible to reduce the number of women further. By custom and order, six wives for each company were permitted to accompany the army and draw rations. The reduction to three was made possible only because fifty men from each battalion were to be left in Canada.

[14] General Philip Schuyler was then commanding the northern rebel army.

CHAPTER 9. "Critical and Conspicuous Services"

[1] Each of these *bateaux* had a crew of four Canadian boatmen who were paid 2/4d a day and received rations consisting of 2lb bread, 10 oz pork, pease and 1/6th quart rum.

[2] Few if any of the German troops brought their wives with them from Canada (there is no mention of them being allowable in the treaty with the Duke of Brunswick). Several Germans probably married during the long dark winter in Canada.

[3] At Ticonderoga on 4 July, a son was born to the wife of Sergt. Major Anderson of the 21st Foot. The child was later adopted by Brigadier Hamilton whose names he took. A commission was eventually procured for him in the 2nd Dragoons (Royal Scots Greys). He rose to command the regiment and was killed, charging at their head, at Waterloo.

[4] Apart from its ten drummers, each battalion had two fifers, who formed part of the grenadier company.

[5] The only practicable alternative was the long swing round to Lake Ontario, Oswego and the Mohawk river.

[6] By Standing Orders the piquet for each regiment consisted of 1 subaltern, 1 sergeant, 1 corporal and 25 privates, with a captain and drummer from each brigade.

[7] Some authors have suggested that the whole German Reserve reached the battlefield preceded by a band. Von Eelking said that Riedesel ordered a band to precede the jägers to give an impression of strength. Riedesel, however, reported that only "a handful" of Germans arrived. The band was imaginary but Anbury speaks of the jägers singing psalms as they advanced and this, combined with the two bugle horns of the jäger company, may have given the impression of a band to the Americans.

[8] Volunteers were candidates for commissions without purchase. They carried muskets and served in the ranks but messed with the officers until a vacancy occurred for an ensigncy.

⁹ Burgoyne's reference in his despatch to Fraser "supposing the German troops to be very near" when he attacked suggests that Fraser had made at least a sharp comment.

¹⁰ Brigadier Hamilton had been left at Ticonderoga as garrison commander. He remained there until mid-August when he was relieved by Brigadier Powell.

¹¹ The British were so constantly being imposed upon by bogus deserters that it is difficult to remember that a very large number of genuine deserters came over to the British side throughout the war. In moments of stress it was, of course, hard to tell which were genuine.

¹² According to Sergeant Lamb, who was present, there were only 190 all ranks. Digby says they were "not above 200". Even allowing that the flank companies, say 110 rank and file, were away with Fraser and that several other detachments had doubtless been made, these figures seem very low for a battalion which had started the campaign with 542 rank and file, about 610 all ranks, and had so far suffered no casualties.

¹³ John Money (1752–1817) became a full general before his death. He was a man of great enterprise and in 1785 made one of the first British balloon flights (two years after the Montgolfier brothers in France). Unfortunately he was blown out over the North Sea from Norfolk and spent seven hours up to his chin in the water before being rescued. In 1803 he proposed to the Secretary at War that balloons should be used for military purposes, especially observation. He wrote, "There are few men, Sir, in this country who know better than myself the use that can be made of balloons in military operations, having been up three times in one, and expressly for that purpose."

¹⁴ The hatred of Burgoyne for the Indians lived long after the campaign. In October 1787, Prince William (later William IV) wrote from Quebec to his father that the Canadian Indians avowed their devotion to his Majesty but "that in the late rebellion the evil spirit had done them harm in the eyes of their loving father . . . The evil spirit is General Burgoyne for whom they have a most singular aversion."

¹⁵ Howe was having the same trouble, and commented that the German officers were "much attached to their baggage, which they have in amazing quantities in the field".

¹⁶ The Fifty Third Foot (less flank companies with Fraser), 462 rank and file, and Prince Frederick's Brunswick Regiment (less grenadier company with German Reserve), 448 rank and file.

CHAPTER 10. "Depending on Adventure"

¹ The date of receipt is printed in HMC Sackville as 18th May. The endorsement of the original in the Public Record Office (CO5/94 6391) is obscure. It could read "R[eceived] 18th May" or "R'd 8th May". Lord George's reply is dated 18th May and since he had, since receiving the letter, consulted the King and, almost certainly, the cabinet, it is most probable that it arrived on 8th May.

² The ship that carried the copy of the orders reached Sandy Hook on 3rd June. The despatch cannot have taken many days to reach Howe from there.

³ In his original (December) proposal for the seizure of Philadelphia, he had proposed taking ten thousand men. In his letter of 2nd April this had crept up to eleven thousand and this was agreed. He actually embarked 13,799 rank and file, probably 15,500 all ranks.

⁴ In mid-July Howe had arranged for a misleading letter to Burgoyne to fall into rebel hands, with the intention of making Washington think the southern army was to move on Boston. The suggestion of planting bogus letters had come to Howe from Burgoyne, who had proposed that a special code sign should be attached to them. (Willcox 165)

⁵ These reinforcements were sent on most reluctantly by Carleton. "I am but barely authorized to send you the additional companies, but as [the Secretary at War] tells me the men were to complete the corps, and the officers to return before the winter, I shall avail myself of that opening and send all those belonging to the corps you took with you."

⁶ It was not only that the dragoons were tired of walking but that under the treaty with the Duke of Brunswick they would receive the higher pay of "light horse from the day they

shall serve on horseback". This would mean almost a shilling a day to the private soldiers, and much more to Riedesel as lieutenant colonel of the regiment.

[7] It is generally claimed that Baum spoke no English. The only source for this assertion is in Hadden's diary and seems to be no more than the uninformed gossip of the army. It is noticeable that Burgoyne's correspondence with Baum was carried on in English although it was usual to correspond with German officers in French, as was the case with letters between Burgoyne and Riedesel, who was reputed to speak English.

[8] The Queen's Loyal Rangers, raised by John Peters, a Yale-educated lawyer from Gloucester County, NY.

[9] Again an echo of Wolfe, who wrote to Monckton on 25th July 1759, "It would be right to preserve some of the milch cows for the young children."

[10] Many of the genuine Loyalists (particularly a party of 90 which had just joined Baum under Lieut. Francis Phister) fought most gallantly. Those who survived and were captured were treated abominably and some, it is said, were shot in cold blood.

[11] These two guns had an adventurous history. They were French-made and captured by Wolfe at Quebec. Lost by Breymann in 1777, they were recaptured by the British at Detroit in 1812, only to be lost again to the Americans at Niagara in the following year.

[12] One of the pieces of folklore that clings to the battle of Bennington is that the dragoons were encumbered throughout the expedition with thigh length boots. They had, in fact, been issued with black cloth gaiters reaching to the knee on arrival in Canada in 1776.

[13] It is hard to calculate the actual loss. Stark claimed 207 "Hessians" dead and seven hundred prisoners. Burgoyne admitted the loss of 26 officers and "about 400 men, killed and taken; but men who were dispersed in the woods drop in daily." The loss of the dragoons is certain, 15 officers and 209 other ranks. The total loss to the Germans during the month was 416, but some of these must be attributed to sickness and other causes. The British loss during August was 75 of which thirty may have been from the Corps of Marksmen at Bennington. The discrepancy between Stark's figures and Burgoyne's, almost five hundred men, can only be Loyalists enlisted during the expedition and staying to fight. Despite this loss the number of enlisted Loyalists serving with the army rose by eighty during August.

[14] Detachments of 110 men from both the Eighth and Thirty Fourth Foot, the Hanau Chasseurs (342 rank and file) and forty Royal Artillery.

[15] The battalion companies of the Fifty Third were in garrison at Ticonderoga.

CHAPTER 11. "The Course of Unsuccessful Events"

[1] Two battalion companies of the Forty Seventh had been detached to Diamond Island on Lake George.

[2] Also spelled Dovacote, Dovegot, Dovogot, and subsequently called Coveville.

[3] General Riedesel was colonel of this regiment, which was commanded in action by its Lieutenant Colonel, Ernst von Speth, Riedesel was also regimental lieutenant colonel of the dragoon regiment with Burgoyne's army which is, consequently, often referred to as Riedesel's Dragoons. Its official name, however, was Prince Ludwig's Regiment of Dragoons, after its colonel, Prince Ludwig Ernst, younger brother of the reigning duke of Brunswick.

[4] It seems probable that these "formed bodies" of rebels were no more than patrols. No mention is made of them by any source except Riedesel, who says that news of the rebel advance in this quarter was brought by Indians "running across the woods and mountains from the right wing". It is hard to see why Indians from the right wing should make their retreat between the British and American lines, cutting across the rear of the rebels at the farm, when they could have fled more easily by the shorter route to the west or north.

[5] This account of the postponement is derived from the account of an American officer who had it from General Phillips. Digby wrote that Burgoyne was reluctant to attack though urged to do so by Phillips and Fraser. Digby was only a lieutenant and would not have been present when the decision was taken and the other account seems better authenticated and more probable.

6 This version of the message comes from Clinton's file copy. When reporting to London he wrote, "I sent a messenger with three lines in cypher. 'You know my poverty, but if with 2,000 men, which is all I can spare from this important post, I can do anything to facilitate your operations, I will make an attack upon Fort Montgomery if you will let me know your wishes.'" The date of this message is doubtful. The date on the file copy was 10th September but it was changed to 11th. In the letter to London quoted above, Clinton says it was 12th September and this was the date on which Burgoyne believed it to have been written.

7 To retreat or to stay and wait until Clinton's attack developed.

8 Field guns of this date had a flat trajectory and could not fire over the heads of their own infantry. It was usual to deploy them in front of the line to get a clear field of fire.

9 Batmen were not officers' servants but the soldiers detailed to look after the baggage. (From the French *bât* = pack-saddle.)

10 Most accounts say that it was a Brunswick battalion which broke, but Pausch's account makes it clear that it was the Regiment of Hesse Hanau. Since Pausch was a Hanauer himself he would not have made a mistake on this point. There were only eighty Hanauers of all ranks present, and it is possible that the detachment from Rhetz on their right also gave way.

11 No accurate return of casualties was made for the battle but the loss of the British and German infantry for the first two weeks of October was 420. Some of these must have been sick and some were wounded in skirmishes. The loss of the artillery, British and German (including the detachment of the 33rd Foot) rank and file for the whole campaign was 161.

12 According to Frau General Ridesel, who had joined her husband at Fort Edward, on the 9th October, "I asked General Phillips why we did not continue our retreat while there was yet time. 'Poor woman,' he answered, 'would you were our commanding general. He halts here because he is tired and intends to spend the night and give us a supper.' In this latter achievement General Burgoyne is very fond of indulging. He spent half the nights in singing and drinking and amusing himself with the wife of a commissary who was his mistress, and who, like himself, loved champagne." This story cannot be true. The troops were far too exhausted to continue on that night. Moreover, apart from the fact that the remarks attributed to Phillips are out of character, he was on that night commanding the rearguard and, since the artillery was still on the wrong side of this Fishkill, he would have been with it. As to the Frau General's accusations about Burgoyne's usual misconduct, it is remarkable that no one else mentioned his behaviour. Few of his real or imagined faults were not paraded in the controversy which followed Saratoga.

13 *Chamade* = the signal, given by beat of drum, for a parley.

14 Major (B/Lt. Col) Robert Kingston, formerly an officer of the 16th Light Dragoons, was Deputy Adjutant General to Burgoyne. Since 7th October, he had also been acting as Military Secretary.

15 James Wilkinson, who in 1813 commanded the United States army at Chrysler's Farm where he was decisively defeated by a smaller British force. He was subsequently tried by court martial but acquitted.

16 When Cornwallis surrendered at Yorktown he omitted to safeguard the Loyalists in his army.

CHAPTER 12. "Ministerial Ingratitude will be Displayed"

1 Burgoyne's use of the phrase "forlorn hope" should not be taken to mean that he thought his task hopeless. It is a phrase from the jargon of siege craft and referred to the small body of men who led the storming party. Traditionally it was the post of honour.

2 There was no need for a physical junction between the two armies. What was essential was that Howe should occupy the Highlands and clear the navigation at least as far as Livingstone's Manor, sending shallow draught gun boats and supplies on to Albany. This would have drawn away enough rebel forces to enable Burgoyne to get to Albany without incurring crippling loss. There is no evidence that he or Germain ever thought an unsupported advance to Albany practicable.

[3] The true story of the cartouche boxes was told by Lieutenant Colonel Kingston in the House of Commons. "On talking to Mr Gates when the King's troops marched by with their accoutrements on, Mr Gates asked me (we were old acquaintances formerly) whether it was not customary on field days for army and accoutrements to go together. I told him there was nothing in the Convention that I agreed to with him relating to accoutrements, and he could have no right to anything but what was stipulated in that treaty. He replied 'You are perfectly right': and turned to some officers in their service nearby and said, 'If we meant to have them, we ought to have inserted them in the Convention.'"

[4] Compare, in the twentieth century, Lloyd George's treatment of General Gough in 1918 and, in 1940, Churchill's treatment of Admiral North.

[5] On hearing of Howe's Long Island victory in the previous year, Fox had written to Burke, 'What a dismal piece of news.'

[6] Burgoyne had sent the first copy of his despatch with Lord Petersham by way of New York. Another copy he sent with Craig to Carleton. The governor forwarded Craig, with his own a.d.c., Captain Foy, to London. By some trick of the wind Craig reached London three weeks before Petersham.

[7] Robert Vyner Jnr, MP for Lincoln City.

[8] The Hon. Temple Luttrell, MP for Milbourne Port, was third son of Lord Carhampton, an Irish peer.

EPILOGUE

[1] Elizabeth Farren was one of the stars of Drury Lane from 1777 until she retired to marry the 12th Earl of Derby, with whom she had been living for some years, in 1797. She thus became Burgoyne's niece by marriage. The first Lady Derby had run away with the Duke of Dorset, Germain's cousin, in 1778. This would have been another factor in turning Burgoyne against Lord George.

[2] Fonblanque says that she played Matilda. The Collected edition of Burgoyne's works says the part was played by Mrs Mountain. Mrs Jordan became the mistress of the Duke of Clarence (William IV) and the mother of a large brood of Fitzclarences.

APPENDIX

[1] Lieutenant Hadden, who served under Captain Jones in the 2nd Brigade, gives Blomefield as commanding the Centre Brigade of the Park and Carter as commanding the whole Park. There seems to be no doubt that Blomefield was Brigade Major RA (he signed his parole as such) and it would be usual for Williams, as senior RA officer after Phillips, to command the Park. As Carter was the only Captain without a command it seems probable that he commanded the Centre Brigade.

Bibliography

(with abbreviations used in the references)

AHR.   *Journal of the Society of Army Historical Research.*
Anburey.   *With Burgoyne from Quebec.* Lt. T. Anburey. Ed. S. Jackman. 1963.
Anderson.   *The Command of the Howe Brothers.* Troyer Steele Anderson. 1936.
Atkinson.   *History of the Royal Dragoons, 1661–1934.* C. T. Atkinson. 1934.
Baroness.   *Letters and Journals relating to the American War.* Baroness Riedesel. Trans. W. L. Stone. 1867.
Bowler.   *Sir Guy Carleton and the Campaign of 1776 in Canada.* R. Arthur Bowler. Canadian Historical Review. June 1974.
Burgoyne.   *The Dramatic and Poetical Works of Lt. Gen. J. Burgoyne.* (2 vols). 1808.
Burke.   *The Correspondence of Edmund Burke.* Ed. George H. Guttridge. 1961.
Burt.   *The Quarrel between Germain and Carleton: an Inverted Story.* A. L. Burt. Canadian Historical Review. 1930.
Carleton.   *Guy Carleton, Lord Dorchester, 1724–1808.* A. L. Burt. 1957.
Channing.   *A History of the United States.* Edward Channing. 1912.
Chatham.   *Correspondence of William Pitt, Earl of Chatham.* Ed. Taylor and Pringle. 1840.
Christie.   *The End of North's Ministry 1780–83.* Ian R. Christie. 1958.
Clinton.   *The American Rebellion. Sir Henry Clinton's Narrative of his Campaigns, 1775–82.* Ed. William B. Willcox, 1954.
Commons.   *The House of Commons, 1754–90.* Sir Lewis Namier & John Brooke. 1964.
Constituents.   *A Letter from Lieut. Gen. Burgoyne to his Constituents upon his Late Resignation.* 1779.
CorGIII.   *The Correspondence of King George III from 1760 to 1783.* Ed. Sir John Fortescue. (6 vols) 1928.
Cumberland.   *Memoirs of Richard Cumberland written by himself.* (2 vols) 1807.
Curtis.   *The Organisation of the British Army in the American Revolution.* E. E. Curtis. 1936.
Digby.   *Journal of Lieutenant Digby. A Journal of the Campaigns against the Americans in 1776 & 1777.* Ed. J. P. Baxter. 1887.
Dobson.   *History of the Parliamentary Representation of Preston.* W. M. Dobson. 1868.
Donne.   *Correspondence of King George III with Lord North.* Ed. W. Bodham Donne. (2 vols) 1867.
Duncan.   *History of the Royal Regiment of Artillery.* Francis Duncan. (2 vols) 3rd Edn 1879.
Fonblanque.   *Political and Military Episodes in the latter half of the Eighteenth Century derived from the Life and Correspondence of the Rt. Hon John Burgoyne.* Edward Barrington de Fonblanque. 1876.

Fortescue.	*A History of the British Army*. Vols ii & iii. Sir John Fortescue. 1910 & 11.
Fuller.	*Decisive Battles of the United States*. J. F. C. Fuller. 1942.
German Letters.	*Letters from America 1776–79. Being Letters of Brunswick, Hessian & Waldeck Officers during the Revolution*. Transl. & Ed. Ray W. Perrengill. 1924.
Gibbon.	*The Letters of Edward Gibbon*. Ed. J. E. Norton. (2 vols) 1956.
Graham.	*History of the Sixteenth, Queen's, Light Dragoons (Lancers) 1759–1912*. Henry Graham. 1912.
Gruber.	*The Howe Brothers and the American Revolution*. Ira D. Gruber. 1972.
Hadden.	*A Journal kept in Canada and upon Burgoyne's Campaigns in 1776 & 1777*. James M. Hadden, Lieutenant, Royal Artillery. Ed. Horatio Rogers. (2 vols) 1884.
HMC American.	*Report on the American Manuscripts in the Royal Institution of Great Britain*. Historical Manuscripts Commission. 1904.
HMC Bathurst.	*Report on the Manuscripts of Earl Bathurst*. Historical Manuscripts Commission. 1923.
HMC Dartmouth.	*Report of the Manuscripts of the Earl of Dartmouth*. Historical Manuscripts Commission. 1895.
HMC Hastings.	*Report on the Manuscripts of the late Reginald Rawdon Hastings*. Historical Manuscripts Commission. 1934.
HMC Knox.	*Report on the Manuscripts in Various Collections. Vol. vi.* Historical Manuscripts Commission. 1909.
HMC Sackville.	*Report on the Manuscripts of Mrs Stopford Sackville*. Historical Manuscripts Commission. 1904.
Horse.	*For Want of a Horse, being the journal of the campaigns against the Americans in 1776 & 1777 conducted from Canada, by an officer who served with Lt. Gen. Burgoyne*. Ed. G. F. C. Stanley. 1961.
Huddlestone.	*Gentleman Johnny Burgoyne*. F. J. Huddlestone. 1928.
Hutchinson.	*The Diary & Letters of Thomas Hutchinson*. Ed. Peter Orlando Hutchinson. (2 vols) 1883.
Junius.	*The Letters of Junius*. Ed. C. W. Everett. 1927.
Lamb.	*An Original and Authentic Account of Occurences during the late American War*. R. Lamb, late Serjeant. 1809.
Last Journals.	*The Last Journals of Horace Walpole during the Reign of George III 1771–83*. Ed. Francis Steuart. 1900.
Last Ten Years.	*Memoirs of the Last Ten Years of the Reign of George II*. Horace Walpole. 1822.
Later GIII.	*The Later Correspondence of George III*. Ed. A. Aspinall. 1962.
Macksey.	*The War for America*. Piers Macksey. 1964.
Mackinnon.	*Origin and Services of the Coldstream Guards*. Daniel Mackinnon. (2 vols) 1833.
Mahan.	*Major Operations of the Navies in the American War of Independence*. A. T. Hahan. 1913.
Marshall.	*Royal Navy Biography*. John Marshall. 1823.
NamierAmr.	*England in the Age of the American Revolution*. Sir Lewis Namier. 2nd Edn 1966.
NamierGIII.	*The Structure of Politics at the Accession of George III*. Sir Lewis Namier. 2nd Edn 1961.
NamierPP.	*Personalities and Powers*. Sir Lewis Namier. 1955.
Nickerson.	*The Turning Point of the Revolution or Burgoyne's Campaign in America*. Hoffman Nickerson. 1928.
Old Westminsters.	*The Record of Old Westminsters*. G. F. Russell Baker & Alan H. Stenning. (2 vols) 1928.
Orderly Book.	*The Orderly Book of Lieut. Gen. John Burgoyne from his Entry into the state of New York until his Surrender at Saratoga*. Ed. E. B. O'Callaghan. 1860.

Osler. *Life of Admiral Lord Exmouth.* Edward Osler. 1835.

Oxberry. *Oxberry's Dramatic Biography and Histrionic Anecdotes.* (5 vols) 1835–36.

Parlhist. *The Parliamentary History of England from the Earliest Times to the year 1803.* 1813–14.

Pausch. *The Journal of Captain Pausch, Hanau Artillery, during the Burgoyne Campaign.* Transl. & annotated W. B. Stone. 1886.

Percy. *Letters of Hugh, Lord Percy from Boston and New York 1774–77.* Ed. C. K. Bolton. 1902.

Palmerston. *Portrait of a Whig Peer.* Brian Connel. 1957.

Ramsay. *The Life and Art of Allan Ramsay.* Alistair Smart. 1952.

Reynolds. *Life and Times of Sir Joshua Reynolds.* C. R. Leslie & T. Taylor. (2 vols) 1865.

Riedesel. *Memoirs and Letters and Journals of Major General Riedesel.* Max von Eelking. Transl. W. B. Stone. 1868.

Rockingham. *Memoirs of the Marquis of Rockingham and his Contemporaries.* George Thomas, Earl of Albemarle. (2 vols) 1852.

Rogers. *Weapons of the British Soldier.* H. C. B. Rogers. 1960.

Sackville. *The Trial of the Rt. Hon. Lord George Sackville at a Court-Martial.* 1760.

Shelburne. *Life of William, Earl of Shelburne, afterwards 1st Marquess of Lansdowne.* Lord Edmund Fitzmaurice. (3 vols) 1912.

Shortt & Doughty. *Documents Relating to the Constitutional History of Canada.* Vol. ii. A. Shortt & A. G. Doughty. 1918.

Smyth. *History of the XX Regiment.* B. Smyth. (2 vols) 1903–04.

Stanley. *Canada Invaded.* George F. C. Stanley. 1973.

State. *A State of the Expedition from Canada as laid before the House of Commons by Lieut. Gen. Burgoyne.* 1780.

Stuart. *A Prime Minister and his Son.* Hon. Mrs E. Stuart Wortly. 1925.

Valentine. *Lord George Germain.* Alan Valentine. 1962.

Victoria. *Victoria History of Bedfordshire.* vols iii & iv. Ed. William Page. 1908 & 1912.

Walpole Letters. *The Letters of Horace Walpole.* Ed. Peter Cunningham. 1906.

Watson. *The Reign of George III.* J. Steven Watson. 1960.

Wilkinson. *Memoirs of my Own Times.* James Wilkinson. (2 vols) 1816.

Williams. *The Whig Supremacy.* Basil Williams. 2nd Edn. (rev. by C. H. Stuart) 1962.

Willcox. *Portrait of a General: Sir Henry Clinton in the War of Independence.* William B. Willcox. 1964.

Wraxall. *Hiitorical and Posthumous Memoirs of Sir Nathaniel Wraxall, 1772–84.* Ed. Henry B. Wheatley. (5 vols) 1884.

References

Prologue
page
1. State lv. Minutes of 1st Council of War.
2. — lvi. Minutes of 2nd Council of War.
2. — lv.
2. — lvi.
2. — lx and HMC American i 140. JB to Howe, 20 Oct 77.
2. — lvi.
3. Osler 39.
3. Orderly Book 132.
4. Macksey 113.
5. Channing iii 244.
5. — iiii 265.
5. Hadden i 315. BO of 19 Aug 77.
6. Fortescue iii 243.

Chapter 1. *Britain in the Seventies*
12. H. A. L. Fisher. History of Europe (1936 Edn) p. 782.
13. CorrGIII. iv 221. HM to North, 14 Nov 78.
14. NamierGIII. 148–49.
14. Parlhist xviii 1291, 21 May 76.
14. NamierGIII. 164.
14. — 131.
14. Speech to the Electors of Bristol, 3 Nov 77.
14. Christie 131. Nottingham Journal 3 Apr 84.
15. Shelburne i 49.
15. NamierPP 72.

page
17. HMC Knox 280 Undated memo by Knox.
18. CorrGIII. iii 477. Robinson to HM, 19 Sep 77.
18. — iii 479. North to HM, 20 Sep 77.
18. Wraxall i 369.
18. Cumberland ii 353.
18. Wraxall i 366.
18. — i 364.
18. — i 361 & 337.
18. Cumberland ii 349.
18. Gibbon ii 66. 2 May 75.
19. Last Journals i 83.
19. Christie 5.
19. Parlhist. xx 948.
19. Hutchinson i 379. Gibbon to Hutchinson, 18 Feb. 75.
20. Burke iii 250.
20. Parlhist xviii. 2 Feb 75.
23. Gibbon ii 9. to Holroyd, 29 Mar 74.
20. Last Journals i 316. 14 Mar 74.
20. CorGIII iii 80. North to HM, 14 Mar 74.
20. Gibbon ii 9, to Holroyd, 29 Mar 74.
20. CorrGIII iii 104. HM to North, 6 May 74.
20. — iii 131. —, 11 Sep 74.
20. — iii 153. —, 18 Nov 74.
24. Gibbon ii 58, to Holroyd, 31 Jan 75.
24. Last Journals i 409. Nov 74.
24. Oliver Goldsmith "Retaliation" i 29.
24. Last Journals i 498.
25. — i. 306.
25. Burke iii 89, to Rockingham, 5 Jan 75.
25. Last Journals i 445.
25. Gruber 15, Barrington to Gage, 31 Jan 75.

Chapter 2. *"They have a great Resource in our Incapacity"*
page
26. Burke iii 278, to Rockingham, 4 Jul 76.
26. Hutchinson i 378.
28. Fortescue iii 169, AG to Irwin, 30 Jun 75.
30. Last Journals i 172.
30. "Of Public Absurdities in England". Prose Works of Jonathan Swift, Ed. Temple Scott (1907) xi 180.
31. Parlhist xvii 949, 26 Jan 74.
31. HMC Sackville i 124, GG to Irwin, 24 Oct 67.
31. Last Journals i 148 (1772).
31. — — i 172 (1773).
34. CorrGIII iii 194, Jenkinson to HM, Mar 75.
34. Quoted in AHR xlv 57 from "History & Topography of Ipswich", G. R. Clark, 1830.
34. CorrGIII iii 255.
34. — — iii 250, HM to North, 26 Aug 75.
34. — — iii 515, — —, 18 Nov 77.
34. — — iii 516, — —, 18 Dec 77.
35. Anderson 265.
35. AHR xlv 242. G. Tylden "The principal small arms carried by the British regular infantry".
38. Letter of Lt. Montgomery. Ed. Sir John Fortescue in "The Times" 31 Jul 1931.
39. AHR. xlvi 196. A/C of Sir John St Clair, quoted in Robert L. Yaple "Braddock's Defeat: Theories and a Reconstruction".

Chapter 3. *Dragoon and Guardsman*
43. Victoria ii 44.
44. Walpole Letters vi 494, 5 Oct 77.
46. Atkinson 181 fn.
48. Mackinnon i 394 & ii 357.
49. Fonblanque 12.
49. — 13.
50. — 13.
50. — 14.
51. Graham 2.
52. Rogers 96. quoted from Hinde "Discipline of the Light Horse" 1788.
52. Fonblanque 16–22.
54. — 84, JB to Viscount Townshend, 1767.

page
56. HMC Sackville ii 110, JB in House of Commons, 26 May 78.
56. Fonblanque 40, JB to Loudon, June 1762.
57. — 40,
57. — 45, La Lippe to Bute, Jul 62.
58. — 47, JB to C Townshend, 10 Aug 62.

Chapter 4. *Honourable and Gallant Member*
59. Commons i 396.
60. Fonblanque 56, Pitt to JB, 1 Jul 66.
61. — 61, JB to Ellyott, 9 Sep 66.
61. — 65–66.
61. — 62–69.
62. — 69–74.
62. — 77–79.
62. — 83, Chatham to JB, 14 Dec 66.
62–65. Dobson *passim*.
65. Junius 303, to H. S. Woodfall, 12 Dec. 69.
66. Walpole Letters vi 494, to Mason, 5 Oct 77.
66. Fonblanque 124.
67. Donne i 57, HM to North, 14 Feb. 71.
67. Last Journals i 304.
67. Parlhist xvii 233.
67. Corr GIII ii 328, HM to North, 12 Mar 73.
67. Last Journals i 80.
68. Parlhist xvii 233.
68. — xvii 535.
68. Last Journals i 199, 10 May 73.
68. Walpole Letters v 463, to Mann, 15 May 73.
68. Last Journals i 201.
69. Last Journals i 201.
69. — — i 230.
69. — — i 231.
69. — — i 231.
70. Constituents 3.
70. Parlhist xvii 1271, 19 Apr 74.
71. ib.

Chapter 5. *"A Professional Tragedy"*
75. CorrGIII iii 131, HM to North, 11 Sep 74.
75. Parlhist xviii 222.
76. Last Journals i 236.
76. CorrGIII iii 59, HM to North, 4 Feb 74.

page

76. HMC Sackville ii 2, GG to Suffolk, 16 Jun 75.
76. HMC Knox 257, Undated memo by Wm. Knox.
76. CorrGIII iii 59, HM to North, 4 Feb 74.
76. —— iii 154, ——, 18 Nov 74.
77. HMC Sackville i 128, GG to Irwin, 28 Aug 68.
77. Last Journals i 433.
77. CorrGIII iii 156, HM to North, 17 Dec 74.
77. —— iii 151, ——, 18 Nov 74.
77. Last Journals i 433.
78. Walpole Letters vi 373.
78. Willcox 37.
78. — 124.
78. HMC Knox 171, GG to Knox, 5 Sep 80.
78. Clinton 18, Clinton to ?, 15 Jun 75.
79. Fonblanque 120.
79. — 121.
79. — 123.
80. — 125.
80. CorrGIII iii 202, HM to North, 11 Apr 75.
80. CorrGIII iii 202, HM to North, 14 Apr 75.
81. Fonblanque 126.
81. Hutchinson i 420, 29 Mar 75.
81. Fonblanque 131.
81. Clinton 18.
82. HMC Hastings iii 156, Rawdon to Hastings, 3 Aug 75.
82. ib.
83. Fonblanque 140, JB to AG, 14 Jun 75.
83. ib.
83. CorrGIII iii 220, Howe to ?AG, 22 & 24 Jun 75.
83. HMC Sackville ii 3, Howe to Ld Howe, 22 Jun 75.
84. CorrGIII iii 220, Howe to ?AG, 24 Jun 75.
84. HMC Sackville ii 3, Howe to Ld Howe, 22 Jun 75.
84. Clinton 19.
84. Fonblanque 157.
84. — 155.
85. HMC Hastings iii 154, Rawdon to Ld Huntingdon, 20 Jun 75.
85. HMC Hastings iii 157, Rawdon to Ld Huntingdon, 3 Aug 75.
85. Fonblanque 147, JB to Rochfort, nd.
85. — 208.
86. Clinton 19.

page

86. CorrGIII iii 220, Howe to ?AG, 24 Jun 75.
86. Stuart 71, Stuart to Bute, 24 Jul 75.
86. HMC Hastings iii 161, Rawdon to Huntingdon, 13 Dec 75.
86. HMC Sackville ii 7, JB to GG, 20 Aug 75.
86. Fonblanque 132.
86. — 202, JB to ?, Sep 75.
87. CorrGIII iii 242, JB to ?North, 10/18 Aug 75.
87. —— iii 224, JB to Rochfort, 25 Jun 75.
87. —— iii 242, JB to ?North, 10/18 Aug 75.
88. Fonblanque 175–77, JB to North, Jul 75.
88. HMC Hastings iii 160, Rawdon to Huntingdon, 5 Oct 75.
88. Oxberry iii 101.
88. Stuart 73, Stuart to Bute, 8 Oct 75.

Chapter 6. *"Unactivity and Want of Spirit"*

89. Wraxall i 385.
89. HMC Sackville i 280, Cumberland to Dorset, 20 Sep 46.
90. Wraxall i 385.
90. Valentine 10.
90. Wraxall i 384.
90. Shelburne i 362.
91. Sackville 342.
91. Last Ten Years ii 417.
91. Sackville 38.
91. Valentine 69.
92. HMC Sackville i 103, GG to Irwin 23 Dec 65.
92. Hutchinson i 294.
92. HMC Sackville i 134, GG to Irwin, 17 Oct 74.
92. Last Journals i 312.
93. HMC Sackville i 137, GG to Irwin, 13 Sep 75.
93. — i 138, ——, 4 Nov 75.
93. Cumberland i 289.
94. Fonblanque 126.
94. HMC Hastings iii 166, JB to Huntingdon, 3 Jan 76.
95. HMC Sackville ii 23, JB to GG, wrongly dated 3 Mar 76. (possibly 13 Mar. Lady Margaret Stanley did not die until 9th March).
95. Last Journals i 523.
95. Fonblanque 212, GG to JB, 1 Mar. 76.

page
96. Parlhist xviii 1148.
96. Fonblanque 142, JB to Rochfort, 25 Jun 75.
96. — 212, GG to JB, 1 Mar 76.
96. Burt 221.
97. Parlhist xvii 1368.
97. Shortt & Doughty ii 583, Carleton to Dartmouth, 23 Sep 74.
97. — ii 584, — to Gage, 20 Sep 74.
98. Stanley 83.
99. Mahan 11, Return of 1 May 76.
99. HMC Sackville ii 26, JB to GG, 31 Mar 76.
99. Osler 12.
100. HMC Sackville ii 26, JB to GG, 31 Mar 76.
100. CorrGIII iii 383, Williams to GG, 23 Jun 76.
100. ib.
100. ib.
101. Stanley 125, Maclean to ?GG, 10 May 76.
101. CorrGIII 355, Williams to GG, 23 Jun 76.
101. HMC Sackville ii 36, JB to GG, 22 Jun 76.
102. ib.
102. CorrGIII iii 406, HM to North, 13 Dec 76.
103. Marshall i 325.
103. HMC Sackville ii 44, Christie to GG, 26 Oct 76.
104. Pausch 82.
104. Mahan 18.
104. Pausch 82
104. HMC Sackville ii 44, Christie to GG, 26 Oct 76.
105. Fonblanque 218, Phillips to JB, 23 Oct 76.
105. Last Journals i 561.
106. CorrGIII iii 386, North to HM, 22 Jun 76.
106. HMC Sackville ii 39, GG to JB, 23 Aug 76.
106. ib.
106. Gibbon ii 125, to Holroyd, 22 Nov 76.
106. HMC Knox 126, J. Pownall to Knox, 23 Oct 76.
106. CorrGIII iii 403, North to HM, ?16 Nov 76.
106. — iii 405, GG to HM, 10 Dec 76.

Chapter 7. *"To Finish the Rebellion in one Campaign"*
page
109. HMC Sackville i 137, GG to Irwin, 13 Sep 75.
109. Last Journals i 592.
109. HMC Hastings iii 188, H. Stanley to Huntingdon, 18 Dec 76.
110. HMC Sackville ii 44, Christie to GG, 26 Oct 76.
110. State vii, GG to Carleton, 26 Mar 77.
111. — ii, —, 22 Aug 76.
111. CorrGIII iii 407, HM to North, 13 Dec 76.
111. Last Journals i 592.
111. CorrGIII iii 407, HM to North, 13 Dec 76.
112. Walpole Letters vi 397.
112. State i, JB to GG, 1 Jan 77.
113. HMC Sackville ii 49, Howe to GG, 30 Nov 76.
113. — ii 49, — —.
113. — ii 56, GG to Howe, 14 Jan 77.
114. Fortescue iii 168.
114. CorrGIII iii 215, Howe to AG, 12 Jun 75. See also HMC Dartmouth ii 315.
114. HMC Sackville ii 9, Ld. Howe to GG, 25 Sep 75.
114. — ii 32, Howe to GG, 12 May 76.
114. — ii 38, —, 10 Aug 76.
115. — ii 52, —, 20 Dec 76.
115. ib.
115. HMC Knox 128, GG to Knox, 31 Dec 76.
116. CorrGIII iii 421, HM to North, 24 Feb 77.
116. State v.
120. CorrGIII iii 443. Unsigned, undated memo.
121. ib.
121. Fonblanque 486.
121. HMC Sackville ii 58, GG to Howe, 3 Mar 77.
121. — ii 52, Howe to GG, 20 Dec 76.

Chapter 8. *"Directed to make a Junction"*
123. HMC Knox 129, GG to Knox, 2 Apr 77.
123. Hadden i 43.
123. HMC Sackville ii 60, GG to Carleton, 26 Mar 77.
124. Hadden ii 433, Carleton to JB, 19 Jul 77.

page

125. HMC Sackville ii 60, GG to Carleton, 25 Mar 77.

126. AHR xxvi 139. C. T. Atkinson, "Some Evidence for Burgoyne's Expedition:", JB to Fraser, 6 May 77.

126. Willcox 135.

126. HMC Knox 277. Undated memo by Wm Knox, written after 1782.

127. ib.

127. HMC Sackville ii 70, Howe to GG, 5 Jul 77.

127. Burt 218, Carleton to GG, 22 May 77.

127. LaterGIII i 146, HM to Pitt, 28 Mar 85.

128. CorrGIII iv 457, HM to North, 2 Jul 77.

128. HMC Knox 132, GG to Carleton, 10 Jul 77.

128. — 132, GG to Carleton, 10 Jul 77.

128. AHR xxvi 139, JB to Fraser, 6 May 77.

128. State xxxi, JB to AG, 19 May 77.

129. — xxx, JB to Carleton, 7 Jun 77.

129. CorrGIII iii 294, HM to North, 18 Nov 75.

130. Anburey 97.

131. State iii. "Thoughts".

131. — x, JB to GG, 14 May 77.

131. — 74. Evidence of Maj. Kingston.

131. — iii. "Thoughts".

131. — x, JB to GG, 14 May 77.

131. — 74. Evidence of Maj. Kingston.

131. AHR xxvi 134. "Memorandum relative to a Corps of Marksmen." 30 Aug 76.

132. Duncan i 208.

132. HMC American i 55, Barrington to Carleton, 23 Aug 76.

132. State xxxii, JB to AG, 11 Jul 77.

132. Anburey 83.

133. German Letters 70.

133. Pausch 124.

133. Orderly Book 5.

133. Pausch 123, 30 May 77.

133. Orderly Book 80.

134. Fuller 28–30.

134. Orderly Book 3.

134. Smyth i 307.

134. Orderly Book 2.

134. Anburey 94 & 57.

135. State xi, JB to GG, 19 May 77.

page

135. Fonblanque 233, JB to Howe, 14 May 77.

135. HMC Sackville ii 65, Howe to Carleton, 5 Apr 77.

137. — ii 63, Howe to GG, 2 Apr 77.

137. — ii 79, — —, 22 Oct 77.

137. — ii 52, — —, 20 Dec 76, (received in London 23 Feb 77)

Chapter 9. "*Critical and Conspicuous Services*"

141. State xxxii & xxxiii, JB to AG, 22 Jun & 11 Jul 77.

142. *Ibid.* xxii.

142. Anburey 126.

142. Fonblanque 490.

142. Last Journals ii 47.

142. Hutchinson ii 155.

143. German Letters 32.

143. Anburey 120.

144. State x, JB to GG, 19 May 77.

144. Orderly Book 17. GO of 30 Jun 77.

145. Hadden i 82.

145. Fortescue ii 335.

146. State xv & xvi, JB to GG, 11 Jul 77.

147. Anburey 134.

147. State xv, JB to GG, 11 Jul 77.

148. *Ibid.* xvi, — —.

149. Hadden i 89.

149. State xvii, JB to GG, 11 Jul 77.

150. Anburey 138.

150. ib.

151. ib.

151. ib.

152. Anburey 140.

152. State xviii.

152. Lamb 140.

153. ib.

153. State 61. Evidence of Maj. Gordon Forbes.

153. Lamb 141.

153. ib.

154. Digby 234.

154. Anburey 140. 12 Jul 77.

154. State xx, JB to GG, 11 Jul 77.

155. Orderly Book 24.

155. State xx, JB to GG, 11 Jul 77.

page
180. Hadden i 165.
180. State 79. Evidence of Maj. Kingston.
180. Hadden i 166.
180. State xlix, JB to GG, 20 Oct 77.
181. State 79. Evidence of Maj. Kingston.
181. Digby 274.
181. Wilkinson i 251.
181. Willcox 177, Clinton to JB, 10–12 Sep 77.
182. Rockingham ii 334, JB to Clinton, 21 Sep 77.
182. — ii 334, Clinton to AG, 13 Oct 77.
183. State 15.
183. — 80. Evidence of Lt. Col. Kingston.
183. State 16.
183. Clinton 63.
184. — 64.
184. — 70.
184. — 70.
184. Willcox 176, Clinton to Howe, 6 Sep 77.
184. Nickerson 341, Clinton to ?, 9 Sep 77.
184. Willcox 175, Clinton to AG, 16 Sep 77.
185. Clinton 379, Clinton to JB, 6 Oct 77.
186. German Letters 103.
187. Anburey 176, 6 Oct 77.
188. Orderly Book 125, 3 Oct 77.
188. State 1, JB to GG, 20 Oct 77.
188. Pausch 160.
189. State 69. Evidence of Capt. Blomefield.
189. Pausch 161.
189. ib.
189. State 162. Evidence of Capt. Money.
189. Pausch 162.
189. State 43. Evidence of Capt. Money
190. Anburey 143.
190. Pausch 163.
191. State li, JB to GG, 20 Oct 77.
191. Anburey 188.
192. State lv. Minutes of 1st Council of War.
192. — xlvii, JB to GG, 20 Oct 77.
193–5. Wilkinson i 299.
195. Orderly Book 134.
195. Wilkinson i 136.

Chapter 12. *"Ministerial Ingratitude will be Displayed"*
199. Fonblanque 316, JB to the Ladies Elizabeth & Harriet Stanley, 20 Oct 77.

page
199. — 313, JB to Phillipson, 20 Oct 77.
199. HMC American i 140, JB to Howe, 20 Oct 77.
200. State liii, JB to GG, 20 Oct 77.
200. Fonblanque 313, JB to Phillipson, 20 Oct 77.
200. HMC American i 140, JB to Howe, 20 Oct 77.
200. German Letters 95, 15 Nov 77.
200. Fonblanque 318, Carleton to JB, 12 Nov 77.
201. HMC American i 143, JB to Howe, 25 Oct 77.
201. Fonblanque 325, Clinton to JB, 16 Dec 77.
201. Fonblanque 322, J. McN. Hayes MD to JB, 4 Sep 78.
201. Lamb 196.
202. Fonblanque 328, JB to President of Congress, 11 Feb 78.
202. — 333.
202. — 331. Riedesel to JB, 2 Apr 78.
203. HMC Knox 131, GG to Knox, 24 Jun 77.
203. — 134, — —, 1 Jul 77.
203. — 134, — —, 2 Aug. 77.
203. — 135, — —, 17 Aug. 77.
203. HMC Sackville ii 70, Howe to GG, 7 Jul 77.
204. — ii 77, — —, 16 Jul 77.
204. — ii 139, GG to Irwin, 23 Aug 77.
205. CorrGIII 471, GG to HM, 23 Aug 77.
205. State xx, JB to GG, 11 Jul 77.
205. CorrGIII iii 480, GG to HM, 25 Sep 77.
205. Hutchinson ii 160 (see also Last Journals 6 Oct 77).
205. — ii 161.
205. Willcox 175, Clinton to AG, 18 Aug 77.
206. HMC Knox 140, GG to Knox, 31 Oct 77.
206. HMC Sackville ii 2, GG to Suffolk, 17 Jun 75.
206. Last Journals ii 69.
207. Parlhist xix 434.
207. Gibbon ii 167, to Holroyd, 2 Dec 77.
207. — ii 168 —, 4 Dec 77.
207. Last Journals ii 80.
207. Chatham iv 77.
208. Hutchinson ii 169.
208. — ii 170.

page
209. CorrGIII iii 514, GG to HM, 15 Dec 77.
209. — iii 520, HM to North, 25 Dec 77.
209. — iii 527, — —, 27 Dec 77.
210. HMC Sackville ii 88. Undated memo written before 1 Feb 78.
210. Last Journals ii 100. i Feb 78.
212. Wraxall ii 450.
212. Hutchinson ii 210, 22 Jul 78.
213. Constituents 8–9.
213. Last Journals ii 176.
214. HMC Sackville ii 10.
214. Last Journals ii 179.
215. — — ii 182.
215. Fonblanque 351 fn.
215. Constituents 21, Barrington to JB, 5 Jun 78.

page
216. — 22, JB to Barrington, 22 Jun 78.
216. State. Dedication i.
217. Constituents 26, Jenkinson to JB, 24 Sep 79.
217. — 27, JB to Jenkinson, 9 Oct 79.
217. — 32, — —, 9 Oct 79.

Epilogue
219. Wraxall ii 45.
219. Burgoyne i 127.
219. Oxberry i 47.
220. Fonblanque 400.
221. Walpole Letters ix 96, to Countess of Upper Ossory, 24 Jun 87.
221. Fonblanque 464.
221. Gentleman's Magazine, August 1792.

Index

249